The Doctoral

The Doctoral Experience presents a vivid picture of the experiences of PhD students and their academic mentors in a variety of different disciplines. It shows how younger academics are socialized into the distinctive sub-culture of their chosen academic discipline, displaying how different disciplines and departments reproduce their specialized ways of conducting research.

The book is based on research involving in-depth interviews with over 200 postgraduate students and academics across the United Kingdom. The issues explored include: how the students deal with the uncertainties of their own research; how they cope with frustration, failure and the intellectual isolation they experience; how research groups can act as socializing environments; and how academic supervisors handle the tensions between the intellectual autonomy of the research student and their responsibilities as intellectual mentors.

Sara Delamont is Reader in Sociology at Cardiff University. She has published extensively on social interaction in schools and classrooms, women's education, women intellectuals, and the anthropology of contemporary Europe.

Paul Atkinson is Professor of Sociology at Cardiff University. His research and publications include work on medical knowledge, genetic science and educational knowledge.

Odette Parry is Senior Research Fellow in the Research Unit in Health and Behavioural Change at the University of Edinburgh. She has extensive research experience in a number of fields, including health and illness, the body, and education in the UK and the Caribbean.

The Doctoral Experience
Success and Failure in Graduate School

Sara Delamont, Paul Atkinson and Odette Parry

Routledge
Taylor & Francis Group

LONDON AND NEW YORK

First published 2000
by RoutledgeFalmer

2 Park Square, Milton Park, Abingdon, Oxon OX14 4RN
711 Third Avenue, New York, NY 10017, USA

*Routledge is an imprint of the Taylor & Francis Group,
an informa business*

First issued in paperback 2016

Transferred to Digital Printing 2005

Copyright © 2000 Sara Delamount, Paul Atkinson and Odette Parry

Typeset in Times by Taylor & Francis Books Ltd

All rights reserved. No part of this book may be reprinted or reproduced
or utilised in any form or by any electronic, mechanical, or other means,
now known or hereafter invented, including photocopying and recording,
or in any information storage or retrieval system, without permission
in writing from the publishers.

Notice:
Product or corporate names may be trademarks or registered trademarks,
and are used only for identification and explanation without intent to infringe.

British Library Cataloguing in Publication Data
A catalogue record for this book is available from the British Library

Library of Congress Cataloging in-Publication Data
A catalog record for this book has been requested

ISBN 978-0-7507-0927-9 (hbk)
ISBN 978-1-138-96788-5 (pbk)

Contents

Acknowledgements		vii
1	Cultures of the Academy	1
2	Researching our Peers	18
3	The Nature of the Quest	34
4	The Appliance of Science: Laboratory Scientists in the Making	53
5	Fieldwork	72
6	Modelling Realities	100
7	Genealogies and Generations	116
8	Supervisors' Narratives: Creating a Delicate Balance	134
9	Pedagogic Continuities	152
10	Disciplines and the Doctorate	173
	Appendix 1: Two Research Projects	183
	Appendix 2: The Policy Context	188
	References	193
	Name Index	199
	Subject Index	203

Acknowledgements

The research on which this book is based was supported by the Economic and Social Research Council (ESRC): 'The academic socialisation of doctoral students in social science disciplines' (T007401010) and 'The academic socialisation of doctoral students in natural science disciplines' (R000233120). We gratefully acknowledge the support of the ESRC. The interpretations offered here are our own and do not represent the views of the ESRC.

In the course of that research we benefited from the help of many academics and research students in a diverse range of British universities. When they agreed to work with us we assured them of confidentiality and anonymity. We have done our best to achieve these. Consequently our thanks must be to unnamed hosts and helpers, to whom we are deeply indebted for their patience and co-operation.

We have already published a very different sort of book from our research (Delamont et al., 1997a). That was an essentially practical book of advice, aimed at supervisors of graduate students. In this companion book we address our materials from a complementary set of perspectives. Here we analyse and discuss the research primarily from the perspective of the sociology of educational and academic knowledge. We draw together threads of analysis from sociological traditions concerned with work and the professions, scientific work and knowledge, educational institutions and academic knowledge. Versions of our arguments have previously appeared in academic journals: *The British Journal of Sociology of Education*, *Studies in Higher Education* and *Teaching in Higher Education*.

Among the many individuals who have provided colleagueship and help in the course of our research and drafting of this book, we are especially grateful to Angela Jones, who transcribed the recorded interviews. We are also grateful to Bob Burgess and Chris Pole, who were responsible for a parallel pair of research projects, and who have exchanged information and ideas over the years. We also thank Geoff Walford and Oliver Fulton for

Acknowledgements

their helpful comments. Early versions of some chapters were word-processed by Rosemary Bartle-Jones.

The chapter epigraphs are all taken from *Homo Academicus* by Pierre Bourdieu (1988).

1 Cultures of the Academy

> Seeking in the social structures of the academic world the sources of the categories of professional understanding.
>
> (Bourdieu, 1988: xii)

Introduction

How does one become a scientist? Obviously there are many answers to that question. We focus on just one crucial step in the process – the work and experiences that go into the period of doctoral research. We look at the experiences of PhD students and their academic supervisors in a variety of sciences – social and natural science subjects – in order to understand how novices are socialized into their respective academic disciplines and cultures. Becoming a scientist – indeed, becoming an academic in any field – is not just a matter of formal learning and assessment in specific domains of knowledge. To become a biochemist, say, involves more than just learning biochemistry. It also involves the acquisition of more general cultural knowledge and personal experience. One must learn not merely *about* biochemistry, one must also learn what it is to *do* the science, and what it means to *be* a biochemist. This depends on socialization into the culture of the discipline. It also rests on a crucial shift from the kind of learning that is characteristic of secondary schooling and undergraduate education.

Academics in higher education rightly make much of the relationship between teaching and research. Research-led universities insist that the quality of their undergraduate education rests on the research activities of their teaching staff. They insist that the most significant feature of their undergraduates' education is the fact that they are being taught by those people who are themselves creating the knowledge. They are probably right to affirm the relationship between research and teaching. Nevertheless, most of the knowledge that undergraduate students are exposed to is pedagogically processed, packaged and controlled in various ways. Knowledge is carefully doled out in the form of courses or modules, course outlines and reading lists, lecture topics and assessment tasks. Students' practical work in the laboratory or 'in the field' is carefully managed and controlled. Students' individual projects are normally tightly bounded and controlled. Laboratory 'experiments' and individual projects are carefully managed, low-risk activities, conducted within tightly defined parameters.

Students' experience of transition to independent doctoral research is marked by a radical break with such knowledge-reproduction. We do not mean that the conditions for doctoral research are uncontrolled, or that students are let loose to attempt high-risk projects without controls or guidance. As we shall see in the course of this book, that is not the case (although it does vary from discipline to discipline). Rather, students now have to learn craft skills and cultural competencies that are not part of the undergraduate experience. They have to learn how to cope when experiments do not 'work' – when failure is not just a matter of things going wrong technically or pedagogically, but has enormous implications for their identity and self-esteem. They have to cope on their own 'in the field', away from the relative safety of the classroom or the seminar. They must rely on their personal resources and, often, on the informal support of other students who find themselves facing similar problems. For the undergraduate, the basic structures of knowledge may be taken on trust. For the doctoral student, the creation of knowledge is a more uncertain process. Research is much less reliable, and the trust of the student is replaced by a different kind of faith that experiments will work 'in the end', that recalcitrant equipment will finally run, that the messy realities of field research will ultimately yield understanding, or that computer models will finally yield adequate solutions. If we are to understand how scientists and scholars are fashioned, then, we need to understand how they acquire the kinds of knowledge and personal experience that allow them to embark on and complete the risky process of independent research. We also need to understand the roles of their academic supervisors and mentors in guiding, helping (and hindering) their junior colleagues in this socialization process.

Academic socialization does not merely produce new recruits to departments and disciplines, it also reproduces the forms of knowledge that are their stock-in-trade. The reproduction of academic knowledge through the socialization of young scholars is a central process to the repeated round of self-recruitment and reproduction of science and scholarship. Doctoral research is a twofold process. It is the key status passage through which young academics gain entry to the academy. It is also a significant aspect of the research process in the academy generally. In that sense, therefore, doctoral research is a key mechanism through which academic knowledge is produced and reproduced.

We explore these and similar problems across a range of different academic disciplines. Our own research is grounded in different academic disciplines, departments and institutions. We range from laboratory research in the natural sciences, through computer-based modelling, to field research in social science. Our disciplines are as varied as biochemistry, physical geography, artificial intelligence, town planning, human geography and social anthropology. Ours is not a comprehensive review of all the natural and social sciences. It does, however, capture features of socialization that are common across all these sciences, as well as fundamental differences in the way such disciplines are organized and reproduced. Through our detailed qualitative research in a number of contrasting disciplines (described in more detail in the next chapter) we explore how academics are socialized, and how academic knowledge is replicated in university departments and their research groups. The academy is far from homogeneous. The process of socialization – or enculturation – is not predicated on a single academic culture. There are, of course, common structures and regulations across the higher education sector, and some pressures exist to promote even greater homogeneity. Nonetheless, there are clearly differentiated and persistent subcultures. Individual departments and institutions have their own local folk ways, traditions and arrangements. More powerfully, there are deeply entrenched subcultures associated with different disciplines. A good deal of this book is concerned with this last level of analysis: how young researchers are enculturated into the distinctive academic culture of their discipline.

The distinctiveness of academic cultures has been noted before, of course, both in the popular mythology and fiction of academic life, and in a small but significant corpus of research literature. Becher (1990) aptly characterizes the divisions of the academy in terms of 'academic tribes and territories'. Becher describes the contemporary university – or at least, the modern research-led university – in terms of marked internal diversity. Contrasting disciplinary cultures reflect different disciplinary commitments – in terms of values and definitions of academic knowledge. The increasing specialization of academic knowledge and research practices implies fissiparous tendencies. While commentators such as Fulton (1996) are right to emphasize that there are other dimensions of contrast in the academy – such as sectoral differences and differences of rank within the profession – and that there are important commonalties – such as conditions of service, pay scales and external regulatory mechanisms – the everyday realities of academic staff and students are strongly coloured by local academic cultures or subcultures. We do not seek to over-estimate these cultural differences. The Carnegie Survey of academics in four Western European countries (West Germany, the Netherlands, Sweden and England [sic]) showed that academics emphasize their disciplinary identity more highly than their identity with their department or their institution (Fulton, 1996), but, as Fulton reminds us, 'to say that people identify with their discipline more than with the immediate organizational context is not the same as saying that they are primarily shaped by it' (Fulton, 1996: 163). We will suggest, however, that a separation between academic subculture and organizational context is hard to sustain when subjected to close scrutiny. The everyday realities of academics and apprentice scholars are grounded in social worlds in which academic, disciplinary subcultures and local organizational practices are closely intertwined. Academic cultures do not exist *in vacuo*. There are close affinities between the social organization of research and the reproduction of knowledge.

There is no doubt that doctoral research produces and reproduces not only knowledge, but social identities as well. As Fulton indicates, there is ample evidence from international research that identities are discipline-specific. Doctoral research is a key stage in the socialization process for academics. It is a relatively prolonged process of status passage. Identification with particular academic disciplines crystallizes at different stages for different subjects (as we discuss in a subsequent chapter), but for virtually all academics and would-be academics, the experience of postgraduate research is one in which identity-formation is especially important. For most students, in most disciplines, the enculturation process involves a degree of identification with their chosen academic discipline. The crystallization of such identities, their form and their acquisition, varies from discipline to discipline. Academic subjects and departments require different kinds of badges and shibboleths. The rites of passage and initiation into the respective mysteries are peculiar to different knowledge domains. Disciplines demand different kinds of loyalty. The criteria for membership are different. We shall explore some of the crucial features of academic status-passage, identity and loyalty in the chapters that follow.

In general, there can be little doubt that universities are major organizations in the modern world, which simultaneously produce knowledge and identities. They are knowledge-processing and people-processing institutions, like many other modern institutions, educational and otherwise. The twin processes of discipline and identity-formation have been studied repeatedly in educational institutions at primary and secondary level, but, with some notable exceptions, less thoroughly in further and higher education. The sociology of education as a discipline has been curiously blinkered in the United Kingdom, North America and elsewhere. All too often 'education' is equated with schooling, and schooling itself is often interpreted in terms of mainstream, compulsory schooling. By contrast, the same processes of knowledge production or reproduction, and the formation of social types through processes of enculturation in higher education remain under-explored by sociologists (or anthropologists) of education. There are, as we have indicated already, some notable exceptions, and we discuss them by way of introduction to our own research before going on to introduce the scope and conduct of our own empirical studies.

The Contest of the Faculties

The most sustained sociology or anthropology of academic cultures is contained in the work of Pierre Bourdieu. His analysis focuses exclusively on academics in France, and most of the empirical detail is specific to the institutions of French higher education. His more general perspectives are, however, of wider relevance and our own approach owes much to his general stance. Bourdieu's analysis is grounded in his more general interest – which pervades his sociological work – on principles of classification. Rooted in his early anthropological work in North Africa, Bourdieu's sociology of knowledge – and of educational knowledge in particular – retains a strong structuralist flavour (Jenkins, 1992: 36ff.). Culture is generated out of principles of difference and discrimination. In Bourdieu's general anthropology, the principles of classification operate reflexively: culture classifies and it classifies the classifiers. In other words, the production and reproduction of culture simultaneously reproduce systems of social difference. Despite Bourdieu's own distancing of his work from a purely structuralist standpoint, it is apparent that this aspect of his sociology owes much to the Durkheimian tradition. It has, for instance, clear affinities with Durkheim's collaboration with Mauss on principles of classification among Western societies (Durkheim and Mauss, 1963). They argued for a sociology of knowledge that was fundamentally sociological, proposing clear affinities between cosmology and social structure. The principles of classification that furnish the major axes of culture are, they agreed, the principles of social differentiation.

This Durkheimian perspective flows through into Bourdieu's sociology of knowledge. Repeatedly, he explores the principles through which social differences and classifications relate to the ordering of culture. In the hands of Bourdieu, this analysis is not based on purely static structuralist displays of homologies and oppositions. The classificatory principles are enacted through the local organization and everyday practices of social institutions. The academy is one set of such organizations, supremely preoccupied with the classificatory ordering of knowledge and culture. The academy is, moreover, equally preoccupied with principles of hierarchy and the differential distribution of status. The classificatory principles that generate culture do not merely demarcate a 'flat' domain of differences and categories. Culture is differentially situated and legitimated. Its logic is one that grants different degrees of legitimacy to different kinds of cultural practices and artefacts. It 'consecrates' some cultural domains, while treating others as essentially profane. Such a distinction again recapitulates a Durkheimian frame of reference. The categories of culture – most notably 'high' Culture in the sense of legitimated and consecrated fields – are thus dependent on systems of differentiation and hierarchical ordering.

Of nothing is this more true than of the academy. Homo academicus (the eponymous character of Bourdieu's most sustained treatment) is supremely

Cultures of the Academy

a classificatory being. Academic knowledge – and 'high' Culture – are especially concerned with activities of discrimination. Specialized, esoteric knowledge and taste are predicated on collective and individual competencies to operate with the socially defined principles of differentiation. The rhetoric and connotations of 'discrimination' (another of Bourdieu's titles) capture the general issues. Discrimination implies two things simultaneously. It refers to the capacity to *differentiate* – to classify – and to be *discriminating* – the competence to apply cultural conventions. A third connotation of discrimination – that of social exclusion – further evokes the key notion of social sorting and differentiation. Institutions of esoteric knowledge and culture are pre-eminently concerned with mechanisms for discrimination.

Bourdieu's account of the cultural distinctions between French academics is concerned with their social background, and their cultural and political preferences, as well as their disciplinary and institutional affiliations (Bourdieu, 1988). He contrasts two bases for the legitimacy of academics: the domain of 'pure' scientific research, and engagement with temporal power outside the academy. He compares and contrasts law, medicine, arts, social science and science. He suggests that the conflict of the faculties is an expression of social class differences – grounded in differences in the social origins and cultural capital between different faculty members. More pertinently for the subject-matter of this book, Bourdieu also considers the processes whereby bodies of knowledge are reproduced through training and recruitment. For instance, with regard to those faculties that are 'dominant in the political order' Bourdieu writes that they have

> the function of training executive agents able to put into practice without questioning or doubting, within the limits of a given social order, the techniques and recipes of a body of knowledge which they claim neither to produce nor to transform; on the contrary, the faculties which are dominant in the cultural order are destined to arrogate to themselves, in their need to establish a rational basis for the knowledge which the other faculties simply inculcate and apply, a freedom which is withheld from executive activities, however expectable these are in the temporal order of practice.
>
> (Bourdieu, 1988: 63)

For all disciplines,

> the surest guarantee of academic order, inextricably social and scientific, doubtless lies in the complex mechanisms whereby promotion towards the summit of the temporally dominant institutions goes hand in hand with progress in academic initiation, masked, in the case of the medical faculties, by successive competitive examinations ... or, in the case of the arts faculties, by the long wait for the doctorate, that is, in both cases, by

Cultures of the Academy

an enforced prolongation of the dispositions which have been acknowledged through the primitive procedures of co-operation, and which hardly encourage heretical breaks with the artfully intertwined knowledge and power of academic orthodoxy.

(Bourdieu, 1988: 105)

It is essentially with aspects of this power that we are concerned. As Bourdieu himself notes elsewhere in *Homo Academicus*, academic life and culture are dependent on the investment of time. The processes of socialization are lengthy. Academics and would-be academics invest time in the acquisition of their cultural (intellectual) capital. The period of doctoral research is one major investment of that sort. The novice or apprentice scholar commits a considerable period of time to the acquisition of the doctorate, and to the acquisition of the competencies peculiar to his or her discipline.

One overall theme of Bourdieu's work is the extent to which 'the faculties' reflect and reproduce specific forms of 'habitus'; that is, habitual patterns of disposition and practice that generate and constitute cultural forms and values. Through our detailed studies of selected academic disciplines, we seek to explore some key features of the distinctive habitus that produces these disciplines and their distinctive, contrasting modes of enculturation and reproduction. Our focus is more narrow than that of Bourdieu himself. As we have acknowledged, he is interested in the relationships between academic authority and temporal power, in the relations between inherited social capital and the acquisition of academic capital. Equally, as we have also suggested, Bourdieu's analysis is weakened by his inattention to the institutional and organizational practices whereby academic culture is enacted. Our analysis focuses on that specific level of social organization. We explore how the distinctive habitus of a given discipline is reproduced through the social organization of doctoral research. What is of importance in Bourdieu's anthropology of the academy is the strong sense he conveys and documents of the differentiation of its cultures, and the recurrent competition for legitimacy. His sense of 'distinction' helps to capture the structures and processes of differentiation together with the academic quest for honour within the university's system of rewards and recognition.

Classification and Identity

Bourdieu is by no means the only author to have drawn attention to the classificatory principles that generate academic or educational knowledge. Bernstein's sociology of educational knowledge and pedagogic discourse draws on the intellectual origins similar to those of Bourdieu (Bernstein, 1975). Mediated in part through the work of anglophone scholars such as Mary Douglas, Bernstein draws on the Durkheimian tradition in order to expose how academic knowledge is ordered, and how that ordering projects and distributes social identities of students and teachers (Atkinson, 1985, 1995).

Much of Bernstein's work has been developed in relation to schooling in the UK and beyond, but its general application is relevant to a wide variety of educational and other organizational settings. At the heart of his classic analysis of educational knowledge are the paired ideas of classification and framing. These complementary analytic ideas are both about the relative strength of boundary, but are also used to exercise control over the contents and delivery of educational knowledge. Classification operates at the level of content – the subject-matter of education. Framing refers to the mode of transmission – to pedagogy and the organization of the educational encounter. When classification is strong, then the contents of educational knowledge are delineated and represented by clear symbolic membranes. Knowledge is typically organized in terms of discrete domains, which may correspond to traditionally labelled 'subjects' (maths, physics, chemistry, history, English, etc.). When classification is weak, then knowledge is ordered with reference to different principles, whereby boundaries between content are weaker and more flexible. Such ordering principles may reflect systems of integration rather than separation (such as integrated humanities, area studies, history of ideas). When framing is strong, then there are clearly imposed boundaries and frameworks circumscribing pedagogy. The ordering, pacing and selection of educational knowledge will be structured and prescribed – either by externally imposed prescription or by the exercise of control by the teacher(s). When framing is weaker, then the pedagogic encounter is more flexible, more negotiable and subject to more local, emergent ordering.

These principles – classification in particular – have significant consequences for the production and distribution of academic identities, and the modes of identification and knowledge domains. When there are strongly classified and demonstrated academic subjects, then that subject-matter – the 'discipline' – becomes the main *raison d'être* of academic socialization in its own right. The learner is gradually initiated into its 'mysteries'. The subject itself may be introduced by means of various kinds of 'recapitulation' – the history of the subject, demonstrations of key experiments, the mapping of key ideas, schools, authors – through which the subject itself is reassembled. (Of course, no educational mapping provides a comprehensive account, even in its own terms; such recapitulations are always selective.) By contrast, under conditions of weak classification, 'subjects' are subordinated to superordinate conceptual justifications, such as 'the scientific method'.

These modes of organization have direct implications for the production of loyalty and identification. Under conditions of strong classification and the separation of subject domains, the educational identities of members of organizations such as schools, colleges and universities become closely tied

Cultures of the Academy

to the discipline itself. Organizations that are structured along clear disciplinary lines encourage loyalty to a chosen subject. This is an organizational culture in which the academic department – associated with a discipline and a disciplinary culture – becomes the main source of identity for students and staff alike.

Although Bernstein's original analysis concentrates on schooling, and changes in the organization of schools and school knowledge, his general perspective is applicable to the institutions and practices of higher education as well. It is especially applicable to our own work on doctoral research. Together with Bourdieu, Bernstein's analytic framework draws attention to the different – sometimes competing – definitions and principles that generate the partition of the academics field. Both draw attention to the ordering principles of differentiation. Each, in different ways, stresses the fact that the academic division of labour reproduces different social identities and types. Each discipline reproduces a distinctive habitus. Under conditions of specialization, identities and subcultures may diverge markedly. Both authors stress that – in highly bounded domains especially – the apprenticeship process is long. There is a protracted process – a series of rites of passage – whereby the novice is progressively admitted into the ranks of the initiated. There is a long process of enculturation during which key features of habitus are acquired.

This is not, for doctoral students, a generalized socialization into a single 'profession'. The academic world is not organized in those terms. He or she may, of course, acquire general experience and skills relating to the politics and procedures of academic life, but these are far less significant than the intellectual competencies and practices that are much more specific to his or her own discipline, and that are grounded in his or her own research activities. In so far as there is an 'academic profession', it is, as Fulton (1996) points out, a highly divergent one.

Professions and Socialization

While the sociology of higher education has paid relatively little attention to the everyday realities of students and their teachers, and the sociology of education in general has paid scant attention to higher education, there is a significant corpus of research literature that is relevant to both domains. It is, however, all too often treated in isolation from both. We refer to the long tradition of sociological work on 'professional socialization'. Often regarded as grounded in the sociology of work and occupations, or the study of organizational life, a great deal of research on professions and their recruits is germane to our interests here. The research has been reviewed and commented on repeatedly, and it is not necessary to recapitulate here in any detail. A number of significant issues should, however, be highlighted.

One of the most consistent perspectives to be found in the research litera-

Cultures of the Academy

ture concerns 'situational learning'. This perspective – associated originally with the Chicago-school studies influenced by Everett Hughes and his colleagues – shows that occupational socialization is not a smooth transition from novice to full-fledged practitioner. Socialization is not a simple transmission of knowledge or values from one generation to the next. Socialization is not, therefore, portrayed in terms of a straightforward incorporation into a fixed body of professional knowledge and practices. In studies of occupations as diverse as medicine and hairdressing, such perspectives have emphasized the extent to which students and other novices need to cope with the everyday realities of being a student. Rather than a simple homology between the knowledge and understandings of established practitioners and their students, this view emphasizes possible disjunctures between the two. The everyday coping strategies of occupational novices, who are often faced with very considerable demands on their time, effort and intellectual resources, may even seem counter to the stated aims and values of senior academics and practitioners. In other words, professional and occupational students, faced with common and recurrent problems, may generate their own subcultural responses. While not necessarily oppositional in form, such subcultures generate strategies whereby students can 'get by'.

One element of such situational adaptation consists of what has been called 'learning the ropes'. That is, students' effort must go into understanding local, organizational routines and requirements, if they are to cope and thrive as medical students or interns, law students, military recruits and so on. From this point of view, then, there emerges a 'hidden curriculum' of everyday practices and perspectives. Students' status passages are actively produced and negotiated. Their practical understandings and perspectives interact with the formal requirements of curriculum and assessment.

One major criticism that we have made about much of the work in this area – especially in its formative years – is its relative neglect of knowledge-acquisition. The early sociological research on professional socialization, for instance, was so concerned to demonstrate the possible disjunctures between 'formal' professional knowledge and informal, situational learning of novices that it failed to address how characteristic modes of knowledge-acquisition and use are actually transmitted in socialization settings (Delamont and Atkinson, 1990). An emphasis on organizational learning tended to strip out any systematic examination of how professional or educational knowledge is transmitted and transformed – either through the manifest curriculum of instruction or through the hidden curriculum of local organization and everyday coping mechanisms. It is, therefore, important that we grasp how the cultures of the academy combine both facets. We must understand how academic cultures and organizational arrangements define and produce the esoteric knowledge that is their *raison d'être*. Equally, we must understand that the practical realities of academic socialization do not rest on the smooth transmission of knowledge independently of the practical and organizational contexts of everyday work in the academy.

There is a field in which the 'great traditions' of academic disciplines intersect with the 'little traditions' of academic departments and research groups, and where encounters between academics and their students are enacted. This is especially true of doctoral research. The doctoral student is engaged directly with the esoteric knowledge of the discipline, often in ways quite different from his or her work as an undergraduate or Masters candidate. Original doctoral research engages directly with the production and reproduction of academic knowledge. Equally, the doctoral student must cope with the practical requirements imposed by his or her supervisor: as a relative novice in an academic department or research group, needing to meet the specific requirements of the doctoral process itself. We have seen that the academy is characterized by different, even competing, domains, each with a distinctive academic habitus. There exist important institutional contexts within which academic work is organized and through which academic work is done. The work of the doctoral student is a significant and integral part of the process whereby the great traditions and the little traditions are engaged with one another.

The Social Organization of Scientific Knowledge

The sociology of knowledge and its reproduction has been addressed most consistently by scholars working on the sociology of scientific knowledge (SSK). The social organization and the exclusive cultures of science provide one of the best documented means for a more general sociology of the academy. Again, we do not attempt to provide a systematic review of this area, but to indicate a number of key themes most relevant to the subject-matter of this book. Sociologists of scientific work and scientific knowledge have repeatedly demonstrated the thoroughly social character of scientific knowledge. The cognitive cannot be devised from the social and cultural contexts in which scientific research is pursued. Scientific research is a collective enterprise. However, the processes and products of scientific work are social. Scientific knowledge is socially produced, while the core assumptions and methods of scientific work are socially shared.

Studies of laboratory life have, for instance, documented the social contexts of discovery work. As Knorr-Cetina (1995) notes, such studies – socially ethnographic in character and conduct – have shown that 'scientific objects are not only "technically" manufactured in laboratories, but also inextricably *symbolically* and *politically construed*' (143). She goes on to say that:

> Another implication is that the products of science themselves have come to be seen as cultural entities rather than as natural givens 'discov-

ered' by science. If the practices observed in laboratories were 'cultural' in the sense that they could not be reduced to the application of methodological rules, the 'facts' that were the consequence of these practices also had to be seen as shaped by culture.

(Knorr-Cetina, 1995: 143)

From this standpoint, the laboratory is not merely an organizational setting for work. Knorr-Cetina suggests that the 'laboratory' itself is a significant agent in the production of scientific knowledge. Laboratories are themselves transformative. In the laboratory, natural objects or processes and human agents (scientists) are reconfigured through specific forms of scientific practice.

The laboratory is an arena for enculturation. The craft knowledge and skills that inform the conduct of scientific research are locally produced and reproduced. As Collins (1985: 55) summarizes it, 'only those scientists who spent some time in the laboratory where the success has been achieved prove capable of successfully building their own version of the laser'. The production of scientific knowledge through the construction of equipment and the design of experiments that 'work' is dependent on tacit knowledge acquired through enculturation into the practices of the laboratory. Groupings and networks of social actors who share common frameworks of understanding and assumption are crucial to the construction of scientific knowledge and the propagation of common practices. The development of consensus, stability and confidence are dependent on the mobilization of networks and 'core sets' of experimentalists and others (Collins, 1985; Pinch, 1986). The research group is one local manifestation of such social relations and organization. Like the 'laboratory', the research group is a social mechanism for the simultaneous enculturation of scientists, physical resources and research problems. Calibration is not restricted to the manipulation of instruments in the research laboratory. Actors are calibrated through enculturation processes and the assimilation of tacit knowledge and skills.

Traweek's (1988) ethnography of high energy physicists provides a telling account of the cultural contexts in which research is conducted. On the basis of cross-cultural comparisons, she shows that there is no single culture of high energy physics, but that in different contexts (USA and Japan) there are contrasting cultures, with contrasting modes of social organization, leadership styles, and assumptions governing scientific work. Traweek's monograph is an outstanding example of research documenting the local production of scientific culture. In a similar vein, Knorr-Cetina (1999) documents disciplinary differences in scientific culture. Knorr-Cetina is one of the few authors in this field to have paid explicit attention to the role of doctoral students in the laboratory. She emphasizes the relative diversity of the sciences with respect to their methods and mechanisms of fact construction. She refers to the production of 'epistemic cultures'.

Cultures of the Academy

Considering the considerable emphasis placed on the social bases of knowledge production in science, and the place of groups, networks and laboratories in the transmission of knowledge, it is surprising that so little attention has been paid to the socialization of scientists through mechanisms such as doctoral research. The simultaneous socialization and calibration of problems, technologies and actors would seem to invite close attention to the processes of formal training, situational learning and assessment that are characteristic of postgraduate research. While one could not seek to commit the genetic fallacy – of assuming one can understand 'science' merely by studying how actors 'become' scientists – the general neglect of novice scientists remains striking. The clear bias in the sociology of scientific knowledge towards scientific discovery and controversy (for all its scepticism concerning 'discovery') has meant that a great deal of mundane scientific work remains under-represented in the sociological literature. This includes the ordinary work of service laboratories as well as the routine work of 'normal' science that goes on in very many laboratories in universities and elsewhere throughout the world.

Hacking (1992) is one of the few commentators on scientific knowledge to have paid attention to general issues of socialization. His particular interest is in the social production of stability in scientific disciplines. In common with others, Hacking argues that scientific work is constructed from a number of different elements, including the social, the material and the conceptual. Scientific work involves the mutual adjustments of these elements. Hacking suggests that scientific stability is maintained because scientific practice is like a rope with many strands. Even if one of the strands is severed, others survive. Science encompasses several traditions, including the theoretical, experimental and instrumental – a rupture in one is not necessarily fatal for the others (cf. Galison, 1987). Moreover, Hacking also suggests that many sciences are 'pedagogically stable': 'We have geometrical optics when young, the wave theory as teenagers, Maxwell's equations on entering college, some theory of the photon in senior classes, and quantum field theory in graduate school' (Hacking, 1992: 39)

Through the stability of pedagogical practice and pedagogical knowledge, taken-for-granted forms and contents of scientific thought are transmitted from generation to generation. Clearly, the enculturation of scientists into the other skills, problems and assumptions of a local research group through doctoral research is a key stage in that process of inter-generational transmission.

The sociology of scientific knowledge and practice thus provides us with key exemplification of academic cultures. The general sociology of science has repeatedly documented the social processes through which specialized knowledge is produced. Equally, specific studies have shown the disciplinary and institutional differences between institutions and cultures. Social networks, research groups and laboratories create social contexts throughout

Cultures of the Academy

which core assumptions and tacit knowledge are produced and reproduced. Doctoral research and doctoral students play a key role in such mechanisms of reproduction. Simultaneously, such students are themselves socialized into the forms of knowledge, practice and social relations that constitute disciplines, departments and research groups.

Disciplines

Hitherto we have referred to academic disciplines. We do not intend to convey that they somehow exist independently of the cultural and institutional frameworks of the academy (or elsewhere). As authors such as Bourdieu and Bernstein forcibly remind us, the symbolic boundaries that define these disciplines are culturally arbitrary. The demarcation of subject domains is itself a major product of academic culture. The cultural or subcultural differences between disciplines are constantly being reproduced and reaffirmed through the everyday work and the shared assumptions of actors in the academy. Although the array of academic disciplines is a matter of convention rather than a reflection of an inherent order, there is a quite remarkable degree of consensus and stability. Universities, learned societies, funding bodies and other agencies consistently deal with disciplinary arrangements that are broadly congruent across nations, educational sectors and the like. Disciplines are not immutable. They rise and fall. By no means all scholarship and research is confined within traditional disciplinary boundaries: contemporary policy and practice consistently promote the virtues of interdisciplinary research, multidisciplinary research teams and the like.

The social reality of disciplines is produced through a variety of arrangements. As we have acknowledged already, the academic department is normally the main unit of organization and is usually the main source of professional identity for academics. Departments are organized primarily on disciplinary lines, although the fashion in the UK for large organizational units often results in groupings that incorporate more than one discipline. Disciplines mean more than just particular subjects. They incorporate a variety of cultural elements: traditions, folk heroes and heroines, myths, key examples, 'sacred' texts, centres of excellence, scandals, cycles of fashion. Members map the internal topography of their discipline in terms of key individuals, locations and texts. They recognize genealogies of influence and inheritance. Each discipline implies its own cultural capital. The competent member will acquire the ability to trade in the cultural goods that are the discipline's stock-in-trade. As Bourdieu and others remind us, the acquisition of cultural capital in academic disciplines is a lengthy process. It is not usually something that can be inherited suddenly. Lengthy apprenticeship is normally a prerequisite for the cultural learning a discipline implies.

Discipline, of course, carries multiple connotations. It means, in broad terms, a field of academic specialization. It also carries implications of the proper conduct of that academic work. In common with more general usages of 'discipline', it suggests that the novice and the initiated must submit themselves to the rigours and demands that are the price of full membership. Discipline, in this sense, reflects the same kinds of regimes of control that constitute discipline more generally. Academic commitment thus implies a disciplined self and a disciplined mentality. The self is disciplined through the investment of time and effort. The apprentice is time-served, the convict does his or her time, and the would-be academic must also put in the time. The pressures of time are great. The individual's commitment of time is not open-ended. Pressure to complete work to meet externally imposed deadlines is ever present. This applies from the everyday work of the undergraduate onwards, and it is especially acute for the research student. The academic and the academic novice alike are *disciplined* by the temporal frameworks of the academy. The relevant timetables are, moreover, discipline-specific. Academics' individual and collective research timetables are, for example, quite different in a laboratory subject like biochemistry (the main focus of Chapter 4) and a field social science such as anthropology (the main topic in Chapter 5). While universities and funding bodies (such as the UK Research Councils and Higher Education Funding Councils) assume and enforce common time frames, the temporal ordering of the research process varies from discipline to discipline. For the laboratory scientist, the research process is cumulative over time, with a day-to-day engagement with research problems, equipment and colleagues in the laboratory. For the anthropologist, the research process includes a one-off commitment to 'the field', which may last as long as eighteen or twenty-odd months. Likewise, the two disciplines project different futures for their respective novices (we return to this in Chapter 8).

The assumptions that underpin research, that constitute 'the discipline', differ markedly. The novice researcher is socialized through the disciplinary constraints of what constitutes appropriate kinds of research problems. Self-evidently, a researcher in biochemistry should tackle a biochemical problem, and a physical geographer should be preoccupied with research in geography. But the definition of what 'counts' as an appropriate kind of research problem, and the kind of activity that implies – these can be strikingly different across the disciplines. If the definition of research problems (what is sufficiently original, what is doable, what is feasible) varies between disciplines, so too does a generalized notion of doctoral research. Disciplines constrain their novices to undertake research that is proper to the discipline they have chosen. We are familiar with the notion of a *paradigm*, as originally formulated by Thomas Kuhn and subsequently incorporated into the history, philosophy and sociology of science (and indeed into more general discourse about science and the academy). A paradigm, in this sense, consists of a package of problems, techniques and examples that frame orthodox opinion in a given research field at a particular time. Disciplines are thus constituted out of the prevailing paradigms. Paradigms demand allegiance. There is a strong element of faith in the promotion of paradigmatic disciplinary knowledge. For the novice – such as a doctoral candidate – the socialization process often depends on the confirmation of an act of faith and personal commitment through the successful enactment of research.

Kuhn himself pointed out that in the process of scientific work there is a constant and – in his terms – essential tension between two tendencies. On the one hand, there is the reaffirmation of paradigmatic, orthodox knowledge. As Hacking's observations on pedagogic stability also emphasize, science depends on the repeated reaffirmation of established and taken-for-granted knowledge. On the other hand, there is a constant imperative for the scientist to innovate and to discover. Discovery must, however, always be accomplished and evaluated against a background of established knowledge. Tradition and innovation are mutually implicative (this is the central theme of Chapter 8).

The essential tension is by no means confined to the laboratory sciences. All disciplines reflect it. None is content merely to recapitulate the received wisdom of earlier generations, and researchers – including doctoral students – are required to achieve originality and innovation in their work. What *counts* as originality, however, is discipline-specific. Likewise, the degree of innovation that is tolerated is likely to be both discipline-related and more locally negotiated. The frameworks of disciplinary knowledge thus inscribe the Kuhnian essential tension. They prescribe certain kinds of knowledge and practice, and simultaneously proscribe others. They set the external boundaries – of what counts as appropriate disciplinary research – and the internal boundaries – of how problems shall be formulated, how inquiry shall be conducted, how success shall be evaluated.

Disciplines – like mechanisms of power more generally – do not only constrain knowledge and practice. They are *productive*. They do not only eliminate what is unthinkable, they also make possible what is thinkable and 'doable' (Fujimura, 1997). Disciplines and their paradigms thus furnish academics and researchers with 'doable' research projects and programmes. They permit individual researchers and research groups to project their own work into wider frames of reference and significance. They link the past, present and future of research in the construction of traditions, schools of thought, research programmes and so on. The form and content of such conformities are discipline-specific.

Disciplines are defined by particular ways of knowing. They are epistemic collectives. They have their own epistemological styles of thought, their own characteristic modes of discourse and their own modes of social organization. They do not constrain their members to such an extent that change or heterodox beliefs are not possible. The relative stability and conformity of a laboratory science, or a discipline like social anthropology does not preclude individual or collective innovation. But innovation, even rebellion, in the academy takes place against a background of taken-for-granted ideas, orthodoxies and traditions. In some disciplines – especially but not exclusively among humanities and social sciences – the avant garde is itself individualized, and constitutes an orthodox tradition in its own right. If our own analysis emphasizes continuity and stability in the disciplines, then, it is not because we adopt an essentially functionalist view of order, but because we recognize that cultural continuity is a prerequisite for recognizable innovation. Moreover, the overwhelming majority of the research students and academic supervisors we worked with were committed to working within well-defined disciplinary boundaries.

The remainder of this book is, therefore, about the cultures and the cultural reproduction of academic disciplines. It is more than an account of how postgraduate students cope or fail in the course of their doctoral research, or how their academic supervisors account for the characteristics of graduate work. It is really about how the tacit knowledge and cultural forms of academic knowledge shape the identities of academics themselves. From this point of view, then, one may think of academic disciplines and departments as 'social worlds' (Clarke, 1998) that generate and are sustained by distinctive folk ways. They are far from static: disciplines and specialisms wax and wane. They can be collectively mobile in the hierarchy of prestige and status within the community. They can become fashionable at one time only to become obscure once more. In the rest of this book we are not concerned primarily with those dynamic aspects of discipline-formation and disciplinary mobility, important though those issues are (Abir-Am, 1982). We are forced to present a snapshot of the disciplines and departments when we studied them. We are, however, able to offer one of the few accounts of academic cultures based on the systematic sociological study of academics and their everyday social worlds.

2 Researching our Peers

> We are aware of the obstacles to scientific knowledge constituted by excessive proximity as by excessive remoteness.
>
> (Bourdieu, 1988: 1)

Research on doctoral students and their academic supervisors necessarily involved us in studying our own peers in the academy. Academics are all familiar with peer review of research and publications, but they are much less familiar with studying one another, or with being studied. Research in universities is not always easy: studying one's own peers, members of the same profession, is not straightforward. Difficulties – practical, theoretical and political – can arise from the tensions between strangeness and familiarity in research sites, and from the tensions that arise from transgressing disciplinary boundaries. When Bourdieu writes of 'excessive proximity' he alerts us to one of the central ambiguities that we faced in conducting the fieldwork on academic socialization. Studying our peers, especially about a key aspect of academic policy such as higher degree supervision, can often be problematic. We should not, however, assume that we enjoy equal 'proximity' to all our fellow academics, or that proximity can be treated as a single dimension. There are many sources of proximity or distance and they are not coterminous. In this chapter we explore some of the key dimensions that informed our research. (The more mundane account of the data collection is given in Appendix 1, in which we outline the extent of our field research and its practical conduct.) We begin by discussing our fellow academics. We introduce the research experience with some brief vignettes that capture some aspects of our research negotiations and relationships. We present them in order to draw out more analytic themes for this chapter. Our main, overarching theme is an exploration of the tensions between Bourdieu's 'excessive proximity' and 'excessive remoteness', as enacted in the field of doctoral research.

The Masonbridge campus is best visited in summer, when its 1960s pastoral style is seen at its best. The trees have matured since it was first built, softening the visual starkness of its academic and administrative

Researching our Peers

buildings. In winter they still cannot prevent the cold winds from sweeping across the campus. The footpaths and walkways become slippery, and on cold days like today they are icy. The unwary visitor can fall in an undignified heap while searching for a way into the building. On a bitterly cold December day, when the undergraduates had all gone home for Christmas, Paul Atkinson tramped across the campus from the bus stop to interview Professor Hurrell, the head of the Anthropology department. He was not apprehensive about the interview. Odette had established working relations with members of the department, and data collection from staff and graduate students at Masonbridge was completed. This was to be more of a courtesy visit to round off our presence at this research site – it was not an access interview – and Paul's biography overlapped with Professor Hurrell's enough for him to expect a useful session. He only got lost temporarily. It seems an inevitable fact of academic life that all universities are inadequately or confusingly signposted (if at all) – at least one wrong turning seems unavoidable, and porters' lodges are always located elsewhere.

Having found him, in the event, Paul had a constructive interview with Professor Hurrell. They discussed various aspects of the research on postgraduate training in the social sciences, and in anthropology in particular. Professor Hurrell was especially explicit about his own discipline's history of suspicion about the training of research students. The ESRC's guidelines and requirements for postgraduate training had been greeted especially negatively by anthropologists in the United Kingdom. Professor Hurrell reflected on how anthropology's insistence on the personal, tacit knowledge of the anthropologist was at odds with the contemporary culture for explicit training in research methods. He explained some of the characteristic paradoxes and tensions within anthropology. It is a small discipline, he said, with strong personal networks between its practitioners. It is at once highly cohesive and internally riven. Anthropologists have traditionally operated with a consensus about the essential features of their shared discipline. They have also fought out bitter feuds and rivalries among themselves. These two aspects of the discipline are entirely compatible: the academics are able to engage in internecine dispute precisely because they have a strong collective identity. There has always been strong agreement about certain taken-forgranted fundamentals about anthropology and anthropological knowledge, and this provides the backdrop for more arcane disputation. In particular, the shared identity of anthropologists rests on the experience of 'fieldwork', usually in a culture overseas. From the experience of fieldwork, and from the unique knowledge that it yields, is derived the anthropologist's authority. That personal authority remains unchallenged even when anthropologists disagree about particular theoretical perspectives and specific interpretations. This unique authority also justifies anthropologists' own sense of collective identity and their sense of difference from other academic disciplines. Professor Hurrell also suggested, however, that in recent years, the authority of the anthropologist's knowledge had been radically questioned and undermined. Epistemological debates had shaken the foundations of modern anthropological fieldwork and the production of anthropological knowledge. Hurrell became particularly forthcoming about the literary turn or crisis of representation in social anthropology. This was a paradigm shift with significant consequences for the conduct and reporting of research. The traditional repository of anthropological knowledge – the ethnographic monograph – and its conventional modes of representing another culture had come into question. The consequence had been, in some quarters at least, a crisis in anthropology more fundamental and more threatening than any passing disputes (about structuralist or marxist analyses, for instance) had ever been. The 'interview' became a collegial discussion about the discipline of anthropology and its recent intellectual history. It was based on shared knowledge about the social sciences and the politics of academic knowledge.

The trip to Masonbridge and the amicable conversation with Professor Hurrell serves to introduce a number of themes that ran through our research, and that appear in various guises in this book. Notwithstanding the number and diversity of universities in the United Kingdom, British circles are quite small. Paul had been acquainted with Professor Hurrell for many years, and they had many academic acquaintances in common. Paul had a first degree in social anthropology, and was familiar at first hand with many of the intellectual issues that Hurrell talked about. Moreover, he had written about very similar issues concerning the textual representation of ethnographic work – from a sociological rather than a specifically anthropological background. The conversation at Masonbridge was a meeting of equals, covering a good deal of common academic ground. In contrast, Masonbridge University itself is quite unlike our 'home' territory of Cardiff. A campus, 'plate-glass' university, it organizes itself very differently from our own institution, and has very different kinds of style and ethos. Local arrangements have significant consequences for the organization of departments and faculties, and for the training and supervision of postgraduate students. While the general features of social anthropology were very familiar, therefore, its local manifestations were not. As a result, familiarity and unfamiliarity were mixed for Paul in his encounter with Professor Hurrell. In particular, he could recognize the generic features of the discipline and its intellectual preoccupations without quite sharing or endorsing British social anthropologists' sense of exclusivity.

On the other hand, the anthropologists' concern with the foundations of fieldwork created the possibility for an uneasy tension in our own fieldwork. Social anthropologists were – in that regard – the least likely of our hosts to regard sociological field research as unproblematic. In a different department of social anthropology, for instance, Odette Parry and Paul Atkinson attended a meeting with all members of the academic staff. This meeting

Researching our Peers

was part of our 'access' negotiations. The head of the department had given his general blessing for our research to take place in the department, but had – quite properly – made it conditional on the approval of his academic colleagues. We had agreed to talk to a staff meeting. When Odette and Paul presented themselves, they were closely grilled about their epistemological, theoretical and methodological positions. These anthropologists, not surprisingly, shared our preference for detailed ethnographic studies and were reluctant to condone research based primarily on interviews. This was less like a normal 'access' meeting with potential research hosts, and more like a *viva voce* examination conducted by a dozen or so examiners. These social anthropologists took a lively interest in the theoretical and epistemological foundations of the proposed research. They explicitly contrasted our own sociological perspectives with their own anthropological approaches – and in some cases were openly contemptuous of our preferences. Having grilled us and subjected us to a version of a degradation ceremonial, they granted us access. Indeed, they were mostly accommodating and helpful. But their own disciplinary interest in social research and its conduct gave them an entirely legitimate interest in our proposed research. To some extent too, this open grilling by the entire department staff reflected something of the departmental and disciplinary culture of that group of social anthropologists. As we discovered, they subjected their own graduate students to similarly rigorous, sometimes stressful, examinations and disputations.

The proximity of our disciplinary interests and backgrounds here made for a much closer and more critical scrutiny of research methods, theories and epistemology than the majority of field researchers expect from their actual and potential hosts. For Paul, it came as little surprise. He was used to anthropologists' disputatious culture, and to their somewhat peevish attitude towards sociologists. Many anthropologists still cling to the idea that sociologists only conduct surveys, while anthropology enjoys a monopoly over techniques such as participant observation. They can, therefore, get especially tetchy when faced with sociologists conducting qualitative research. In our own access negotiations, therefore, we appeared to be proposing a double encroachment – studying them and their students, using their own techniques. It was little wonder that they subjected us to an inquisitorial hearing. For Odette, however, it was very novel. Her own training had been in sociology at Cardiff, which does not have an anthropology department. The culture of anthropologists was a 'strange' one for her. The self-presentations of the anthropologists were new. She would become fascinated by social anthropology as the research progressed, precisely because of its mix of familiarity and strangeness.

Many of our hosts and informants were wary of us. Typically, we would be carefully screened for technical competence and ethical responsibility. Our potential hosts were rarely directly hostile to us, but they were cautious and careful. It was, for example, a hot day in September. Paul Atkinson and

Researching our Peers

Odette Parry were ushered into a small, scruffy seminar room, with the sunlight playing on the film of chalk dust. Posters were curling up on the notice boards. The blackboard had a half-erased announcement about 'Exam Revision', apparently left over from June. Five men and one woman sat in the room – about half the geography staff at Boarbridge University. They were not hostile, but they were wary. We wanted their permission and co-operation in interviewing the academic staff in Human Geography and their PhD students. They wanted to find out what we were like: Could they trust us? What did we really want?

They were by no means unfamiliar with our own interests in qualitative research: they themselves had run a research group that used ethnographic and similar approaches to the cultural analysis of spaces and landscapes. They were, however, edgy with regard to our more general research agenda. They thought of themselves as among the elite in their discipline; Boarbridge itself is a high-status institution, located within the metropolitan 'golden triangle' of English institutions. At least some of the senior staff among the geographers felt bruised by the Research Council's policy concerning research students and their training. They seemed to feel that the implicit criteria of excellence and the elite apprenticeship their students enjoyed were being undermined by the imposition of more formal training requirements. They also felt that the Research Council was the tail wagging the dog: they had many more students than were funded by the Research Council, yet the latter was felt to be imposing its own requirements across the sector as a whole. Odette and Paul were thus subjected to cross-questioning about their own position vis-à-vis the Research Council. They were funding our research, and were also promoting the most far-reaching innovations in research-student training. Paul and Odette had to offer clear and repeated assurances that although the specific project was obviously initiated as a response to policy changes, our research was fundamental in nature, and was not intended to promote the short-term policy interests of the Research Council. Equally – and just as importantly – we had to reassure them that our own research project was not a surrogate departmental evaluation. We had to offer clear reassurances concerning the anonymity of the department and its members, and the confidentiality of the information we would be gathering. Here our own perceived proximity to the policy-makers created a potential problem, and we had to work at distancing ourselves from them. To some extent the elite character of Boarbridge constructed a particular kind of relationship between the researchers and the researched. We felt that we approached our potential hosts as equals, and they were certainly not trying to impose some sort of snobbish superiority over us. But their own sense of institutional status and esteem affected their initial attitudes towards our research. In the event, they granted us access to their department, and – like all the academics we approached – were highly helpful and co-operative.

The easy assumption of elite status in the discipline, and location within an institution that enjoyed high prestige gave the Boarbridge geographers a particular set of perspectives on their graduate students and their apprenticeship. This stood in sharp contrast with the kind of access negotiations we experienced in Urban Studies at Chelmsworth University, which had been a very successful polytechnic, and was now one of the new universities with a considerable track record of success. Its history did mean, however, that it had considerable experience in dealing with the old Council for National Academic Awards (CNAA). The CNAA had for a long time operated on the basis of documentation and administrative detail that were alien to the older universities. The old polytechnics were accustomed to spelling out their policies and practices explicitly; the culture was at variance with the tacit, implicit criteria that were taken for granted at places such as Boarbridge – and, indeed, Cardiff at the time. It was, therefore, characteristic of our access interview with the head of Urban Studies at Chelmsworth that he should structure a good deal of his account of his department and their graduate provision in terms of documentation – descriptions of modular programmes of research training and the record of their validation, annual scheme review and so on. In the past few years this approach to academic provision has become much more widespread. It is certainly no longer confined to the new universities. As part of a tradition and an institutional ethos, however, it was very distant from our own institutional culture, and was far removed from that at a university such as Boarbridge. The head of department was not wary of us. Indeed, he seemed very secure in the achievements and symbols of his own institution and the disciplinary culture of a professionally oriented department concerned primarily with town planning.

We have already alluded to Bourdieu's contrast between proximity and remoteness. It relates in turn to our own reflections on familiarity and strangeness in educational and other social research (Delamont and Atkinson, 1995). We have illustrated some of these in the brief examples we have already offered. Rather than being a simple dichotomy, differences of strangeness or proximity must be understood to have several key dimensions in relation to our own research. They include differences and commonalities that are geographical, institutional, disciplinary, methodological, epistemological, personal and experiential.

As we attempted to undertake data collection in universities in Wales, Scotland and England, some research sites were geographically close, while others were geographically remote from our Cardiff base. For some sites, therefore, our own fieldwork meant intensive periods of data collection while staying locally. Other, less distant, sites could be researched on the basis of 'day return' visits. Of course, mere geographic location close to or distant from Cardiff is arbitrary. Distance had practical consequences for the fieldwork, however. 'Distant' sites could not be researched on the basis of short visits or daily commuting. To some extent, therefore, Odette had to approach our further research settings on the basis of short but intense periods of immersion. Sites closer to hand were more readily encompassed within a normal life based 'at home'. A more significant aspect relates to the social location of the university and its department. Social location, as we have suggested already, can reflect spatial location – for example, the elite universities within the 'golden triangle' of England and in the metropolitan urban centres in Scotland. Likewise, the social standing and the spatial location of the older 'redbrick' provincial universities are closely related, as are the cultural and physical locations of the newer campus universities. The university sector is far from uniform, and to some extent the social distinctions and discriminations mirror the geographical dispersion of the institutions. Our own research approach attempted to capture some of those dimensions of contrast in our selection of research sites. In a similar vein, some of those research settings were personally familiar to us, others less so. Inevitably, some universities were already known to us: one or more of us had connections there as external examiners, or from previous research projects, or some other academic business. Others were unknown to us: remote in the sense that none of us had been to the campus, or were acquainted with the people there, or had any particular knowledge of the institution and its organization. Some of the disciplines were familiar to us, and we had friends and colleagues in some of them, while others were entirely strange. Our sense of familiarity with particular disciplines could, of course, be a 'false friend': a discipline changes in twenty years, and personal friendships do not guarantee accurate understanding. Some degree of prior acquaintance did, however, help us to identify lines of inquiry that we might not have recognized in totally unfamiliar fields.

Disciplinary proximity is not necessarily the same as methodological or epistemological proximity. Some of our disciplines, or some sub-specialisms within our disciplines, shared a broad epistemology with us. We conceived the project as an interpretative, social constructivist one, blending sociological approaches to knowledge-reproduction with ethnographic interviewing of an interactionist kind. This epistemology was most commonly recognized (with considerable reservations about our own version of it) in social anthropology, and in *some* sub-specialisms within human geography, urban studies, area studies and development studies. It was least understood in the sciences, where our approach was most 'alien' to the informants. For instance, at one of our biochemistry departments we were invited to address a gathering of all the academic staff. For the most part they heard us quietly and sympathetically. But – perhaps unsurprisingly – we were challenged vigorously by a minority of the academics as to the scientific validity of our proposed research, based as it was on detailed case-studies, without explicit evaluative intent and even without specific hypotheses that we were intending to test. The assumptions informing the 'scientific' method in the laboratory sciences – or at least its common rhetoric – were clearly at odds with our own exploratory approach to understanding social actors and institutions. Again, we survived the public inquisition, and were able to allay any overt or unspoken hostilities. Our intellectual differences did not prevent the research from taking place, and the culture-clash between the disciplines was hardly surprising. Indeed, exploratory qualitative research is often met by the same lack of comprehension in many social domains; it is certainly not confined to the laboratory sciences. This example of intellectual distance does, however, serve to remind us of how diverse our 'peers' in the academic profession really are. It is also a sharp reminder of the importance of intellectual boundaries that define academic differences and distinctions – in many ways the subject-matter of the research itself.

In studying graduate students and established university teachers, we found ourselves studying our peers: members of our own profession in departments across a variety of UK institutions. Furthermore, we were initially studying them at a time when the organization and funding context of doctoral research in the social sciences was an especially sensitive issue. The Research Council Training Guidelines and recognition exercise had recently been introduced, and some departments and individuals were feeling bruised by this process and its outcomes. (The immediate policy context of the research is outlined in Appendix 2.) The fact that we were funded by the Research Council's Training Board meant we were looked upon with some suspicion by those we approached to participate in the study. Although all the departments we asked did agree to take part, the nature of our funding may have been a powerful factor in this decision. We must accept that some departments may have felt obliged to participate, while not totally reassured by our explanations about motives and the outcomes of the study.

In negotiating access with potential 'host' departments, we were aware of the importance of getting across the independence of our research interests. To this end, it was necessary to convince academic gatekeepers, such as heads of departments or deans, that we had no hidden agendas and that the research was not a *sub rosa* form of evaluation or departmental review on behalf of the Research Council. We shared with them the research proposal to reassure them that the study was not intended to inform policy, but was strategic research couched in terms of basic research interests.

We also assured host institutions and departments of confidentiality and anonymity. Although such assurances are standard research practice (or should be), in the study of one's peers, and at such a juncture in time, ethical issues were especially pertinent. As our prospective host departments and their individual members were well aware, honouring these assurances would not be easy. Within the tightly knit networks of UK academic communities it is particularly difficult to ensure anonymity and confidentiality. Although we never disclosed our research sites, we could not stop members of our

Researching our Peers

host institutions talking. It was always possible for groups or individuals from different institutions or departments within institutions to compare notes, and so determine precisely where we had been. Equally, where departments are relatively small, it would be possible for individuals to identify one another – or at least to think that they could do so. For example, when Paul went to Rushberry to see Professor Borringer, a very senior figure in his university, an ethical issue arose. He wrote:

> I arrived just before 9.30. While I was waiting to be picked up in the reception area Jeanne Tesiliko – one of our Cardiff Business School's PhD students I had taught on a diploma option – passed by. She asked me what brought me to urban studies at Rushberry, and I realised she was now working there. I mumbled, smiled, and avoided the question.

Given that it is relatively easy for people to disclose themselves as part of such a study, we have done our absolute best to conceal locations and individuals. We have attempted to do so in several ways. Each university which participated has been given a fictitious name. Where we studied more than one department in the same university they have been allocated different fictitious university names. In an attempt to mitigate the effects of self-disclosure by academics and departments we have been deliberately vague about precisely how many departments we collected data in. So, for instance, when we say we have studied 'not less than' two departments in a given subject, this means that even if two members of different universities know that they were interviewed, and that their departments must have been research sites, even they cannot know if there were yet other research sites in the same discipline. The fact that there were similar projects going on as part of the general Training Board initiative helped to muddy the overall picture of the coverage of the research. The UK team from the Spencer Foundation five-nations project on PhD students (Clark, 1993) were also doing their fieldwork – on physics, history, and economics – at the same time.

The ethical issues do not end with disguising places and people by pseudonyms. There were also the questions of intellectual biography and academic specialism. Academics are highly individual in their unique intellectual interests and careers, and in documenting how they talk about their own academic pursuits, their research interests, their background, qualifications and career paths, they each describe a unique social actor. Through such accounts individuals could easily be identified. We have taken practical steps to conceal individuals in our other publications and in this book. As well as the pseudonym, where absolutely necessary we have falsified biographical details of our informants and made plausible changes in their accounts of their research. In a few cases this has necessitated some creative editing of the data extracts that we use to illustrate our analysis. This has been done in the interests of research ethics and confidentiality and not gratuitously or to make the data 'fit' some analytic preconception of our own.

Not all of the access negotiations were demanding and stressful. Indeed, the majority of our chosen research sites were perfectly willing to allow us to be guests among them, and for us to conduct interviews in their respective departments. This did not mean that each individual was equally at ease with the research process. Approval for access did not necessarily reflect the wishes of all departmental members, some of whom were clearly wary about the research motives given the climate of postgraduate research described earlier and the identity of our funders. Some, we suspect, consented to be interviewed in compliance with department heads' wishes rather than their own.

Reluctant informants could display their hostility in quite subtle ways. For instance, while interviewing an experienced supervisor Odette asked what kinds of skills the supervisor expected her students to acquire as part of PhD work. The supervisor replied to the effect that she expected the student to learn to be a competent interviewer and by way of explanation she listed some skills. These included: the ability to conduct research in hostile situations, where there may be an element of mistrust about the motives of the research or a suspicion of a hidden agenda; to smooth over the distrust and awkwardness and make the respondent feel at ease; to engage with issues that perhaps the respondent has not consciously confronted but which are very pertinent to her interests; successfully to probe for information which the respondent may prefer to conceal and which she wishes in retrospect that she had not revealed. The PhD student must, explained the senior staff member, learn to do all this, as a matter of course, in a friendly unthreatening, non-intimidating way and then smoothly move on to the next respondent. She then looked Odette straight in the eye and said, 'In fact to be competent in those skills that you are using in this interview, Odette'. It was clear to Odette that her informant intended her to understand that this was itself a 'hostile situation', that she did harbour suspicions of a 'hidden agenda'. The backhanded compliment was clearly intended to make Odette feel ill at ease.

The most difficult of our informants seemed concerned that the research findings might jeopardize the relationship of their department with the ESRC or their personal relationships with department heads. Some also seemed to harbour insecurities about their professional competencies. Some seemed anxious about submitting their supervisory practices to peer scrutiny, particularly where alternative and contrasting accounts of these practices might be given by current PhD students whom they supervised. Among the most difficult interviewees were the supervisors who did not have a PhD themselves, more often found in the more vocational or practically oriented departments, such as town planning and development studies. There was a tendency towards defensiveness among these supervisors, which suggested that they felt vulnerable about the omission. More often than not it was the supervisor who raised the issue, providing spontaneous lengthy explanations to unasked questions about their suitability to supervise. The worth of the PhD as both a research experience or learning process was often seriously questioned and undermined or dismissed in these accounts. For example, Mr Sopwith, who taught town planning at Chelmsworth, said that a PhD was 'not a qualification that will get you anywhere in practice, because people will ask you what you've done, what schemes have you produced'. He was not alone in implicitly disparaging the PhD, and in legitimating his own lack of a doctorate. Informants who were relatively hostile or defensive about the doctorate itself were also among the apparently hostile informants: perhaps they felt the subject-matter of our research, coupled with the more general salience of postgraduate training at the time, to be an implied criticism of their own academic credentials. It should go without saying that we had no such intention: indeed we had deliberately chosen town planning in order to explore the relevance of the PhD in an environment where professional and academic interests come together.

New recruits to departments were also among the most difficult informants, especially if they were younger members of staff near the beginning of their careers who had completed their doctorates comparatively recently. Their newness and inexperience led some to adopt defensive strategies in the interviews, and at times these were quite disruptive. On one occasion a female member of an anthropology department, after agreeing to participate, gave Odette such a hard time about her own professional competencies that the respondent/research relationship was affected to the extent that the interview was prematurely terminated.

In studying our peers in the academy, we have benefited from the opportunity to develop an essentially comparative approach. In particular, we have been able to trace the differences – some subtle, some marked – between different academic disciplines. The task of the researcher includes the ability constantly to 'fight familiarity' (Delamont and Atkinson, 1995), or, as Bourdieu puts it, challenge our 'excessive proximity'. We cannot afford to take for granted the familiar academic cultures in which we ourselves have been socialized. It is always necessary for us to achieve a freshness of vision – by questioning what we ourselves find familiar, and by investigating cultural practices that we find more strange. The variety of disciplines we studied, and the consequent ability to compare and contrast between them helped us to establish and maintain 'anthropological strangeness'. Ironically, perhaps, social anthropology was one discipline in which initial familiarity was a danger, as Sara Delamont and Paul Atkinson had first degrees in that discipline, and had a high degree of familiarity with its subculture. Luckily Odette Parry did not have any prior exposure to anthropology, and found it a fascinating discipline – differing in critical ways from her own training in sociology, despite many surface similarities (Parry, 1990). Similarly, Sara

Delamont had spent some time working in a department of artificial intelligence, but the other two had not and so had few preconceptions concerning that discipline. At the other extremes, we had no prior direct experience of biochemistry, town planning or geography. Our general understanding of academic life could thus be set against the particularities of the various different disciplines. The fact that we collected data across the range of different subjects helped us to maintain analytic distance from and between our various research sites. The same is true, of course, of different institutions of higher education. We had a thorough knowledge of our own university and our own department. It would have been all too easy to make assumptions about procedures and practices had we not encountered a much wider range of institutional arrangements and practices. By studying our disciplines across institutions of different sorts, we were able to maintain the right analytic distance and critical perspective on the departments we studied.

Researching academics is a good antidote to any lingering, romantic images of the researcher confronted by 'naive' informants. Our research 'subjects' were, of course, intelligent and well qualified. They were for the most part articulate and knowledgeable. While there is no guarantee that academics will be more reflective about their work than members of any other occupational group, the climate of accountability and the recent changes in training requirements had made explicit many issues concerning postgraduate research and supervision. Many of the academic supervisors we talked to may not have been exactly 'reflective practitioners' in the fashionable sense of that term, but they were certainly capable of reflecting on their own practices, and of reflecting back on their own experiences as graduate students themselves. The doctoral students we interviewed approached things from a somewhat different kind of perspective. Again, they were far from being naive informants. They were, of course, highly knowledgeable about their own work, and many of them were able to talk quite explicitly about it. In the nature of things, their accounts were more biographically grounded, but such accounts were far from being 'raw' personal experience. Both students' and supervisors' accounts were thoroughly informed by their disciplinary backgrounds and identities. The nature of research, what counts as research, and the kinds of intellectual or personal experiences that are recounted are constructed within the cultural frameworks of academic cultures.

Our informants, then, were all enculturated within their disciplinary frameworks of knowledge. The graduate students were still 'learning the ropes' to a greater or lesser extent, and the professional experience of supervisors was also highly variable. We do not wish to imply that disciplinary cultures are monolithic structures. Clearly they are not. Yet it is striking that within each discipline we studied, academics and students shared common frameworks of understanding and assumptions about what constituted knowledge, and what counted as research. There was not perfect consensus, of course, and there were always possibilities of confusion or misunderstanding. Graduate students, in particular, could display differing degrees of sophistication and explicitness in their understanding of departmental and wider academic life: they displayed different propensities to seek out and make explicit the ground rules for success in their chosen field.

We explore these and similar issues substantively in the chapters that follow. Here we are drawing attention to the fact that, in common with many professional and epistemic groups, our informants had highly developed vocabularies and interpretative frameworks within which they couched their autobiographical accounts and their reflections on academic life and work. In some cases too they were as sophisticated as we were – if not more so – about research and its conduct. To that extent, our own research activities were not innocent transactions with naive hosts. The entire research process is more accurately thought of as a series of cross-disciplinary encounters between our research assumptions and interests, and those of the students and academic staff whom we encountered.

Student Informants

Hitherto we have really been talking about researching the academics – the supervisors of postgraduate students. Here we turn to consider data collection from the students. As a rule, PhD students were easier to interview than members of academic staff, and here the biography of the field researcher is particularly important. Odette had finished her own PhD in the mid-1980s and shared a particular empathy with those in the throes of completion. She conducted virtually all of the student interviews herself. In terms of age and professional status she was rather closer to the research students than were Sara and Paul. Odette's reflections on the interviews suggest that the students, unlike staff members, did not feel threatened by the researcher, seeing her more as an ally than a potential critic or adversary. The problems associated with the student interviews were most often practical ones. Many were difficult to contact (the majority of the initial arrangements were made long-distance) especially where fieldwork was part of the research. Nowhere was this more of a problem than in anthropology. Space was another factor. The majority of students did not have access to a private room in which the interview could be carried out, and departments during term time were pushed to find space which was not reserved for teaching. Once these practical problems were resolved, students were eager to talk about their PhD work. On the whole, students appeared very open in the interview and trusted their confidences would not be betrayed. Although obviously having a vested interest in what their supervisors might say about their competence, they accepted that this was a subject out of bounds.

However, the relationship of empathy and trust which developed between

Odette and many of the PhD candidates was not without penalties. Situations arose where accounts given by supervisor and student about the same piece of work, or the same individual, differed to the extreme. There were instances, for example, where the student conceptualized his or her work quite differently from the supervisor, was adopting methodological and theoretical positions other than those attributed to the student by the supervisor and saw him- or herself at quite a different stage of thesis preparation. Sometimes this happened where a student was jointly supervised by two individuals who had quite different conceptualizations of the project. But on other occasions it happened between a supervisor and a student who thought they were in agreement. These situations were psychologically difficult for Odette to deal with because, given the remit of the research, she was powerless to intervene.

An extreme example of student-supervisor discord involved a mature, part-time PhD candidate who was interviewed shortly before submitting his thesis. In separate interviews both student and supervisor appeared fairly confident that the thesis was ready. Three months later Odette received a telephone call from the student who said that the thesis had been failed and that he had been awarded an MPhil. The student faxed Odette a copy of the supervisor's comments about the thesis. In this account the supervisor wholeheartedly agreed with the external examiner's opinion that the thesis was not ready and stated that he had advised the student against submission. The supervisor also agreed that the student should not be allowed to resubmit for a PhD. At this point, Odette went back to her transcripts, which demonstrated the extent to which the supervisor had apparently revised his opinion about the readiness of the thesis after the unsuccessful submission.

Another situation where staff accounts differed from those given by graduate students was in a department where the head claimed a 100 per cent success record, in that every thesis completed in his department had been submitted within four years of registration. No ESRC sanctions had been applied, therefore. On talking to postgraduates, however, it transpired that students were compelled by the department head to submit within four years, irrespective of whether or not they were ready, on the advice that if the thesis was not ready it would merely be referred for adjustments. In several cases it was apparent that this advice had backfired on the student because the thesis was not referred as expected but failed. Understandably, there was bad feeling among these candidates, who had not wished to submit but had succumbed to departmental pressure to do so. Situations like this can and did place a strain on the researcher, who was unable to feed back to either students or supervisors information which was often extremely pertinent to them. Furthermore, being in a position to compare accounts using, in some cases, 'guilty' knowledge about individuals raised issues of personal ethics.

The data collection from students raised another issue of proximity versus remoteness – experiential proximity or remoteness. We mean here particularly the experience of success and failure as a graduate student. Undertaking a PhD is a high-risk activity for a student – investing three or more years of one's life for an uncertain outcome. Odette had successfully completed two research degrees – an MPhil and a PhD; Sara and Paul had both completed PhDs. We were all therefore much closer to the successful students, whose own data collection had been productive, who were writing up fluently, than to those who were in deep trouble. We have had to learn to experience the sense of failure or potential failure, and empathize with the troubles and fears of the student whose work is going badly. Of course, nobody's doctoral research is without problems. We could often empathize with students who were struggling – whether or not they finally completed their PhD successfully – on the basis of personal experience. The vast majority of academics bear the scars of their postgraduate research. Indeed, many of our academic informants structured their own accounts of higher degree supervision precisely in terms of such memories and experiences. This is the theme of Chapter 8.

Academics also face failure, or the possibility of failure, in their careers as supervisors. Here too we could draw on our own experiences of the elation when a research student achieves a breakthrough, and the sadness when they encounter problems. Sara and Paul, as experienced graduate supervisors, were familiar with the fear of failure and many of the other problems reported by our informants. As with all the experiences of this research project, therefore, we approached this issue with a mixture of familiarity and strangeness, drawing on and distancing ourselves from our own biographies and academic careers.

Finally, we must acknowledge a major area of paradox in the conduct of this research. All three of us are known for doing and writing about ethnographic research, with considerable emphasis on participant observation. In the ideal world we would have spent more time at fewer research sites, conducting ethnographic fieldwork on the academic subcultures of university departments, research groups and laboratories. We would have observed more of the seminars and other academic or social occasions that took place in our chosen departments. Equally, we would have been less reliant on interviews with informants. To a considerable extent, the overall shape of our research was set by the requirements of the first project we undertook – on social science disciplines. The project was part of a wider research programme, initiated by the ESRC's Training Board. They were keen to see the projects they funded cover a range of disciplines, in a number of different institutions, representing universities of different types. In order to meet their general requirements, we were forced to rely less on intensive field research and more an extensive coverage of informants by means of interviews. Our second project – on natural science disciplines – was more under

Researching our Peers

our own control. We were therefore able to select fewer research sites and focus on them rather more intensively. But the general format of the research was largely determined by our original research design. All three of us have also written on research methods and ethics (e.g. Hammersley and Atkinson, 1995; Delamont, 1992; Parry, 1983), which makes our accounts of our own data collection, analysis and text production subject to greater scrutiny. But if we describe our research methods too carefully and too explicitly, then we may blow the cover of our informants, who are more vulnerable to 'discovery' by a readership of academics than informants from many other backgrounds. In this chapter we have worked especially hard to disguise and protect our informants – particularly those whose research was not going well, or who were reluctant or even hostile participants in the research.

We are conscious of the fact that we have written this book, and our other publications from the projects, in a very plain and straightforward way. Although we are well aware of the variety of representational styles and genres open to sociologists, anthropologists and others, we have not attempted to engage in any experimental writing here. The only example of more innovative forms of representation deriving from these data is to be found in Coffey and Atkinson (1996), where one informant's account of her PhD viva is turned into a poem. We are, therefore, conscious of the fact that, notwithstanding our own methodological interests and commitments, this particular book does not reflect or represent them fully.

3 The Nature of the Quest

> One person's pedigree can become another's mark of infamy, one's coat of arms another's insult, and vice versa ... the university field is, like any other field, the locus of struggle to determine the conditions and criteria of legitimate membership.
>
> (Bourdieu, 1988: 11)

As Bourdieu points out, academic life is contested, and there are struggles for legitimacy. In this chapter we try to show what the PhD is in the various disciplines we studied: what the PhD student is aiming for, and what the goals of the supervisor are. A PhD is a badge of legitimate membership: a badge to be worn by the student, helped by the supervisor and tested by the examiners. We explore how the students saw the quest, how the supervisors viewed the PhD, and how staff who had been examiners characterized what they looked for in a PhD. We do not talk about the processes of supervision here, because that is the focus of Chapter 8, nor about the everyday life of the PhD student, because that is the topic of Chapter 9. In this chapter we concentrate on the dreams, the quest, the vision, the grail – or even the Sampo of the Finnish epic, the *Kalevala* – and the examination at the end of the quest.

The Sampo is a serviceable metaphor for the contemporary PhD. It is central to the national epics of Finland, collected from traditional folk singers and published by Lonnrot in 1835 and 1849. In his introduction to his English translation Bosley (1989: xxxix) irreverently summarizes the story:

> The Sampo is forged, a rogue screws;
> There's a wedding, a murder, the blues;
> A serf bites the dust, the Sampo gets bust,
> And Finland receives the Good News.
> (By permission of Oxford University Press)

Scholars disagree as to what the Sampo was: it gets made or forged, it is stolen, and it is lost in battle. There have been speculations that it was a

The Nature of the Quest

magic grain/money mill, an idol, a treasure chest, a sacred tree, a stolen Byzantine mint, or a model of the cosmos. Bosley says his readers must be content to leave it as 'a mysterious object'. In canto 10, the Smith, Ilmarinen, has several attempts at making the Sampo. First, his forge produces a crossbow, then a boat, then a golden calf, and then a golden plough. All these are broken and pushed back into the forge before the mysterious Sampo emerges and is taken away in triumph by the hag of the North. The labours of Ilmarinen, forging something mysterious, and rejecting his early attempts, will serve well as a metaphor for the quest we describe: the attainment of a PhD in contemporary Britain. It takes a good deal of hard labour, and no one is quite sure what it is.

We begin the chapter with the end of the quest: the examiner's judgement. During the interviews with supervisors we asked them if they had examined any PhD theses, and, if they had, what criteria they used to judge them. Some of our supervisors had never examined a higher degree thesis, others claimed to have examined a great many. As the material on how examiners judged theses is presented, it will become clear that Bourdieu's concept of legitimate membership is an apt one: examiners are indeed testing the students' attempts to join the world of autonomous scholars. The criteria used are a mixture of what Jamous and Peloille (1970) call technical and indeterminate qualities, similar to the mix found in most occupations and professions. See, for example, Atkinson et al. (1977) and Atkinson (1981, 1996) on medicine, and Delamont (1989) on science. The technical skills have to be there, and have to be adequately described in the thesis, but there are also indeterminate qualities which examiners can recognize but not itemize precisely because, by their very indeterminacy, they are resistant to precise explication. Indeterminate qualities are those which result from cultural capital, and are found by examiners in the theses of those novices who already share the habitus of the discipline. The data make this point very clearly. The early quotes discussed are from departments of town planning, urban studies and development studies – interdisciplinary social science departments where there is consensus on what makes a good thesis.

Examiners' Views of the PhD

We asked our staff respondents if they had examined any theses, and if so, what they looked for. In their answers we obtained some of the clearest ideas about what a PhD was. For example, Professor Paget, a town planning expert at Portminster, said:

> I've examined an awful lot of PhDs. ... A whole variety of things. Substance again I think is important. I do think it needs to be a fairly meaty document – I don't mean tomes and tomes. I've had some two-volume 800 page jobs, and frankly I think they're nightmarish. So topic

is important. The conduct of the thesis – an understanding of literature, of method and its limitations and strengths, an application of general research methods. Best PhD I've ever read, it was beautifully presented, rigorously argued, delightfully researched, the literature was bang on, theoretically very competent, methodologically very competent – in essence it seemed to me to be honest.

In an allied social science discipline, urban studies, Dr Ridgeway from Rushberry was about to examine a PhD, and so he was able to give a concrete, explicit account:

> I'm quite nervous about examining this PhD. ... Looking for originality and excitement, critically. A PhD has to have something about it that's theoretically exciting, and original, without being world-shattering. ... But I think originality is the critical thing. And excitement. Something that grabs you. It's not just a competent pragmatic piece of work. There's something behind it that shows the person is engaged in the debate.

In these two comments we can see the indeterminate criteria. Dr Ridgeway looks for 'originality' and 'excitement', summed up as 'something that grabs you'. Professor Paget wants honesty and something 'meaty' (which does not just mean long). Professor Paget does also mention technicalities – 'beautifully presented', competent use of methods, and a well-conducted review of the literature, but these too are located in indeterminacies. A literature review that is 'bang on' and a 'rigorous' argument are both indeterminate qualities. We have argued elsewhere (Delamont et al., 1997a: 100–16) that learning how to exercise academic judgement in the discipline is the most vital task the student faces. A range of ways in which supervisors could encourage their doctoral students to acquire judgement was suggested.

In the following data extracts other experienced examiners elaborate on the technicalities and indeterminacies involved in judging a PhD. We present four different views, and then explore what criteria emerge. Professor Woodrose, a development studies expert at Latchendon, said:

> I guess there's a minimum level. At a minimum level I'm looking for a good understanding of the state of the literature. I'm looking for total confidence in the application of research methodology. And I'm looking for anything that allows me to say 'There is a contribution to knowledge'. I guess if I'm going beyond that I'm looking for the kind of PhD that one hopes produces papers or a book. I'd like to see something that looks original – a true contribution to knowledge. It's something about the scope of the exercise, that they've really bitten off something – either to apply a set of methods to a new country, or to a new sector, or that

The Nature of the Quest

they've applied them in a rather distinctive way.

Professor Portland, a town planner at Portminster, gave a concise checklist of his criteria:

> Clear specification of objectives of research, careful design of research, good literature review, well structured not rambling, fair amount of precision in thought, good strong use of theory, picking out of appropriate propositions which are being tested. Good ability to manage data handling. Good writing style and clear conclusions.

Dr Wishart, who was in development studies at Latchendon, was equally concise, but used a vocabulary of skills that a student should have acquired and should then display in the thesis itself:

> I see the PhD as incorporating a number of skills. You've got your research skills, your analytical skills that are brought together, then you've got the pure administrative skills of actually writing, ensuring that the references are correct, making sure your section heads are appropriate – the actual putting together of the thesis itself.

Dr Wishart also used the criteria that a thesis should be 'up to date', show a 'critical perspective', display 'thoroughness' and 'coherence', that it should show 'a picture being built up' and that there should be 'a systematic progress through the thesis'.

The criterion of coherence was also emphasized by his colleague Dr Wynyard:

> I guess coherence to start with – is there a defined topic, a defined problem, have they been able to cut that problem up into a set of hypotheses and have they been able to operationalize those hypotheses, are they testable? Have they been able to relate that to the literature on the field. ... Next, fieldwork – have they been able to conduct fieldwork, have they used their methodology as planned, have they been able to cope with problems in the field which inevitably arise? Can they present the data clearly and can they then tie their data into their actual hypothesis?

These four scholars add some new criteria to those offered by Paget and Ridgeway, but the emphasis on indeterminacy remains. Professor Woodrose is committed to originality, but adds the criterion of potential publication. Professor Portland adds 'good writing style'. Dr Wishart's list is more technical: correct references, appropriate types of heading and subheading, but his criteria of 'analytical skills' and 'coherence' are largely matters of judge-

The Nature of the Quest

ment. Dr Wynyard also wants coherence, and evidence that the student has 'been able to cope with problems', which is an archetypal indeterminate quality. (It is a quality in particularly high demand in anthropology and qualitative development studies, as we show in Chapter 5 below.)

None of the six examiners quoted thus far has made a specific point about originality, although this is often mentioned as a criterion for the PhD. Our next informant did stress novelty, linked to a personal experience of the examiner. Dr Savanake, a town planner at Chelmsworth, suggested:

> In a PhD you are looking for a development of ideas, methods, concepts beyond the current literature, into a new area which excites the examiner and the supervisor and in which the student feels perfectly assured. Just that – if it extends me in some way.

Here Dr Savanake introduces another variation on the originality and excitement criterion: extending the examiner.

For social scientists, the originality of a thesis was frequently seen as an issue of theorizing. A good PhD is one in which the candidate is making a contribution to the theoretical advance of the discipline. Dr Ramilles, a social policy researcher in an urban studies centre, makes this point:

> How clear is the analytical framework that is being used, and is it being used to illuminate a particular theme, or thesis, or is the substantive area being investigated being used to test the robustness of the theory? I clearly feel more comfortable if I see some theory testing going on and some contribution to theory – I'm very pleased when I find it. If there has been a good coverage of the previous literature, theoretical and substantive, and there has been some well-conducted fieldwork that further illuminates the theory, then if that is well done, written well – that for me is a PhD.

Here Dr Ramilles is stressing that the theoretical work of the thesis is vital for its success – and, of course, judging *theoretical* adequacy is a classic indeterminate criterion.

So far we have been drawing on our social science informants. Before moving on to the scientists, we need to show that the indeterminate nature of examiners' judgements can render them opaque to students. We can illustrate this with the apparently simple criterion of length. We quote a colleague of Dr Ramilles from the same urban studies centre (at Rushberry) who provides a typical set of criteria. We then treat as problematic one of those criteria – that of thesis length. Dr Rowlandson said that he would be looking for:

The Nature of the Quest

A coherent argument. I look to see what they are setting out to do, I look to see whether they've done it. I look for a decent chunk of empirical work which relates to the argument and supports it. And I look to see whether there's a spark of something original which makes something more of it than just putting together a literature review and empirical material – not something desperately new, but evidence of original thought. I weigh it as well. If it's more than 80,000 words – brevity is something I look for, economy, let's say, not brevity – there isn't more there than there needs to be.

With Dr Rowlandson the criterion of 'brevity' is highlighted. This echoes the complaint by Professor Paget about 'nightmarish' theses that are too long. For supervisor and student judging the appropriate length – not nightmarishly long, not too short and skimpy – is a classic dilemma. A student in anthropology at Kingford, Colin Ives, who came across in his interview as the most cue-deaf student in our study (see Miller and Parlett, 1976; Eggleston and Delamont, 1983; Delamont et al., 1997a), revealed in a complaint about lack of guidance on length that he actually knew nothing about the nature of the quest itself. Whereas an experienced supervisor, like an experienced examiner, 'knows' that there is an appropriate length for a particular thesis – not skimped, not nightmarish, but appropriate – a novice such as Colin Ives does not 'know' what length his PhD needs to be to meet this implicit criterion. As Colin himself told us:

A lot of mistakes I've made are the result of me not asking questions and people not putting me right – they presume I must know. ... I didn't know the PhD was meant to be an argument, as Dr Durham said, it's meant to say something. I thought it was meant to be one of those old-fashioned monographs, a collection of information. When I was an undergraduate I used to think a PhD was one of those articles you get in *Man* [Journal of the Royal Anthropological Institute] or something, a 10,000 word article, I used to think 'they must be PhDs'.

Colin discovered what a PhD was, not by reading some in the Kingford library, but, 'I just happened to be reading a book, the prospectus, one day, and saw 100,000 words and thought "That's really long" and nobody bothered to tell me, and nobody has told me.' Note that Colin did not *ask* about thesis length, but waited to be told by 'someone'. He had not read any recent theses in the library, nor been briefed on the requirements. He was in his third year when we interviewed him. He was therefore ignorant of the technicalities of presenting a PhD in anthropology at Kingford. However, his comments reveal that he was equally ignorant of the indeterminate criteria that would be brought to bear on his work – not just the technical rules as to length, but the judgements about what needed to be said about his Tunisian

The Nature of the Quest

pilgrimage study to show that he could claim legitimate membership of the disciplinary and university communities.

Not all staff seemed to be aware of the indeterminate criteria. A few seemed to be as unsighted as Colin Ives. Dr Silva at Chelmsworth, a town planner, answered Odette's question about the nature of the PhD by reading aloud to her from the institution's regulations, which were modelled on those of the CNAA (Chelmsworth being a former polytechnic with CNAA-validated higher degrees). It is possible that he was a reluctant informant who did not really want to be interviewed, but our judgement was that he simply had not realized that the criteria for success and failure in the PhD cannot be reduced to a set of written rules, however explicit (as shown by the experienced examiners in his discipline, whom we have already quoted). Dr Silva was not alone in his emphasis on the technical. Dr Snow, his colleague, included one equally technical criterion:

> You have to look first of all at whether they have done a sufficient amount of work in the time. Have they coped with the literature reasonably well, have they produced ideas which make some interesting contribution [and] complete the cycle of feedback from the work.

Here Dr Snow juxtaposes some criteria which match those already cited with an apparently naively technical one: 'has the student worked hard for three years?' This is a paraphrase of one of the old CNAA criteria, but it should not, of course, be treated literally. It is actually invoking a rather subtle judgement on the part of the examiner.

Before moving on to the scientists, there is one further criterion found among our experienced examiners that is deceptively simple. Dr Gaisbrook, in development studies at Gossingham, articulated it for us in this way:

> I guess I look for, increasingly, a sense of intellectual modesty about the contribution of their particular research to knowledge. An understanding of the fragility of understanding anything through social science, and therefore a willingness to make tentative claims, to be very explicit about the way to approach different alternative answers, weaknesses with the data – that approach is more than any other thing what impresses me. I tend to look for fluency in writing, presentation and argument [with] definite linkage to an existing body of theory.

The idea of 'modesty' is again deceptive. As Mulkay (1984) shows in his reconstruction of a Nobel Laureate's acceptance speech, 'modesty' in academic rhetoric is a far from simple matter. Clearly a doctoral thesis that was totally unassuming and reticent would enter no claims as to its significance, and would probably fail as a consequence.

The criteria used by social scientists were both technical and indetermi-

The Nature of the Quest

nate, with the latter predominating. The natural scientists used exactly the same criteria – originality, appropriate data collection and a proper relation to existing knowledge. For example, Dr Mandrake – an engineer in the environmental sciences department at Ottercombe, telling Odette about the best PhD he has examined, said: 'I knew from the start. It was looking at a fundamental research problem, possibly developing new techniques, possibly challenging two or three different theories, and that it was an original piece of work.'

The scientists only differed from the social scientists in drawing a distinction between the level of success that was needed to get a student a PhD and that which was needed for subsequent publication. Such a distinction was never drawn by a social scientist. Professor Gantry, of Baynesholme, summarized this point:

> They need some results. The SERC [Science and Engineering Research Council] need results and they make that quite clear. In an ideal world negative results should be OK, and you may be able to write it up for a PhD, but no one will publish negative results. And of course it's important to get published, and if you can't it's not a fat lot of good.

Similarly, Dr Dewry at Ribblethorpe, discussing one student who was halfway through his three years:

> You've got to apply the techniques and that takes a lot of preparation. He's written a paper; writing papers is very important because it's one criterion for theses to be acceptable, they should be of publishable quality. And what better way to show it than having published part of it?

Supervisors are, therefore, in broad agreement that, while there are technicalities which must be correct, the real role of the examiner is to judge whether the student has mastered appropriate indeterminate skills and displayed the right indeterminate qualities. In the next section we focus on what supervisors try to achieve while supervising: what their goals for the student are. Supervisors are, in many cases, thoughtful and reflective about their own roles and behaviours as supervisors, and we have devoted a chapter to those reflections (Chapter 8). In this section we report and discuss what they hope their students will achieve, but we do not discuss the specific techniques of research, which are the focus of Chapters 4, 5 and 6.

Supervisors' Views of the Quest

Professor Brande, a quantitative geographer at Hernchester, expressed the task of the supervisor as follows:

The Nature of the Quest

> I think the most important thing you can do as a supervisor is to really give them a love – it sounds curious, that word, but I think it's the right word – of what they're doing, and a sort of motivation, because I think that research is a desperately lonely business.

Professor Brande is one of Britain's most distinguished scholars, and his words are an excellent evocation of the intellectual loneliness of the social science student, and also capture our 'quest' metaphor. A scientist, Professor Mardian, in environmental sciences at Ottercombe, had a vivid metaphor for a modern quest:

> It's a little bit like driving on the motorway without brakes. ... You have a PhD student you have to motivate them and hope that they will return their thesis at the right time and at the right standard.

His colleague Dr McQumpha, a marine biologist at Ottercombe, echoed Professor Brande:

> Ideally, to have an enjoyable three years and have mastered a reasonably functional science, able to formulate scientific data successfully, actually carry out the practical work, doing the research. That would be the ideal ... they also plan how to identify the research questions ... play a substantial part in the creative work.

Dr McQumpha also introduced the crucial issue of developing the student's judgement: 'It's no good having good data if they aren't right, and the student needs to be able to distinguish what sort of questions need to be asked.'

The supervisor can guide the student towards developing the academic equivalent of 'good taste' (Bourdieu and Passeron, 1977, 1979). The research student has to develop the skill to judge when an experiment has worked and when it has not, when an analysis is 'correct', when a reading is plausible, when the null hypothesis has been falsified, and so on.

The experienced supervisors all talked of how doctoral research tested whether the student could learn to exercise the discriminations needed by the fully accredited scholar in the university field. Successful students learned to discriminate – in their own work and in that of others. Such judgement is a vital part of being a fully accredited professional. As the biochemist, 'Spender' (a pseudonym) in an interview with Gilbert and Mulkay makes clear: 'If you are an experimenter you know what is important and what is not important' (1984: 53). Similarly, a physicist interviewed by Gumport said of PhD supervision:

The Nature of the Quest

> I try to teach them a set of skills. The biggest one is to know when you're right and when you're wrong. It's common for them to miss it when they're wrong. After a while they can see it. It's intuitive partially.
>
> (Gumport, 1993: 265–6)

Judgement is a crucial issue in doctoral supervision. Both parties have to develop judgement. The student has to learn, over the three years, to judge his or her own work by standards appropriate to fully independent research, rather than undergraduate student standards. The supervisor has to learn how to judge not only the student's current work, but also the potential for further improvement, while at the same time helping the student develop his or her own skills.

This is a complex area, particularly so because it deals with the indeterminate, tacit and implicit aspects of a particular academic discipline. It is much easier to teach technical, explicit things than the indeterminate, implicit ones. This is very clear from the literature on occupational – especially professional – socialization, particularly that on medicine (Becker et al., 1961; Atkinson 1981, 1984, 1996), nurses (Olesen and Whittaker, 1968), lawyers (Granfield, 1992; Phillips, 1982), schoolteachers (Atkinson and Delamont, 1985) and even apprentice musicians (Kadushin, 1969). However, we do not know very much either about how apprentice scholars learn the necessary discriminations in their discipline or sub-specialism, or about how established scholars exercise discrimination in their own work. The literature on academics (e.g. Ashmore et al., 1995; Becher, 1989, 1990; Bourdieu, 1988; Evans, 1988, 1993; Latour and Woolgar, 1986; Lynch, 1985) has not produced an easily transferable 'model' of how academic judgement is exercised because such a model is of course inconceivable. Experienced academics 'learn' how to judge research and publications in their field over the course of their career, without explicit instruction for the most part, as the American physicist already quoted has stated.

Two biochemists from Ribblethorpe, one a senior scientist, one a new postdoctoral researcher, express the same view about the PhD in that discipline. Dr Morton Stayman, the postdoc:

Odette: So would you say the PhD is more about learning techniques than getting the bench work done?
MS: And also designing experiments, learning how to handle yourself in a lab, learning how to do experiments and learning how to write scientific reports.

Similarly, Dr Dewry, the head of the lab at Ribblethorpe, said:

> The subject of a project is defined by its interest value. If we find it boring we shift our focus, or if we don't get any results we change direc-

The Nature of the Quest

tion. PhD research is supposed to provide novel data and also PhD work is supposed to modify techniques. It's not all spade work but at the same time if you want the PhD to be wholly novel you'll be in danger of nothing working.

If the quest for a PhD is a lonely one, the supervisor needs to choose students who have 'the right stuff' – the necessary qualities to succeed. For instance, Dr Quayne, a biochemist at Forthamstead, described the characteristics he looked for in a potential PhD student:

> Now if you want to know what I'm looking for, first of all I want to make sure they're intelligent, and in a way the two-one or first will take account of that, but I'm looking for someone with a personality, who's enthusiastic, who's got a lot of staying power, because I think 90 per cent of a PhD can be hard work and 10 per cent initiative.

Dr Quayne stresses the qualities of perseverance, enthusiasm and intelligence. Dr Durtham, an anthropologist at Kingford, adds two further qualities:

> PhD students can be good in all sorts of different ways. We all like students who do go away and write. The ones who are difficult to deal with are the ones who you seem to get fixed on Wednesday and come back unfixed on Friday, where the supervision doesn't seem to help.

Then he used Giselle Dumont as an example of an 'outstandingly good' PhD student:

> She'd done very good fieldwork – very original material to work with. She works damn hard, she reads extremely widely. She has had problems in conceptualizing how the whole argument was going to work, and sometimes in getting the precise phrasing she wants, but she takes her work extremely seriously, she's quite easy to work with. She's on a very steep learning curve, every piece of work is better than the last piece of work.

Giselle was contrasted with the man, Colin Ives, we have already described as cue-deaf, of whom Dr Durham said, 'He's going to have to write things and we will find out eventually how it's going.' Here Dr Durham was raising doubts about whether Colin Ives had 'the right stuff', and whether he would actually get a PhD. Another anthropologist, Mr Fitton at Kingford, in describing the characteristics needed by a successful candidate, said he looked for 'clarity of vision' and students whose work had 'some sort of trajectory' and who 'can address the multiplicity of theoretical issues', while

The Nature of the Quest

surmounting 'surface obstacles'. He also wanted to find students he 'could engage in a good dialogue with'.

In anthropology, and other disciplines which require long periods of overseas fieldwork, supervisors are especially concerned about students' capacity to survive. As Dr Drummock explained to Odette: 'The student has got to be balanced from the point of view of personality to begin with, to put up with this isolation.' He then described the views of the distinguished British anthropologist Mary Douglas on fieldwork in anthropology.

> She regarded this isolation in the field as a very important part of the training of an anthropologist, because one is on one's own. She has this idea that it was a sort of *rite de passage*. One is going through a period when one is marginal, on the borders of one's career, but also involved in another society.

For many of the supervisors, the easiest way to explain what the PhD is, and what they looked for in potential students, was to present stories of failure. Supervisors told us about students who had not finished, or whose theses had been failed. We have not used those data here, because all our supervisors told us about their failures in confidence and exhorted us not to publish those data. It is likely that in the smaller disciplines, the failures would be recognisable. When Dr Drummock described his first few students as 'an absolutely disastrous lot', and remembered that 'I felt it was like sweeping water trying to get them to work', partly because they lacked enthusiasm, it tells us a good deal about how Dr Drummock sees the nature of the quest. For Dr Drummock students who got 'depressed', diverted by 'non-academic alternatives', or were 'lackadaisical' were unlikely to achieve doctorates.

Pierre Bourdieu alerts us to the contested nature of the academic field. One aspect of the supervisor's duty is to train his or her own successors: to produce researchers whose achievements will surpass one's own. Two of our scientists explained the exultation they felt when their students were successful and became autonomous researchers, even challengers in the academic field. Dr Maitland-Maine, an Ottercombe environmental scientist, said:

> The most satisfying kind of teaching is the postgraduate teaching because at the end of the process the teacher-pupil relationship, in an ideal case, is destroyed. And what you end up with is much nearer to the colleague relationship – among equals. They might not be equal in all respects, but certainly within the area of the student's own PhD subject. The student should leave here feeling they're equal.

He used the specific example of a student from a Saudi-Arabian background who had come to Ottercombe and discovered he needed to be 'able

45

The Nature of the Quest

to tackle scientific research in a way schooling and universities in Saudi Arabia had totally not prepared him. When he left he said "Oh, I have learnt to fly" so that was marvellous.'

Similarly, Dr De Manuelos of Ottercombe said:

> after the initial guidance, the students then can take it on board and start running with it, and can develop in their own ideas and inevitably hopefully will go beyond what I've ever thought previously, otherwise I would have done it. And that's the originality we're looking for.

Before moving from how the academics see the nature of the quest to the views from the students, there is one particular feature of the supervisors' opinions we need to mention here, while we are embedded in our quest metaphor. In fairy tales the hero or heroine who sets out on a quest has typically been equipped with some magical aids or special skills. In the *Kalevala*, Vainamoinen and Ilmarinen set off to steal the Sampo with a marvellous sword and a talking boat, and during the journey they make the first *Kantele* (a stringed instrument). For a PhD student the equivalents might be a good grounding in research methods, writing skills, and developing cue-consciousness.

One of the key themes of recent debates in the UK about the future of the higher degree (a debate explained in Appendix 2) has focused on postgraduate *training*: what tools are students given to equip them for the quest? We return to this in more detail in Chapters 4, 5 and 6, but one of the important dimensions is how far academics in the different disciplines believed that students should acquire methods while on their quest, and how far they should be taught them before they set out – allied to an analysis of which qualities are seen as tacit and personal, and which as technical or explicit.

What was particularly striking about both supervisors and students among the anthropologists and the human geographers using qualitative methods was their belief that qualitative methods are part of an individual's personal, indeterminate repertoire, and are not technical skills that can be taught or learnt in class. It is rather as if the heroine of the fairy tale – the plucky woodcutter's daughter about to set out on the quest to rescue the sleeping prince from the witch's castle – is offered seven league boots, a magic flute and a talking cat by her fairy godmother, but refuses them. These beginners about to set off on their quests reject the idea that anyone can teach them any useful skills, and their supervisors also reject the idea that such skills *could* be taught in the abstract.

As long as PhD students believe that they have to do it all alone they are accurately reflecting the culture of the lecturers in their disciplines – for staff also believe research skills cannot be taught – but at the same time they are making it harder for themselves. Their successful socialization into the

The Nature of the Quest

cultures of anthropology, development studies, and qualitative human geography was achieved by accepting a doctrine that qualitative researchers in geography learn their craft unaided and alone. This is a major theme of Chapter 5, and so we have quoted only two students here, both anthropologists. For instance, Howard Creigton, of Southersham: 'I'm not entirely sure what you can teach people about fieldwork; you can learn a bit from their particular experience or they can tell you what to read.' Janet Lundgren at Southersham offered a forthright view of the essentially practical and personal basis for anthropology: 'The anthropology fieldwork year involves just getting out and doing it.'

We now turn to the students' views of the quest: what they are doing and why they are motivated to do it. We begin with the geographers, because they were the most lyrical, and yet had the most trouble defining the object of their desire: geography was as vague as the Sampo.

Students' Dreams

The majority of the student informants saw the quest for a PhD as an opportunity to pursue a subject they loved: to spend three years full-time as apprentice researchers in 'their' discipline. Some of the students were converts to a new discipline – having done a Masters course after a first degree in something else – while others were pursuing a subject they had been doing since adolescence. The geographers exemplify the latter with particular force and clarity. Rick Moliner, a PhD student at Boarbridge, when asked why he wanted a PhD began his reply with, 'It sounds a bit daft really. I've just got a thing about geography. I love the subject.' Jason Ingersoll, also at Boarbridge, expressed the same view. 'I've always loved geography since school, and I've always wanted to carry it on, go as far as I can with it.'

Part of the students' quest is motivated by this love of subject: a desire to push the borders of the subject outwards because they loved it. The geographers were the most lyrical about this passion: this love of geography which reverberates through the interviews with students from all our sampled departments. Jason's interview went on: 'I can't think of anything I enjoy more than geography, I just love all sorts of geography.' Students from other universities were equally enthusiastic about the discipline. For example, Sam Verney, at Tolleshurst, said he had 'discovered geography was the thing I really wanted to do', and that led him to do a PhD. When doing a PhD was good it was wonderful, as we were told by Murray Upton: 'I've found it a very enjoyable experience, doing a PhD – the most enjoyable of my life so far.'

The geographers had all studied the subject at school, and all had done it as their main undergraduate degree course. Their autobiographies stressed a passion that had already lasted a decade. In contrast, almost all our respondents in artificial intelligence (AI), and the majority of our anthropologists (fourteen out of twenty-three) were postgraduate converts. They had done first degrees in something else, and then found, and fallen in love with, AI or anthropology. These converts were doing PhDs in their new discipline with all the fiery zeal of new believers.

Illington is a world-famous centre for AI with a conversion MSc that attracts students from all over the world. Many of the PhD students Odette interviewed waxed lyrical about how that course had changed their lives. For example, Celestine Mallory had a first degree in a bioscience, and after some years outside higher education came to Illington to do the MSc.

> It's a very hectic and intensive course, and about half-way through I discovered I was actually enjoying it, and I thought why not see if I can do a PhD. My idea of fun is poking about with things so therefore I wanted to do robotics. I think it's fascinating.

Similar comments came from Ted Kanelos: 'I chose AI because the subject promised to be interesting and because of the study of intelligence and the fact it cuts across biology and psychology.' Fran Pendleton had also come to the conversion MSc at Illington: 'Once I started I really liked it, and I decided to stay in it.' Salvatore Ianello had done well on the MSc and it fired his love of AI: 'I wanted to do a PhD because I was always interested in science, and I wanted to stay in science, I wanted to do research.' Virginia Kaltenbrun:

> I felt that if I got interested in robotics, and I knew that there was lot of work going on down here, and it seemed like a good way to get into it, I was quite eager to go into research, and I wanted to do a PhD. [It was] the natural progression.

For two of the respondents – Julie Kylie and Wilma Ross – AI was not only intellectually satisfying, but also met their emotional needs. Julie Kylie, for example, told Odette:

> It was absolutely brilliant. I was so, once I'd got here and been here a little while I was so glad I hadn't gone to the States because it's a brilliant course here, it's absolutely wonderful. So yeah, I really felt like I'd landed on my feet, and that I was finally doing something that I really felt happy doing. I love the fact that it's multidisciplinary – that rolled even more of the strands of my life into one.

Wilma Ross expressed similar enthusiasm for the intrinsic interest of the field:

So I did the MSc and that was brilliant, I really enjoyed that, that was quite intellectually stimulating, and it was a good crowd of people. ... I wrote my thesis and I really enjoyed that, and it was the most enjoyable thing I've done since, since I'd left my undergraduate degree so I sort of carried on to do a PhD because I was sort of fired up by my interest in what I was doing.

The converted anthropologists were just as enthusiastic. Louisa Montoya had originally done philosophy. She explained her conversion:

The interest really grew out of a philosophical interest. I was interested in different belief systems. I realized that I liked philosophy and was good at it but I'm not happy with just working with ideas, sitting at my desk, juggling with ideas, I wanted to have a practical aspect as well. I'm very much someone who thinks that fieldwork is very important.

Giselle Dumont:

I read geography at Hadleigh, and decided in my last year that I enjoyed research, I'd done an undergraduate project in Venezuela, which I thoroughly enjoyed, and thought that was something I wanted to do more of. I knew I wanted to get into rural development kind of work. ... I decided to make a switch to anthropology and so the conversion course.

Janet Lundgren had converted from sociology at Southersham: 'I felt much more comfortable in anthropology.'

The students we have just quoted were stressing to Odette how they adored their subject and how doing a PhD was an emotional and intellectual quest for personal fulfilment. It would be naive to accept such accounts at face value, because the same students saw a PhD as a vocational qualification: they wanted to be university lecturers and career researchers. Many also wanted to avoid a routine job, or to escape back to university from a routine job. A few wanted to be in a particular city, and were offered a PhD place before they had found any other source of income. However, the dominant motif in the student accounts is one of enthusiasm for the ideal of the PhD, even if they faced difficulties with specific aspects of it.

The quest has stages: planning, data collection, analysis, writing up. All these stages have their problems and their pleasures. One of our students, Eunice Lester, who was in the final stages of her PhD, told us:

I'm constantly amazed because at each point of the research process somebody will come along and say this is the worst part of the whole process – from research question formulation right up to now! And somebody just said to me they felt really sorry for me because this is the

The Nature of the Quest

most demoralizing and lonely part, etc. etc. etc. And it has been a lonely process. There are ups and downs. There are times when I'm sick and tired of reading my own prose, I don't want to do it anymore. But I'm feeling positive at the moment.

Eunice Lester's comments could be echoed by any of our students in the final year. However, the contrasting disciplinary cultures make students' experiences at each stage rather different, as we show in the chapters that follow. Students whose work was empirical faced different problems from those who worked on theoretical topics.

The last theme that cross-cuts all the disciplines, and that needs to be explored here, is the contrast between successful and unsuccessful students. The specific examples we draw on are from social anthropology, where Odette was able to trace and interview students facing failure: we did not manage to find such unhappy people in our other disciplines. However, because the indeterminacy of the quest is particularly evident in social anthropology these quotes are illuminating in themselves. We begin with two students who had understood what the PhD in social anthropology is: both very successful students who got their PhDs and then lectureships. They had, in Bourdieu's terms, achieved legitimate membership, and brought home the Sampo. Their clear statement can be contrasted with the sad reflection of Colin Ives, who had discovered himself to be a victim of symbolic violence – a casualty of the struggle on the university field. Harry Kettering, at Kingford, said a PhD should be two things:

> It should show you have the capability to do research and to organize collection, interpretation of data, which is one of the aims the ESRC sees, but I also believe that if possible, it should also be an original contribution to knowledge, so that at the same time it's an end in itself, a means to other ends, a means to pursue a career in which you continue these research skills.

Louisa Montoya also said the PhD was two things:

> On the one hand it's simply a title, on the other hand it is major academic work. You do this fieldwork and then you come back and get this title which enables you to get on in your career.

These two students, who got their PhDs – one a British man, the other a woman from overseas – had been successfully enculturated into British social anthropology. Their matter-of-fact accounts are those of the successful: the quest is over, and real professional life can begin. In contrast, Colin Ives, struggling to write up his overdue PhD, and recognizing his failure, sees the symbolic violence that is enacted on PhD students: 'I felt that I was certainly being tested somehow, there was a feeling that I was going through this thing, and you have to come out in the right shape.' Colin did not enjoy his fieldwork, disliked many of his informants, and did not intend to stay in anthropology, because

> I've come to recognize more and more things like class. I come from a working-class background. I was the first person from my very extended family to get to university and I never really thought of class being at all important. But since I started doing the research I realized just how much submerged knowledge there is that presumes some kind of middle-class background. ... I've gained a sense of where I come from. In fact there's a lot of things I didn't know, which I ought to have, and that is something that isn't spelt out at all for the sake of maintaining the right image ... so the idea of staying in social anthropology and being an anthropologist – it's a different social world, it really isn't for me.

The Personal Quest

In the course of this chapter we have explored a number of themes, derived from academics and their graduate students, concerning the PhD. It is apparent that there is no single definition of the personal, intellectual quest on which doctoral students embark. Indeed, we should not expect there to be one. It is apparent that the process of academic socialization, of which doctoral research is an integral part, is often diffuse and complex. Judgements of originality, quality and so on escape the formulae of purely 'technical' specifications. Scientific and academic knowledge does not rest on a purely mechanistic set of definitions and requirements.

We do not believe that this represents a fundamental weakness in the process of doctoral research and supervision. We have not raised these issues in order to raise the spectre of academic quality assurance which can be guaranteed through ever greater explication of procedures, expected outcomes and assessment criteria. It is clear that scientific and academic knowledge is not created or evaluated like that. There are significant elements of tacit, indeterminate knowledge, and academic socialization implies a good deal more than the mere technical accomplishment of a particular piece of academic work. (This relates to a generic problem with many contemporary approaches to 'quality' in UK higher education, which treats tacit cultural knowledge as a dangerous residue to be eliminated rather than an intrinsic feature of all knowledge production and reproduction; a detailed critique along those lines is, however, beyond the scope of this particular monograph.)

Likewise, academic socialization goes beyond the conduct and successful completion of the PhD itself. The experience of postgraduate work involves

The Nature of the Quest

a process of social learning. It is a matter of enculturation into the culture or subculture of the academic discipline. Moreover, the nature of 'knowledge' itself is highly specific to particular disciplines and specialisms. Each discipline creates and re-creates itself through particular forms of intellectual work, and through distinctive forms of social relationship. The three chapters that follow explore some of the specific aspects of disciplinary culture. We explore three different ways of knowledge reproduction, which in turn illuminate more general features of disciplinary culture. We discuss the conduct and social relations of laboratory science – illustrated from our work in biochemistry. We explore the nature of field research, with particular reference to social anthropology and human geography. We then move on to discuss modelling and computational research, drawing on our work in artificial intelligence and physical geography. Each discipline displays a different way of organizing and generating academic knowledge. Each is grounded in a distinctive way of reproducing and representing the natural or social world. The graduate student becomes immersed in these characteristic ways of knowing and doing in the course of academic enculturation.

4 The Appliance of Science
Laboratory Scientists in the Making

> The scientific ambition ... aims to reinsert the extraordinary event into the series of ordinary events within which it finds its explanation.
>
> (Bourdieu, 1988: 161)

This chapter examines socialization in biochemistry, and to a lesser extent the other laboratory-based sciences we studied – physical geography and environmental sciences. We discuss the social context in which that socialization takes place and the production of knowledge in science at doctoral level. To this end we explore how scientific knowledge in biochemistry is defined, produced and reproduced in sites of academic socialization and how this knowledge is characterized and transmitted. The choice of topic was prompted by a notable absence of ethnographic work on 'becoming a scientist' (Delamont, 1987; Ashmore et al., 1995).

We carried out thirty-seven ethnographic interviews with academics and PhD students in British university biochemistry departments. Of those thirty-seven, eight were interviews with the heads of laboratories or research groups who supervised biochemistry PhD students in their labs. The remaining twenty-nine interviews were with biochemistry doctoral students and postdoctoral researchers. In addition we carried out interviews with technical staff at selected laboratories. We also made fieldnotes based on our observations at selected sites. This comprised observation of students at the work bench and in the laboratory, and observation of supervisor-led research group meetings for laboratory members. All the informants quoted in this chapter are biochemists unless we specify otherwise. In this chapter we have also drawn on our interviews with physical geographers and environmental scientists who worked in laboratories or fieldsites: these informants are identified with their respective disciplines. (Physical geographers and others who based their work primarily on computer modelling techniques are discussed in Chapter 6.)

The focus of this chapter is how students of science come to terms with the vagaries of experimental research without abandoning the notion that science is for the most part a very stable and highly convergent activity. Our

53

The Appliance of Science

starting point lies with this 'stability' which derives from our understanding that most science is not in fact revolutionary. On the contrary, a great deal of scientific work concentrates on addressing problems which arise out of, and are solvable within, the existing framework of research (Fleck, 1979). Despite enthusiasm for refutation and revolution, most scientific activity leads to a large amount of relatively stable knowledge, devices and practice. In addressing these issues we draw eclectically on contemporary sociology of scientific knowledge (SSK). There are several sub-groups within the constructivist sociology of science (see Hess, 1997, for an amusing anthropological account). We do not seek to differentiate between the various theoretical and epistemological positions here. We have drawn from a variety of different authors, representing somewhat different orientations – including Collins and Pinch (1993, 1998) and Clarke (1998). We also draw on the work of Hacking. Hacking (1992) offers one explanation for the relative stability of scientific knowledge and practice, in that science is a 'self vindicating' activity. As a science matures it develops theories, apparatus and types of analysis which are adjusted to each other. The different components are mutually dependent because the theory is tested with apparatus that has evolved in conjunction with it. The data are then analysed in accordance with procedures which likewise are inseparable from the theory and apparatus which they support. In this way, scientific work is a creation of its own devices, developed and measured by the very instruments which it has spawned. Even when science progresses it cannot escape its own mature, intellectual and experimental framework (see also Clarke and Fujimura, 1992).

While a great deal of scientific activity is non-revolutionary, every so often one scientific tradition is rejected in favour of another, and when this happens traditional techniques and beliefs are abandoned and replaced by new ones. The question arises of how, when the bread and butter of science is rooted in traditional commitment to a set of beliefs and practices on which the stability of the discipline rests, can one paradigm be suddenly rejected in favour of another. An 'essential tension' described by Kuhn (1977) captures the apparent contradiction here. That is, only research which is firmly located within the current scientific tradition is able to break that tradition. It is beyond the scope of this chapter to grapple fully with the implications of this contradiction, which has consumed the attention of those working from within the social science of knowledge (Pickering, 1992). Our interests, however, do reflect upon issues related to 'essential tension' to the extent that science neophytes are exposed to these contradictions early on in their doctoral careers. Doctoral science, it transpires, is quite removed from undergraduate experiences where results are predictable and outcomes certain (but see Delamont and Atkinson, 1995; Tobias, 1990). PhD students find that their experiments go wrong all the time and that successful conclusions, rather than being the outcome of a unitary process, are only achievable through the mutual adjustment of ideas, instruments and activities.

The analysis presented here owes much to the account of science practice developed by Hacking (1992). It is Hacking's contention that scientific culture is made up of a multiplicity of components (material, conceptual and social), which stand in no unitary relationship to each other. The outcome of scientific practice is achieved through the convergence of these disparate elements. In observing this multiplicity he develops an alternative paradigm of scientific practice to that favoured by SSK. The SSK position holds that scientific culture is a single unitary entity, or an 'open conceptual net' where nothing within the net decides what happens in the future. This leads SSK to the conclusion that it is interest which determines closure of the net (Pickering, 1992).

In rejecting the 'conceptual net' thesis, Hacking considers the multiplicity of cultural elements involved, any combination of which beside interest may determine closure. He argues that any single cultural element may be open-endedly extended, but that the task of fitting various extensions together, or of combining disparate elements, is not. Therefore the convergence of elements is a product of successful engineering, which itself may determine future scientific practice. Hacking suggests three reasons for the appearance of relative stability and continuity in scientific practice. First, he suggests acts of collective reconstruction of past work: research in the past is implicitly rewritten to correspond with contemporary practice. This retrospective reinterpretation of history always tends to create the appearance of stability rather than discontinuity. Second, he suggests that scientific practice can be likened to a 'rope with many strands'. At any given time there are many traditions in play – theoretical traditions, experimental methods, established instrumental environments and traditions. These are mutually supporting. One can be disrupted, however, without totally damaging the overall intellectual project. Third, he refers to the 'black boxing' of experimental techniques, so that successive generations may, for practical purposes, take for granted the innovations and instrumentation of their predecessors.

All of these are relevant to an understanding of the pedagogic continuity of a discipline such as biochemistry. Students inherit and take on trust a good deal of knowledge, and research problems, that derive from previous generations. The work of immediate predecessors is incorporated into graduate students' own projects, as topics are cascaded down successive generations in the research group. In the following sections we present an account of the ways in which biochemistry doctoral students are socialized into scientific practice, based upon data collected during the course of our own research. Our account focuses upon the contradictions which doctoral students experience as a consequence of the 'essential tension' fundamental to experimental scientific research. Through the accounts provided by postgraduates and their supervisors, the paper explores how science training is able to sustain a 'pedagogical continuity' through which effective socialization in biochemistry is realized at doctoral level. Where appropriate, we also deal with the geography and environmental science laboratories.

Recognition of Incongruity

Commentators from Getzels and Jackson (1963) to Tobias (1990) have argued that education in science prior to doctoral level tends to emphasize convergent thinking and evaluation, and that this is often at the expense of divergent thinking. It would seem that until research students are ready to start work on their own projects they are neither expected to attempt innovatory research nor exposed to the immediate products of original work done by others (Kuhn, 1977). To this extent early entrants into science are cocooned within the confinement of a discipline that largely protects neophytes from the vagaries of scientific uncertainty. The conservative journalist Simon Jenkins, addressing the 1998 annual meeting of the British Association for the Advancement of Science in Cardiff, quoted Claude Bernard, the nineteenth-century French medical scientist, who said, 'Science is a superb and dazzling hall, but one which may be reached only by passing through a long and ghastly kitchen' (Jenkins, 1998). This is, of course, a metaphor redolent of its time: only white middle-class males could so readily enjoy the splendours of the hall while avoiding the toil below stairs. But it also captures the sense in which scientists can become initiates while being protected from the realities of human labour that underpin the science itself.

As a consequence, before entering the laboratory as researchers, many students have experienced sciences as pedagogically stable. These early experiences of the discipline lead to expectations that goals of laboratory experiments are realizable and that scientific outcomes are certain. However, as noted by Delamont and Atkinson (1995) and by Collins and Pinch (1998), experiments that are carried out as a routine component of education and training address questions to which the answers are already known and which are constructed to produce only successful conclusions. As new entrants into the world of postgraduate science, PhD students find themselves experiencing a 'reality shock' as the protective cocoon which guided them through undergraduate study is suddenly whisked away. Despite, or rather because of, the confidence instilled by practical experience gained through laboratory-based projects in the final year of undergraduate study, many are ill-prepared for the vagaries of experimental research. Contrary to their prior experience, experiments can and do go wrong, things do not work as anticipated, and outcomes are far from certain. The incongruity between doctoral research and the science education which pre-dates it is recognized by those supervising PhD students as a function of, first, the limited exposure to laboratory work which undergraduates receive and, second, the

The Appliance of Science

deceptive nature of the little laboratory experience which they have received. As one supervisor, Dr Dewry at Ribblethorpe, explained:

> In their undergraduate training they get very little laboratory experience – in their final year project they get a feel and that's all. At undergraduate level the experiments are designed to work, that's why they're chosen. Someone once said if you took every thing that worked in the lab over the course of a year it would be two weeks' work in the lab.

At undergraduate level students expect their experiments to work; at postgraduate level they can make no such assumption. The postgraduate students we interviewed acknowledged their lack of preparation for doctoral work, and talked openly about their feelings of despondency and sometimes panic when experiments consistently failed. As Dr Garnette at Baynesholme suggested:

> That's the most useful thing about bull sessions, I think. It's people thinking about why it doesn't work. I think everybody who does biochemistry accepts that it's like that. ... If you call your time 100 per cent, 85 per cent of the time things don't work, and 15 per cent perhaps do. And the frustration really starts when you have several 85 per cents put together before you manage to generate any 15 per cents.

As Morton Stayman, a postdoc at Ribblethorpe, explained to Odette:

> You either learn to accept things not working nine times out of ten in lab work, and if you can cope with that you'll be all right. Some people it takes longer to realize that, it's a terribly demoralizing process, something they all seem to realize. Some of them are having a terrible time [sequencing DNA]. They've been doing it for over a year now with no successes. There is only one more direction to follow. If that fails they'll have to cut their losses.

And in much the same vein is the account from Lucinda Asmara, from Ribblethorpe:

> Actually day to day at the bench everything I'd learned as an undergraduate was completely unrelated to what it was like actually to do those things at the bench. I don't think there's any way you can go straight from doing it once in an undergraduate practical to actually being competent at the bench.

The realization that the outcomes of laboratory work are by no means certain accompanies a growing concern among new postgraduates that there

The Appliance of Science

is nothing predictable about doctoral study and that there is no guarantee that PhD requirements will be met. This is when the panic begins to set in and the doctoral students acknowledge 'it's suddenly for real', 'it's completely open-ended', and 'there's no guarantees'. In terms of their schedules of study, the students were equally aware how three years' work, in their own words, 'could easily go down the toilet'. Given their paucity of laboratory experience prior to doctoral research, perhaps it not surprising that PhD students experience initial difficulties in producing results. Indeed, popular explanations (among practitioners) for scientific error and inaccuracy often have recourse to 'non scientific' factors (Gilbert and Mulkay, 1984). In other words those experiments that are successful are judged to reaffirm nature and those that are not successful can be accounted for in terms of human error (Collins, 1985; Barnes, 1974; Bloor 1976).

To this end, supervisors stressed the necessity for selecting doctoral candidates who were 'lab wise' and who were good at '*do* [sic] things, rather than *think* things', as Dr Dewry put it. Being 'good at the bench' was seen as a necessary prerequisite for successful experimental research. However, while there is an obvious logic to this, it still stands that, however accomplished the neophyte becomes, 'nine times out of ten things don't work in the lab'. However much effort goes into controlling the conditions under which experimental research takes place, successful outcomes are never assured. Just because an experiment has worked once, there is no guarantee that it will work at any time in the future. We also learnt that once a particular experiment has worked, 'then in most cases it always works', and then again, 'sometimes you'll do something for the first time [and] without any rhyme or reason it will work, and other times things that should work won't' (Dr Danberry of Ribblethorpe).

Despite their recognition that 'nothing about research is predictable', biochemistry PhD students continue to expect, and indeed do produce results from their experiments. Scott Wenzel from Baynesholme said:

> For the first fifteen months nothing worked. I didn't panic too much, although it is very disheartening, as everyone gives you a lot of reassurance and support. It always comes together in the end. That's what everybody tells you. And it did.

Despite such frustrations and expressed shortcomings, research students in the laboratory expect to complete their PhDs. This prompts the question: How, when scientific work is apparently so capricious in nature and unpredictable in outcome, can doctoral candidates predict the successful outcome of their labours?

The Construction of the Doctorate

Experimental scientific work is unpredictable, but doctoral candidates (and their supervisors) expect successful outcomes. Contrary therefore, to the notion that all science activity involves the open and long-term commitment to and pursuit of discovery we find that the PhD is not open-ended. It must be constructed in such a way as to ensure eventual success, or at least to minimize the risk of failure. As Knorr-Cetina (1981) puts it, PhD students cannot commit themselves to a journey of unknown destination. Rather, like seasoned practitioners 'they choose a known destination at which it seems likely they will arrive not only on time, but ahead of anyone else' (Knorr-Cetina, 1981: 59).

The construction of feasible problems rests on the fact that 'not all science activity is about nature' (Latour and Woolgar, 1986: 243) but rather is about the construction of a reality through the manipulation of representations and versions of natural phenomena. Within this construction PhD work involves the grasping of necessary conditions which make those versions of reality possible. It includes what Fujimura (1997) refers to as the construction of 'doable' problems. This goes beyond the technical specification of equipment and bench techniques, and includes the more diffuse skills of allocating time and personal resources, articulating a student's own work with that of the research group, and a general commitment of faith to the research process. Of that less visible work Fujimura herself says of her research on oncogene scientists:

> Training in basic research laboratories emphasizes experimental techniques and not articulation work. Students are explicitly taught how to clone genes and grow cells in culture. They are also taught which materials are easier to manipulate for which purposes and which machines can take care of which tasks. Students may even be taught theoretical problem design, although this is usually learned by example. There are fewer explicit lessons on articulation work.
> (Fujimura 1997: 185)

The construction of a PhD project involves the identification of realistic goals. Furthermore, these goals must be realizable within the allotted period of time for study. None of the doctoral candidates whom we interviewed was responsible for identifying their initial research topics nor the outline structure of their intended study. This task had been accomplished by the supervisor who assumed full responsibility for the identification of projects and attracting necessary funding. Prospective candidates were attracted to departments that contained academic staff working in their preferred area or to particular supervisors who were advertising suitable positions. Although many of our PhD respondents claimed to have a reasonable amount of freedom in their everyday work, i.e. in following their own leads,

The Appliance of Science

the reality was that they worked with a fairly tight research agenda from the outset. We discuss this issue in more detail in Chapter 9, when we elaborate on the social relations of doctoral research in different disciplinary contexts.

In order to effect successful outcomes, PhD students need to achieve results. We learnt how the course of a PhD student's research could change drastically in the pursuit of results. As a supervisor explained:

> Where experiments, or an experiment is not working my attitude is 'don't flog a dead horse'. So change the obvious things and if that doesn't work either we switch to another sort of experiment. For example, if they have to purify enzymes, they may not be able to do it. They need a second chance to get results. And they need some results.

Results were uppermost in the minds of the doctoral students we interviewed. Accordingly, students learn to structure and restructure their own research work on a day to day basis:

> I work at the bench most of the day. I always start off between 8 and 8.30 in the morning and stay according to how much I've got to do. Usually I stay all day and sometimes much longer. You can't plan very much what you're going to do ahead because you may start an experiment and then things could go very wrong. So I couldn't plan over the next week, because my plans will change according to how successful my experiments are. Also if I have a positive result to an experiment I may change my mind as to what I'll do next. That would mean I'd have to alter my plans.

Supervisors and students must make a series of choices throughout the duration of the research which will inform and effect this outcome. This process of decision making can lead to some cynicism on the part of students who see their study determined by the ability 'to (a) pick the right experiment and (b) know when to give up', as one of them put it to us. Supervisors we interviewed also explained the importance of understanding the nature of experiments and getting results. For example:

> We've been talking a lot about experiments that work and don't work but in a sense every experiment works. if they drop the test-tube and it smashes that experiment has worked. I mean, in a very silly sense you know the gravity has taken over when the tube hits the floor, it smashes, and there's no experiment actually that doesn't work, that's almost the faith in which we put in science. When they've done the experiment if the student comes to me and says 'look the experiment didn't work, I'm doing it again' I never let them go and do it again. We go through the experiment because it has worked. What they mean is it hasn't given

them the results that they predicted, and that is very, very important. I think so-called failures are often more important than the experiments that give you the result which you predicted.

Doctoral students must grasp that although they are encouraged to produce successful conclusions to their experiments, failed experiments are both scientifically interesting and valid. In the initial stages of PhD work this in itself is a source of relief to students who are failing to achieve their desired results. That 'you don't have to get results to get your PhD' and that 'all results are scientifically important' lend comfort to the depressed, anxious and disillusioned. Needless to say, however, the objective of biochemistry doctoral students is to produce usable, meaningful results, every time.

Coming to Terms with Problems

Preparation for failure constitutes an important aspect of science training at doctoral level. Doctoral students learn that they cannot expect experiments to work; indeed, they learn in most cases that they won't work. It is only when PhD students first begin to produce results in the laboratory that their previous worries and insecurities are overshadowed, and despondency gives way to a growing conviction that that ultimately their experiments will work:

> One of the things that's very frustrating is when your experiments are not working. When I came here to begin with I had great aspirations for achievement. I had good ideas about what I'd do and that I'd get lots of results. Then in the first few months nothing does work and you get really worried about it. But then when it does work you get really excited. You probably get more excited with the first results than any you get after. You're really pleased. And slowly you come to terms with things not working.
>
> (Suzanne Deladier, Baynesholme)

Once students come to accept the unpredictability of scientific research it becomes a manageable component of their work. When they first plan an experiment, 'it's always on the basis that everything will work, which of course it doesn't'. After a while they learn to rationalize this failure in terms of likely outcomes: 'at the first attempt there's a fifty-fifty chance it will work, but that's being generous'. Whilst in the long term it is probable that many more experiments will fail than succeed, doctoral students come to understand this as part and parcel of the laboratory experience. At this point they stop attributing failed experiments to personal inadequacy: 'PhDs get bad patches when things don't work out in the expected way. They can't see where it's going wrong and they don't have any results. They mostly

The Appliance of Science

appreciate that this does happen and not just to them' (Dr Duval, Ribblethorpe).

So whilst experimental laboratory work is frustrating because initially 'you can't get something to work' and 'you can get to your wits' end trying to get something to work', PhD students gradually develop confidence in their endeavours. Doctoral students come to accept that 'everything goes wrong but you have to remember that's not all the time'. When experiments do 'work', then students gradually develop confidence in their developing competence. They can start to sense that they have the right personal skills and tacit knowledge.

In the early stages PhD students are painfully aware of their lack of laboratory experience. They recognize that this experience will be necessary for them to conclude their study successfully. 'Being good at the bench' is viewed as a determining factor in the eventual outcome of research. However, graduate students also recognize that bench skills can be as elusive as the phenomena that they are studying. They are not, for example, seen as teachable or even particularly learnable skills. In essence, they defy translation into standard formulae; they are grasped and intuited as much as they are 'taught and caught'. Initiates therefore talk about the combination of both learned experience and the 'gift' of excellence in the laboratory:

> You get a feel for working at the bench and you get a real feeling for it. We deal with tiny amounts and you need confidence in dealing with that. You have to overcome being tentative, and it's a well known saying, 'being good at the bench'. People who are good at the bench take a protocol and fiddle around with it and they will get it working. Other people are really cack-handed. It's a knack and it's virtually impossible to teach. Some people who are good at the bench seem to do many things wrong and yet their experiments work. And some appear to do it perfectly and it never works. There was this one person here known as the cowboy, but his stuff always worked.

This account from a postdoctoral researcher lends credence to the proposition that because of it's 'capricious' and 'tacit' nature, the transmission of scientific knowledge is seldom straightforward. Mastery of the techniques through which 'tacit' knowledge is grasped depends upon the ability to perform skills without being able to articulate how they are actually done (Polanyi, 1958: 67). 'Tacit knowledge' can be juxtaposed against knowledge that readily lends itself to explicit formulae and can be taught by 'chalk and talk' techniques. Whereas 'tacit knowledge' (the 'enculturational' model) relies upon social skills, the 'algorithmical' model is transmitted through formal instructions (Collins, 1985). We have already introduced the complementary concepts of *indeterminacy* and *technicality* (Jamous and Peloille, 1970; Parry, 1994; Atkinson et al., 1977; Coffey and Atkinson, 1994).

The Appliance of Science

Technical knowledge is constructed as amenable to documentation, prescription and explicit formulation. Conversely, indeterminate knowledge is personal and tacit, constructed as defying translation into techniques, skills and formulae. Whereas technical knowledge is believed to lend itself to formal instruction, indeterminate knowledge is felt to defy translation into explicit transmission. Indeterminate knowledge is thus believed to be 'caught' rather than 'taught', transmitted via personal experience rather than by systematic instruction.

Academic disciplines are characterized by a tension between tacit and technical knowledge, and the former has been described as a crucial component of all scientific work (Collins, 1985; Pinch et al., 1996). It has also been argued that the extent to which tacit knowledge characterizes a discipline informs the methods by which disciplinary knowledge is transmitted (Parry, 1992). Previous research on the transmission of knowledge (Collins, 1985: 56) suggests that the flow of scientific information travels best where there is personal contact with an accomplished practitioner, and where it is already tried and tested. The application of research techniques is not acquired simply from reading textbooks or research papers. As Gilbert and Mulkay explain:

> Methods sections give the impression that the application of methodological procedures is a highly routinized activity, with little room for individual initiative and variability. Informally, however, scientists stressed that carrying out experiments is a practical activity requiring craft skills, subtle judgments and intuitive understanding. They talked of particular researchers having 'good hands' or 'a feel' for laboratory work.
>
> (Gilbert and Mulkay, 1984: 53)

Spender, one of the distinguished biochemists interviewed by Gilbert and Mulkay explained: 'You get a feel for what you read. ... Dr X was not an experimenter and no longer does any. If you are an experimenter you know what is important and what is not important' (Gilbert and Mulkay, 1984: 53).

Pre-established Knowledge

Doctoral work in the laboratory sciences is thoroughly dependent on what Hacking (1992) describes as pre-established knowledge. Scientific research comprises ideas, materials and skills, all of which inscribe pre-established knowledge. Pre-established knowledge is available to students by virtue of the way in which doctoral work is structured in the laboratory. It comprises the body of scientific theory and knowledge, which provides the context from within which research questions arise and are addressed. It includes the accepted methods and tools of scientific procedure, and the way in which doctoral students learn to carry out their research tasks (Galison, 1987).

Doctoral socialization in biochemistry is mediated through laboratory arrangements which both afford the students contact with accomplished practitioners and are firmly located in the context of existing research. To reiterate, it is the supervisor rather than the student who identifies the research topic and provides the structure of the research that is to be carried out. Doctoral supervisors in biochemistry see 'creating the possibilities for other people to do (research) and trying to shape the direction of what gets done', as their primary function and students are expected to seek supervisory assistance on a day to day basis elsewhere. As one established scientist, Professor Gantry from Baynesholme, told us:

> Well what I like to do with students – when I was a postdoc in the lab I liked to work very much on my own. Because it suits me. So I encourage people to do the same, I give them their own head. Because of the numbers I couldn't always be looking over their shoulders anyway. If they need day to day help there are others like the postdocs in the lab and they can help them. I tend to give specific advice to students. They have a definite programme. I'm not there to tell them how to use an instrument. They can find someone else for that.

Laboratory research revolves around a supervisor or research director with doctoral students and postdoctoral researchers working in his or her area on topics that are to some extent related. Supervisors or research directors tend to have several PhD students at any one time and talk about the concept of 'team work' in relation to laboratory activities (Becher, 1989). Supervisors take a back-seat role in regard to practical day to day supervision of students, who tend to rely upon postdocs and doctoral students more advanced in their study. For instance, the following extract from an interview with Giles Perrin conveys a sense of those relationships:

Giles: [...] does seem to do a lot of lab work. ... He's always around. We talk at least once a week, we all have our individual day when we talk to Prof.
OP: So you see him once a week by yourself?
Giles: By ourself [sic]. I mean we're always talking in the lab. For the actual techniques we've fortunately got qualified postdocs all of which have got a lot of detailed knowledge. So you simply go and ask them. You don't go to one person.
OP: And you have a weekly meeting?
Giles: Yes, we have a weekly meeting.

The Appliance of Science

When we interviewed Professor Barsington, a physical geographer at Hernchester, he was in charge of a group of nine people – six research students, one postdoc and two technicians – running two projects, which shared a 'common mathematics', as he put it. The research students were expected to help each other and to rely on the technicians for day to day direction. Barsington saw the allocation of specific topics to his doctoral students as 'a student protection element', because students expected to get their theses completed on time in his research team. He used the metaphors of 'a chain letter' and a 'relay race' to capture the transmission of research problems within the group: 'It's like a baton in a relay race, it's like a baton, passed on to the next student. To maintain knowledge you have to have overlap.'

In this process of transmission, postdoctoral researchers and experienced technicians are crucial intermediaries, ensuring the smooth hand-on from one generation to the next by overseeing the mundane practicalities of laboratory research. Postdoctoral researchers see postgraduate supervision as part of their responsibilities, and in doing so reproduce the conditions under which they themselves were trained. They see their experience as qualifying them to supervise, and claim an expertise in 'generat[ing] a feeling for what is likely to make the difference between something working and not working'.

The research laboratory operates upon the principle of reciprocity, whereby members take an active interest in the activities of their colleagues. At the same time, members of the laboratory pursue their own objectives and recognize that the interests of PhD students differ from those of the postdocs:

> I tend not to differentiate between them, although what you have to keep in mind with the student is that the student has to write a coherent thesis at the end. But I guess, OK, they're more inexperienced, the students are than the postdocs, but everyone works as a team, and if the postdoc is good then that postdoc will actually stimulate and help look after the students, and get credit in due course.
>
> (Dr Quayne, Ribblethorpe)

Our observations of supervisor-led research meetings confirmed the way in which laboratory members (supervisor, postgraduates and postdocs) provide assistance and support for each other through the sharing of experiences. In the following extract from our fieldnotes, based on observation of Professor Gantry's group, a doctoral student, Charles Albright, outlines a particular problem that he has experienced in the preceding week. The notes summarize the interaction, and are reported in indirect speech:

Supervisor: Asks Charles about the progress of his cells.

The Appliance of Science

Charles: He says his cells are OK. He then explains he's been taking them from the parent cultures and subcultures every day and that they've started to grow. He's been taking samples and looking at them under the microscope. However he has to take another subculture sample as he doesn't think he's got enough cells.
Supervisor: Asks Charles whether the cells are clumping together.
Charles: Confirms that there are still a lot of aggregate cells.
Elissa Tyrone (PhD student): Says that in order to try solving this problem Charles should try passing them through the tip of a needle several times, put them through a syringe five times and then count them.
Dr Fouteaux (postdoc): Asks if Charles has got anything in the suspension medium to stop them clumping: 'We always use BSA to stop clumping.'
Supervisor: Stresses the importance of getting the cells multiplying and dividing.
Ian Angelworth (PhD student): Explains it's standard to get clumping, because after all Charles wants to avoid stabilizing the cells.
Supervisor: Agrees that there is a danger of altering the metabolism.
Charles: Refers to another experiment where he had quite different results. Because of this he's not sure whether it's just a one-off.
Ian: Asks what stage the culture is at.
Charles: Says it's the same.
Supervisor: Asks if the duplicates are the same.
Charles: Confirms that they are.
Supervisor: Explains that's the trouble with doing an experiment again several months later. He says as a result Charles will probably have to repeat the experiment again.
Ian: Says Charles should check the levels.
Supervisor: Agrees with Ian. Charles must get the method sorted out. Then he asks Charles if it's the final experiment for the paper which he's writing.
Charles: Confirms that it is.
Supervisor: 'That's sod's law!'

In this encounter members of the research team apply themselves to solving Charles's problem of clumping cells. They do this by providing him with examples of the ways in which they have dealt with similar problems and offering suggestions that may assist Charles to overcome the difficulties he is experiencing. They then move on to discuss Elissa's experiment.

The team approach to supervision provides doctoral students with a buffer against isolation and can also help to rescue the PhD when relationships between the student and supervisor break down. The scientists talked about 'pulling together', 'digging ourselves out from a dodgy situation' and

The Appliance of Science

'collective survival, in the face of a staggering lack of supervision' (Earl Mohr, Ribblethorpe). In less extreme situations, and when PhD students are experiencing despondency due to initial difficulties in getting their experiments to work, other members of the group are supportive. In the following extract from the fieldnotes taken at a research team meeting, ten days after the one noted above, Charles (the PhD student) expresses concern because the cultures which he is working on are infected:

Charles: I've got an infection in my suspension cultures.
Supervisor: All of them?
Charles: No, I started two off on Friday.
Supervisor: They can get an infection when you open the container.
Dr Garnette (postdoc): It's a bad time of year for that.
Supervisor: It's the particular cultures too.
Dr Garnette: What's the temperature?
Ian (PhD student): Is it cloudy?
Charles: One is.
Ian: It could be that something has come off the glass.
Dr Garnette: I used to get mould problems.

Other members of the team here offer advice to Charles and also reassurance that the problems are usually something simple, sometimes due to circumstances beyond the student's control and also routinely experienced by other team members. We do not mean to imply Charles Albright was a poor student by citing two examples of his research problems. As we have indicated consistently, problems with equipment and experimental procedure are 'normal' for postgraduate students generally.

As well as experience, laboratory research work revolves around the mutual support and sharing of materials, skills and equipment:

> We're all working on the same sort of areas, we use a lot of the same assays and substances ... a lot of the substances I make will be used by other people as well. If I invent a method to make something easier then they'll use it as well.

An important feature of laboratory work is a continuity of practice so that skills, equipment and topics are passed down through the ranks of postdoctoral researchers and research students. Doctoral students describe their research as 'taking further' and 'building upon' the work of others. They often know these individuals, who may be employed as postdocs in the laboratory after completing their own PhD work:

> The way that it actually happens, is that someone has done a purification of an enzyme and characterized it and then has finished and then

the next student takes it on. What I tend not to do is have two people working on the same enzyme so one does the purification which can be very routine and then another one does the exciting things which can be done once you've purified it. That tends to set one student against another, so we run projects in series in any particular area rather than in parallel.

(Dr Quayne, Forthamstead)

Reliance upon pre-established knowledge can, however, be problematic. The process of passing down 'old' skills and equipment means the production of 'new' science must depend to some extent upon the mastery and reproduction of 'old' equipment and techniques. Despite the fact that equipment and techniques are 'tested and 'proven', doctoral students experience considerable difficulties in reproducing outcomes. Initially it can take them several months, and in some cases it can take 'most of your PhD' to produce the same results as their predecessors, despite using the same materials, equipment and methods. The problems they encounter mirror uncertainties routinely encountered in scientific work. That is, contrary to common sense or lay expectations, the reproduction of experimental results is far from straightforward. Even within the established scientific community, practitioners who independently produce identical outcomes incur professional scepticism from their colleagues (Traweek, 1988; Collins, 1985; Pinch, 1981).

Doctoral students also draw on the published findings of previous research, of course. It is from within this body of 'accepted' science that theoretical traditions are developed, methods ratified and future research initiated. Because of this, scientific publication has beciome a focal point of social science inquiry, although the driving force of its assumed importance is contested. The urge to publish has been explained in terms of 'normative' science practice (Hagstrom, 1965), which facilitates a professional exchange process whereby practitioners 'read' and are in turn 'read' by their colleagues. Bourdieu (1975), on the other hand, suggests that normative behaviour is the outcome rather than the cause of scientific activity, and thus interprets exchange in terms of the accumulation and investment of resources. The actual cause of social activity, according to Bourdieu, is the set of strategies adopted by investors wanting to maximize their symbolic authority. However, neither explanation is sufficient to tell us why scientists are compelled to read each other's work (Latour and Woolgar, 1986) and both explanations have been criticized for failing to tell us anything about the production of scientific value (Callon, 1986). An alternative approach, favoured here, interprets publication as an essential component of a process of reification whereby tacit skills, material and equipment (often the products of grant funding themselves) become the acceptable tools of other laboratories. It is this reification process that enables both the maintenance and expansion of scientific activity (Latour and Woolgar, 1986).

The Appliance of Science

As doctoral candidates, students are immersed in established science from day one of their research. The research topic or problem which they address will be firmly located within, and a product of, scientific tradition. Publication is an intrinsic element of this tradition and the production of papers is an essential component of science activity (Myers, 1990). Members of laboratories, including PhD students, are expected to publish on the basis of their experimental findings:

> Publishing is essential for funding. My lab publishes about 4, 5, 6 papers a year. PhD students publish less because they're training although they may publish a couple of papers in their final year. It's the post docs who are most productive.
>
> (Dr Duval, Ribblethorpe)

The pressure to 'publish or perish' is alleviated to a degree in that laboratory members collaborate in the production of papers. Students publish jointly with their supervisors, other postgraduates and postdoctoral researchers. Publication is seen as a joint responsibility which provides the less experienced with practice and the opportunity to 'get their work in print':

> We've got one paper published, one in press – one I've written and has been past John [supervisor] and Clive [second supervisor] and is now with Chris [postdoc] in biology. With this project we haven't published anything yet, but John likes us to go to the Biochemists' Society meetings and to publish a poster so we get a minor publication from that.

Doctoral students begin publishing by producing posters presentations for conferences (Whittlesea, 1995). (The genre of conference posters is a much more common mode of academic dissemination in the sciences than in the humanities or social sciences.) Conferences are seen as a crucial part of doctoral training, and funding to attend is built into PhD studentships or available to students either through departmental resources or the Biochemistry Society. Without exception the PhD students we talked to had been to or were planning to attend conferences many of which were international. (We expand on this in Chapter 9.) Supervisors felt it crucial that 'scientists go to conferences early in their careers' to make and nurture career-building contacts, and to keep abreast of latest developments in the field. In the bull sessions, students are also exposed to the peer judgement of other researchers' publications. In one of Professor Gantry's bull sessions, for example, Charles explained a difficulty he was having. Professor Gantry suggested 'Make cultures derivative from the olive cultures first', and asked if anyone had made such cultures before. Matt Ferguson said 'Yes, I've got a paper on it by the group at —'. Prof Gantry replied, 'Ah, that's the paper with the paragraph written by —. We'll treat *that* paper with suspicion.'

The Appliance of Science

There is general laughter. Here students glimpse the personal side of scientific knowledge rather than the depersonalized accounts of published journal papers (cf. Gibert and Mulkay, 1984: 59–60). In the bull session, and encounters like them in other labs, students are admitted to private, sometimes 'guilty knowledge' about what 'really goes on' in the world of scientific research.

Becoming Scientists

We have explored how doctoral students in laboratory disciplines come to terms with the uncertainty and unpredictability of scientific research. An important aspect of this process is highlighted by the 'reality shock' that students experience when their experiments fail initially, and the ways in which they learn to incorporate notions of uncertainty and unpredictability into their view of science as a stable activity. We have drawn on Hacking's (1992) notion of 'pedagogic stability' in focusing on the social relations of knowledge reproduction. We have stressed the inter-generational transmission of scientific research problems, and the processes of enculturation whereby intermediaries such as postdocs act as cultural relays. We found the structure of PhD science research functioned to maintain this stability through continuity and mutual dependence, two elements highly visible in biochemistry research at doctoral level. Using Hacking's analogy of the rope we could see how the interests of group members are mutually intertwined in a diachronic process through which the work of individuals is shaped and developed.

An important element of doctoral socialization is the way in which continuity is maintained through the reliance upon pre-established knowledge. PhD topics arise out of, and are addressed from within, the existing body of scientific theory and knowledge. PhD students rely upon previously published research work and are in turn expected to add to this body of knowledge through the publication of their own results. They are encouraged to attend and contribute to conferences and, in so doing, keep abreast of current scientific activity and develop future career building contacts. Furthermore, the equipment and instruments which they use are those which have been developed and tested within the scientific community.

The fact that scientific knowledge is experienced as both capricious and tacit has implications for the way in which knowledge and skills are transmitted in the laboratory. PhD students acquire research skills through their close association with other practitioners, and through a team approach which has both sharing and caring functions. Team members share their materials, equipment, skills and experience, and also create a mutually supportive environment for when things do not work out as anticipated. We have explored the production of those elements which together constitute scientific research at doctoral level. We have examined the ways in which

The Appliance of Science

students master the hard and uncertain creative work of combining instruments, phenomena and interpretations, and, in so doing, both produce and reproduce scientific knowledge. In this sense, we have interpreted the socialization experience as one element, in its own right, contributing to the reproduction of scientific stability. The research group, the laboratory and the inter-generational exchange of research activity are powerful social mechanisms for the reproduction of stable science and for the mobilization of scientific consensus. They also embody highly successful means of academic enculturation.

5 Fieldwork

> Allowing themselves to be guided ... by a system of implicit criteria.
> (Bourdieu, 1988: 137)

Introduction

Fieldwork is a dominant mode of data collection in several major disciplines. It means different things in different academic contexts, of course, and we do not mean to imply in this chapter that there is one single 'fieldwork' approach to research. It is of particular significance to the discipline of social anthropology, and in this chapter we focus particularly on the place of fieldwork in the socialization of anthropologists. Field research of a broadly similar nature is also significant for at least some students in other disciplines – including human geography, development studies and urban studies. In this chapter we have attributed a discipline to non-anthropologists who conducted fieldwork; quotes without a disciplinary attribution are from anthropologists. Field research stands in contrast to the work of the laboratory scientists that we outlined in the previous chapter, but there are also some general similarities and continuities in the personal and intellectual experience of individual research, whether in the laboratory or in the 'field'.

Fieldwork is not merely a means of data collection in social anthropology. It is part of the collective tradition of the discipline, and a key element in the personal development of the individual anthropologist. In his general overview of British anthropology, Kuper suggests that:

> British Anthropology is not merely a term for the work done by British or even British-trained anthropologists. The phrase connotes a set of names, a limited range of ethnographic regional specialities, a list of central monographs, a characteristic mode of procedure, and a particular series of theoretical problems.
> (Kuper, 1973: 227)

Fieldwork

The conduct of ethnographic fieldwork is part of that 'characteristic mode of procedure', and is in turn closely linked to the notion of the 'monograph' as text and the range of regional ethnographic specialisms (Jackson, 1987; Fardon, 1990). Fieldwork provides a way of working as well as an academic identity that is every bit as distinctive as laboratory work for the natural scientist.

Anthropology is marked by strong academic allegiance among its academics and graduate students, and this promotes a notable sense of disciplinary identity among its numbers and converts. We use the term 'converts' here because the majority of PhD students we talked to had converted to anthropology after completing a first degree in another discipline. The term also captures the sense – which was strong among many of our informants – that they experienced a personal 'conversion' to social anthropology. In the following sections of this chapter we examine some aspects of anthropological work which contributed to 'anthropological identity' and which our informants – established academics and students – took to be fundamental to the formation of the discipline and their academic identity within it. Fieldwork is virtually a *sine qua non* of anthropological membership – just as laboratory research is a taken-for-granted facet of the natural scientist's academic socialization. Both processes foster distinctive kinds of academic knowledge – and equally distinctive claims to personal competence. The laboratory scientist works with sometimes intractable and unpredictable natural phenomena in order to make experiments – and so the laboratory – work, while the field researcher has to make sense of a complex social world. The natural scientist is likely to stress bench skills, as well as less determinate craft knowledge. The anthropologist is likely to stress the personal qualities that are called upon to survive the demands of fieldwork. The form and content of research differ markedly between the laboratory and the field. Both, however, demand a blend of the personal and the intellectual, of formal research skills and tacit personal competences.

Fieldwork and Identity

Social anthropology, whether pure or applied, is marked by the strong empirical base of the discipline and a dependence upon fieldwork (Grillo, 1985). The symbolic and individual value of anthropological fieldwork goes well beyond the strict requirements of 'research methods' and 'data collection' (Fardon, 1990). Generally, fieldwork was described as the essence of anthropological work, distinguishing anthropology from other disciplines in the social sciences. This is described below, first by a member of staff and second by a PhD student:

Fieldwork

> The main problem with anthropology – and this is something which differentiates anthropology from sociology – anthropology is of course almost always based upon fieldwork to do with alien cultures.
>
> (Professor Feering, Kingford)

> I think the most important thing to ask people [is] why anthropology is different from other subjects and what they think is special about it. Because it does present special problems of which, as a PhD student, fieldwork stands as the central difference with other subjects.
>
> (Douglas Travers, Southersham)

Because anthropology is a small discipline, in which most people are very familiar with each other, *and* because many of our informants were bitterly opposed to the new compulsory training, we have in this chapter carefully disguised the biographies of staff and students.

Intriguingly from our own point of view, the claims for the distinctiveness of anthropology, and the defining character of ethnographic fieldwork, extended to repeated claims by our informants concerning the essential difference between their discipline and sociology. Notwithstanding the quite remarkable preponderance of qualitative, ethnographic research among contemporary British sociologists over the past two decades or so, the anthropologists we interviewed consistently affirmed the special, even unique, role of field research in anthropology. This, indeed, seems to constitute one of the clearest symbolic boundaries constructed to demarcate the discipline of anthropology. The image of the sociologist whose research is driven by surveys and quantitative techniques of data analysis remains a negative reference point for anthropologists.

Fieldwork, of course, is not conducted just 'anywhere'. Social anthropology is grounded not only in a general method, but in distinctive regionally defined traditions (Fardon, 1990). The regional specialization of social anthropologists is a crucial part of their identity. Of the twenty-four students we interviewed, all had a clear regional orientation. Even those who had not yet undertaken their fieldwork were already certain about which area of the world they would work in. The overall pattern of anthropological fieldwork appeared very traditional: most of the British students were heading for third-world countries, while overseas students researched aspects of their own societies. Very few were intending to or had pursued fieldwork in the United Kingdom. Despite the fact that recent years have seen an increased interest in 'anthropology at home' (Strathern, 1981; Cohen, 1982; Jackson, 1987; Chapman, 1992; Rapport, 1992; Cohen, 1992; Douglass, 1992), apprenticeship in the discipline is still grounded firmly in research away from the UK. One established anthropologist we interviewed had conducted doctoral research in the UK, and expressed how such fieldwork 'at home' can be regarded in British anthropology:

Fieldwork

The PhD was done in Britain, which was extremely unusual at that time in anthropology, and it arose out of my extremely fumbling attempts as a neophyte in anthropology to try to act on my sense of discontent with the theoretical basis of the subject. So I chose to work in Britain because I had a very strong view that the notion of anthropology being about overseas was not adequate. But at the time the various ways in which I'd been trained, given that at that time I only had an undergraduate degree in anthropology, meant that I couldn't take my criticism very far. So that in retrospect I felt that I'd been very bound by, not so much the theoretical assumptions of the discipline, but by its methodological assumptions. So what I did was I studied a rural community in Ayrshire and I did what would now be seen to be an ethnography – although I have a very strong drive to make analytic innovations in the work that I do – so I did an ethnography looking at kinship, class and many other things. ... But I also did a lot of theoretical work as well, in terms of what kinds of concepts are appropriate to describe social process, and what we used to call 'social structure'. So the thesis was quite wide-ranging in those things. Almost immediately after I'd done the research in Britain I felt – which I think most people feel who've worked in Britain – that that kind of work was not particularly regarded by the British anthropological establishment as proper anthropology. So I felt it didn't do what I wanted it to do – to insert me into the profession at all. That I did this very interesting and well-received piece of work, but that actually it was only well received by my external examiner, and I wasn't able to insert it properly in anthropology. That's because it's always seemed to me that the anthropology of Britain has always been extremely marginal.

(Dr Herrick, Masonbridge)

Dr Herrick's autobiographical accounts captures the sense that anthropological fieldwork in the UK is not quite proper, and can give rise to a sense of spoiled academic identity. The same is even more true for doctoral research that is not based on any anthropological field research at all. Nigel Barley (1983) makes the point (while mocking the attitude) in the opening chapter of his funny book for the intelligent lay person, *The Innocent Anthropologist: Notes from a Mud Hut*. Barley had done his PhD in the library from published sources:

The profession is full of devoted fieldworkers, skins leathery from exposure to torrid climes, teeth permanently gritted from years of dealing with natives, who have little or nothing of interest to say in an academic discipline. The whole subject of fieldwork, we effete 'new anthropologists' with our doctorates based on library research had decided, had been made rather too much of. Of course, older teaching staff who had

Fieldwork

>   seen service in the days of empire ... had a vested interest in maintaining the cult: they damn well suffered trials and privations of swamp and jungle and no young whipper-snapper should take a short cut.
>
>   (Barley, 1983: 7)

From among our own informants, Dr Gideon, at Masonbridge, said: 'This is anthropology. It has a strong tradition of empirical work. There have been people who do library theses, but I wouldn't take one on.'

The period of intense fieldwork – which may be a protracted one – provides the foundation for more than the PhD itself. This is especially characteristic of British social anthropology, but has similar significance elsewhere. Of the USA, for instance, Clifford suggests that 'Fieldwork in anthropology is sedimented with a disciplinary history, and it continues to function as a rite of passage and marker of professionalism' (Clifford, 1997: 61). Clifford also suggests that most of his colleagues would not grant validity to doctoral research in anthropology which was not based on conventional fieldwork (such as autobiographical writing or intensive and protracted research conducted via the Internet). One reason why fieldwork assumes so much importance in the discipline, particularly at PhD level, is because doctoral study affords a period of time which individuals can devote to the selection and exploration of a given society. This provides a stock of knowledge and experience that lasts the anthropologist a long way into his or her career. John Campbell (1992), for example, studied the transhumant shepherds (Sarakatsani) of Northern Greece in 1954–5. His distinguished career at Oxford, and with UNESCO, was rooted in that fieldwork, which he was able to use for a respected paper in 1992. (We return to this point in Chapter 8.) The period of doctoral research can thus form the basis of specialization on which the anthropological career is built. The investment of time and personal commitment to the fieldwork is transformed into cultural capital from which the academic anthropologist can draw in the years ahead. One academic expressed it explicitly in those terms: 'Anthropologists only know one culture well. And you're investing that capital for the better part of ten to fifteen years. ... The PhD is about acquiring this body of cultural capital' (Professor Feering, Kingford).

The few anthropologists we encountered with no fieldwork experience reported feeling marginalized within the discipline (Barley, 1983). This category included students and supervisors who were completing, or who had completed, theoretical or library theses. Because successful fieldwork completion signifies membership of the discipline, students at the pre-fieldwork stage of research did not see themselves as full members of the anthropological community. The anthropologist quoted below describes feeling that their work had been trivialized because it was not empirically based. The following account refers to the experience of presenting a paper to an anthropological audience in a department other than their own: 'It

Fieldwork

was quite difficult because Tim Scott-Windlesham, the chairman, kept suggesting it wasn't proper anthropology, and surely I couldn't get rich enough material if I wasn't sitting at the end of a market square somewhere' (Dr Gilchick, Masonbridge).

Although attitudes to non-empirical work differed, generally it was felt to be the exception rather than the rule, something was at best tolerated rather than celebrated:

> There are some seminal anthropologists who did library theses, or who've never done any fieldwork since, and I think there can always be room for the great stylists, if you like, in the discipline. Because there are some awful, boring theses that just entail going somewhere that somebody hasn't been. It's a matter of balancing the two, I think. I know that non-fieldwork theses are discouraged because they're harder, because when you have new data it's easier [for it] to seem an original piece of work. When you're dealing with stuff that's been written, it's harder to give an original imprint to it. But I wouldn't discredit that route.
> (Dr Talisman, Southersham)

For the majority of anthropologists the successful completion of a major ethnographic project, based on intensive fieldwork, is a major claim to disciplinary membership and respectability. (The geography PhD students whose views we quoted in Chapter 3 made the same point.)

This does not mean that fieldwork results in empiricism divorced from theoretical concerns. But theory was seldom mentioned in isolation. It was always related directly to empirical field research. The grounding of theory in the personal and intellectual commitment of ethnographic fieldwork was stressed. As one anthropologist explained:

> It's impossible not, I think, to be influenced by the theoretical developments in anthropology in recent years. They provide the concepts of the language in which we think and write. On the other hand, the best work, the best texts, come out of very solid fieldwork and if the fieldwork is poor there's no overcoming that.
> (Dr Fustian, Kingford)

This view was also reflected in supervisors' accounts of PhD work. For instance: 'In this department generally [we tend] to pride ourselves on our theoretical advances. Yet when it comes to students writing their theses, then there's something of a seepage and the concern becomes with the fieldwork itself' (Dr Fitton, Kingford).

In those few cases where PhD students were completing non-empirical work we found they were required by supervisors to demonstrate explicitly how the research related to the discipline of anthropology:

Fieldwork

> At the end I'll write comments like 'this is fine and good and I can see how it links to anthropology, but you need to make your links clearer'. ... I want Viv [the student] to accentuate and show by her particular form of research, which isn't strictly fieldwork, that Viv can use that research to inform the ideas of what anthropology is [and] why it is that fieldwork is held in such high esteem.
>
> (Dr Fitton, Kingford)

Given the importance which our informants placed upon fieldwork, we were interested in finding out the ways in which the essence of anthropological work differed from other disciplines. Eliciting respondents' descriptions of anthropology was a plausible request because the researcher herself was not an anthropologist. Here, for instance, a PhD student uses an empirical example to describe anthropological work:

> If you take a thing like pig husbandry, you would think it was a very straightforward thing. As an agriculturalist or an economist you will think there is such a thing as pig husbandry, and we do it in a certain way and they [the 'others' of the fieldwork] do it in a different way. I'm going to find out how they do it. And I think as an anthropologist you have to do this, but you have to go one step further in trying to understand why they do it in the way they do it – their rationale behind it and what kind of model of husbandry they have. And this is not done by any other discipline even if they work with the same issues on the ground. The anthropological understanding goes beyond that.
>
> (Louisa Montoya, Southersham)

The uniqueness of anthropology, and the uniqueness of fieldwork in anthropology, was stressed repeatedly. For instance, one of the students suggested that:

> It's a unique subject in that you do get sort of sometimes to central Glasgow, sometimes to Somalia, sometimes to places in between, where for a year or more you sit *on your own*, organize your own research very much. ... It is very much like that in the sense that before you go away you are just one of the kids and are treated as such, but when you come back you can be talked to like an adult. You have passed your initiation – well, you've undergone it – whether you've passed it or not you'll find out later – but that's the most important thing about talking to anthropologists. It's such a strange subject in that you have to do this fieldwork.
>
> (Douglas Travers, Southersham)

We quote Douglas Travers here and extensively elsewhere in this chapter.

We do so not because he was unique in his views, but because he was especially articulate in expressing the kinds of perspectives held by very many of his peers at his own university and elsewhere.

Because the fieldwork itself is such an important part of 'initiation' into the discipline, there is a clear contrast in graduate students' career between the pre- and post-fieldwork phases. Until a student has proved himself or herself in the field, membership of the profession and the capacity to complete a PhD is highly provisional. The vocabulary of anthropology itself, especially the notion of *rites de passage* – with preliminal, liminal, and postliminal phases – is frequently invoked here by anthropologists themselves, as in the quotation from a supervisor citing Mary Douglas's use of the term in Chapter 3 (p. 45). The metaphor of East African age-grading systems, in which PhD students are either 'here' in a pre-fieldwork cohort, 'not-here' in a fieldwork cohort, or 'back home' in a post-fieldwork cohort, was also applied by some members of the discipline.

The return from the field may be a disruptive one. The transition from fieldwork back to the routines of academic life in the department and the university is described as problematic. For instance:

> There's a real feeling, especially among those who've returned from fieldwork and are writing up, and the younger members of the teaching staff, that coming back from fieldwork is a strange experience. You feel lost, and to get on with academic work again, and the arduous job of writing up – there's a lot of support for people. The young members of staff that we're getting in at the moment are especially useful for this – it's really nice to have them around.
>
> (Douglas Travers, Southersham)

Douglas went on to express similar feelings about the process of 'return', stressing the individual nature of the problem, and the need for the student and the supervisor to deal with them:

> The psychological problems of being back from your fieldsite, and change of perspective, I think these are very hard to deal with in any kind of course, or through groups. You really depend very much on the goodwill and understanding of your supervisor, and his or her ability to deal with personal problems.
>
> (Douglas Travers, Southersham)

Despite the practical and symbolic significance of fieldwork, prior socialization rarely involves any practical field experience. Students are not, for instance, required to undertake small-scale projects in preparation for their long period in the field. The work of the first year normally includes advanced coursework, language-learning, seminar programmes and the like.

Fieldwork

Fieldwork itself is treated as indeterminate – based essentially on experience, rather than explicit research skills – and therefore as part of an unpredictable future rather than something that is susceptible to preparation and anticipation. Certainly, the core element of anthropological fieldwork – participant observation in a social setting – is often treated in such terms. Indeed, preparation can be seen as a hindrance rather than a help. Again, Douglas Travers's account illuminates the issue:

> It's common to find that until you get to the field you don't know what you'll be doing. ... I think if you're too primed to do fieldwork that can backfire; you can plod along on your own course and be less receptive to the way things are going. It is a problem with the requirement to go and immerse yourself into a society for such a long period of time – you really have to be flexible about your work, and if you're too prepared and you have too many methods you want to employ, if you've structured your time too much before you arrive, you can mess it up by not being receptive enough.
>
> (Douglas Travers, Southersham)

This student, in common with others, stressed the notion of fieldwork as 'immersion', suggesting that: 'you just get in there and participate in the social life of the place as much as possible and observe'.

It is believed that on the path to anthropological understanding there are no explicit techniques and methods. The accounts from both supervisors and PhD students emphasized tacit knowledge and shared understandings rather than explicit criteria. The subject-matter may be described as intangible, and the anthropologist's understanding of them as matters of interpretation. For example: 'As an anthropologist I have my focus basically on things which are intangible ... how people generate ideas and how they communicate them' (Louisa Montoya, Southersham).

Dr Geodrake at Masonbridge, describing his supervision of a very successful student, Rowland Walworth, said he had to point out that the data analysis and the draft 'need to become more anthropological'. However, since Rowland got an academic job 'he's become more of an anthropologist when teaching than when he was writing up'. Just what 'being anthropological' means in such contexts remains implicit.

Students and supervisors talked about how this had implications for the evaluation of anthropological research: 'In the English system there is a lot that is so diffuse and the criteria you see people operating with are more cultural – unconscious criteria are used much more than objective academic criteria' (Dr Jannerat, Masonbridge). Giselle Dumont, of Kingford, claimed: 'I think it's a discipline that rests very much on opinion and interpretation and very little on established methodologies. So there aren't any

Fieldwork

criteria for judging anyone, except what you personally feel about their work'

Fieldwork, then, is seen by the majority of anthropologists – staff and graduate students alike – in terms redolent of 'traditional' images of social anthropology. Theoretical development and disciplinary changes remain predicated on fieldwork and its unique personal and intellectual challenges. This does not mean that doctoral students in anthropology do not complain about a lack of preparation. Some do give accounts of their own fieldwork that reflect a lack of prior preparation:

> Very, very strongly I felt that theoretical bias got in the way. If you go along to a couple of research methods classes – and they were all textbook issues – like how not to ask loaded questions, that kind of thing – and what I wanted to know, and I asked both my supervisors and neither of them gave me an answer, was, 'What actually happens when you get there?' You step off this plane, and what on earth do you do? And nobody would tell me, because I got the impression that they all presumed that I must know. If I'd come this far I must know. And it was actually only when I got there. I was very lucky, I actually managed to affiliate with a research institute in Tunisia, which just happened to be headed by an anthropologist who took an interest and showed me what I ought to be doing – a mixture of attending pilgrimage events, interviewing people, talking to and recording people and events. Before I went, I didn't get anything on that at all. I wasn't sure what living arrangement I should have, if I should live with a family, if it's OK to stay in a hotel for a couple of weeks, or what. I really couldn't get any response from anyone, even direct questions were met with a load of theoretical waffle.
>
> (Colin Ives, Kingford)

Graduate students undertaking field research in other disciplines also related problems as a consequence of poor preparation or lack of training. Some students reported that they had gone into the field well prepared, but others, in this example Glen Madson, a town planning graduate at Portminster, found out the hard way that they lacked skills or experience.

> I know I made one major cock-up in the first year by approaching a particular firm about its relationship to its union. And if I'd had any kind of research training I wouldn't have done that. It was innocent, but it wasn't interpreted that way and it cut off my access to that firm completely. And because I really wanted to do that firm, it was important, I was really upset. It had taken me six months to get some kind of access and I blew it. OK it was common sense, but common sense that had to be learned. It's difficult doing research in organizations and in

Fieldwork

retrospect I was very sloppy but that's because I didn't have any training.

Fieldwork and Indeterminacy

The ways in which our informants talked about fieldwork highlighted a number of issues relating to research techniques and training. The first point was the way in which issues of cultural difference bear upon fieldwork preparation:

> The qualitative methods used in anthropology are specific to this discipline. Because of the setting – either in your own culture, or [you go] to a different social group in your own culture, or to different social groups than the one you grew up in, or you go to a totally different society – and also because of the kinds of questions you will be asking.
> (Louisa Montoya, Southersham)

Anthropological methods were described as contextually dependent and research strategies as:

> mainly determined by constraints in the field, because when you go in and choose one subject as an anthropologist, you don't always find that is relevant to the people among whom you're living, and you don't always call the tune as part of your methodology.
> (Barry Loomis, Kingford)

Flexibility was encouraged in the departments which we visited and was seen as an essential quality associated with 'good students'. A good student was seen as someone who was open to what he or she might encounter in the field, and who was intellectually adaptable. Similarly, good research projects developed in the field through the experiences of the fieldwork, rather than being predetermined from the outset: 'Now that's what I call a good research project; something that's stimulated and developed *in situ*. And that's quite likely to happen in anthropology' (Dr Drummock, Kingford).

The flexibility required was something which concerned PhD students waiting to go into the field not only in social anthropology, but also in qualitative human geography, development studies, urban studies and area studies. Compare the following comments, one from an anthropologist, and the other two from a geographer and his supervisor:

> There is a course on fieldwork methods. I didn't attend that one much but I don't think I missed much because the fieldwork side of anthropology, the ethnography, is hard to teach. In fact I think there's a bias

against teaching fieldwork methodology to any great extent. You just get out there and do it.

(Douglas Travers, Southersham)

> *LF:* Dr Challoner was one of the reasons I came here. Because she's very good on qualitative methods.
> *OP:* Is there any organized teaching?
> *LF:* No there isn't. But to be honest I don't think much teaching is needed. You have an idea of where to pick it up, and you just go to your supervisor to sort it out.
>
> (Lewis Frome, human geographer at Tolleshurst)

> Students come to recognize what skills they need through a process of interaction with their supervisor. Doing a PhD is a creative, imaginative sort of process. ... I expect my students to develop interpersonal skills – that's the nature of the work they do.
>
> (Lewis Frome's supervisor, Dr Challoner)

As a consequence of this view, Dr Challoner was totally opposed to the idea of training in qualitative methods. Like most of the anthropologists, she treated the conduct of qualitative fieldwork as a matter of personal competence, tacitly acquired, rather than as technical skills instilled by explicit instruction.

The anthropologists' beliefs about fieldwork had powerful implications for their views on research training. They repeatedly emphasized the significance of practical experience in the field, the centrality of tacitly acquired competence, and the irrelevance of explicit training in techniques of data collection and analysis. For instance, Dr Fustian of Kingford University said:

> All this business of training I think is largely spurious. It's something that's learnt by the experience of doing it. It's rather like teaching music; you can't teach people how to play without a piano. It's only by playing they can learn, and I think fieldwork is like that.

It is revealing that Dr Fustian's analogy, if taken literally, would imply that learning music was only about performance 'by ear'. And while that would be a very inaccurate picture of musical education – in music, of course, theory and technique are of fundamental importance – it is a good way of capturing anthropologists' insistence that fieldwork is almost exclusively improvisational. Dr Talisman offers an account that locates such views in a recent past, and talks of change. But he also likens the field research to an artistically creative process that finally escapes prescription:

Fieldwork

> I feel that since I grew up in the age of fieldwork mystique, if you like it was an ordeal by fire, you can't experience it beforehand. It's a matter of sink or swim when you're there. It's changing now but the tradition was that it was something you did. But you didn't – you weren't up front about it. You didn't explain the niceties of how you got accepted, or what status you had in the field, or how you left, or what work you did. These were more anecdotal things, and what you wrote about was the data you'd collected. In recent years, of course, there's been a revolution in the way we look at the data we come away with. It's recognized much more now as far more attached to the object you're viewing and particular circumstances of immersion. So it's been necessary to say who we are and who they thought we were in the field and how we gathered data. But initially fieldwork was just something you did and you couldn't explain it any more than you could explain how you keep your balance on a bicycle. You learn how to do it and you keep upright and you learn it by doing it. Having been through that, there's still a part of me that wants to say in the same way that I find the notion of learning to write creatively ... that seems a contradiction in terms to me, that you can teach creative writing. And something of the same anomaly seems to me to pertain to the teaching of participant observation, teaching how to be perceptive, teaching how not to put your foot in it socially, teaching how to be subtle. Because all these notions are culturally specific.
>
> (Dr Talisman, Southersham)

Elizabeth Bettman, a graduate student at Kingford, was critical of the socialization she had experienced, and the consequent lack of preparation prior to doing her fieldwork:

EB: It's a very negative kind of upbringing, I think. Nobody gave me any useful advice at all. They just said 'Go out there and hang around and see what you come across'.

OP: In the pre-fieldwork year did you do anything about research methods?

EB: We went along to a couple [of classes] but they were absolutely useless. They did something on questionnaire construction. They covered the main methods, but it's always a negative appraisal; they encourage you not to use anything else but participant observation. ... They ought to have a more practical approach to gearing people up to going into fieldwork.

These views, and others like them, highlight a recurrent paradox in the enculturation of young anthropologists: explicit instruction is sometimes given in research methods – such as survey design, sampling and question-

Fieldwork

naire design – that are themselves devalued, while the research approach that is celebrated is treated as indeterminate, and hence is not part of research training.

Our anthropologists talked about unanticipated uses of research skills in the field. They also claimed that such skills are beyond those normally expected in other disciplines:

> And what skills do you need for anthropology? You see some skills you need for anthropology that you wouldn't imagine you'd need. Scuba diving is something I needed to know before doing my fieldwork. Sometimes there's not very much you can teach an anthropologist because you won't know what you'll have to do.
> (Dr Feste, Kingford)

Dr Godlee, of Gossingham, also talked about the unanticipated variety of work required of the anthropologist:

> We go through an initial process of trying to define a problem and work out a methodology, but invariably when students go off to do their data collection the problem in the field appears in a lot of different lights.

In the same vein, Dr Harcourt – a development studies expert at Gossingham who said 'I love working with anthropologists' – talked about the unpredictability of field research: 'It's terribly hard to plan fieldwork sitting in Britain. It's even hard to decide what your hypothesis is, because when you're confronted with the reality of it you have to change your entire research proposal.'

These ideas were clearly taken on board by the PhD students to whom we talked:

> The tenor of anthropology compared to sociology is that you go and find out about things without knowing what questions to ask. So there is the image of you jumping in the deep end which is meant to start your ideas and your thinking, and I think there's a value in that. And that's why in a sense there's an argument for not having much training before the fieldwork. And you can see by the way anthropologists write completely different things on the basis of one piece of fieldwork – some of them do it thirty or forty years afterwards. It's not that the experience has got to come before you write and analyse it, it's a basic premise. It's almost antithetical to be too organized in terms of what you're going to do before you get there, because you may have decided on a framework for understanding things and so on which may not fit.
> (Harry Kettering, Kingford)

Fieldwork

The unpredictability of the field and the emergent character of the research process – even of the research questions – lead some anthropologists to discount, or even reject explicit research training. Specific research skills are valued less than the more tacit ability to conduct fieldwork and make anthropological sense of the chosen setting. In some cases – for instance, where PhD students returned from the field to find the data they had collected inadequate or inappropriate – such an absence of fieldwork preparation was highlighted:

> I think there's a bias against teaching fieldwork methodology to any great extent. There's an idea that you just get out there and do it, and that from reading anthropology you should have ideas about what you're interested in, and that everybody had to find their own way of doing it, so why should they tell you?
> (Nina Yeager, Kingford)

Another example was reported by a fellow student about a graduate who had overrun the four years and was struggling to write up: 'She feels her fieldwork wasn't good enough to support the work. And she blames that on the training you get here, which is pretty minimal' (Emily Coughlin, Kingford).

In the narratives supervisors told about failing students, the failure was usually attributed to the students' inability to conduct fieldwork. They had not come back from the field with data that they could use to produce a thesis. An outsider reading the quotation above might think that Emily was agreeing with her friend that she had suffered from insufficient training. In fact, the supervisor is exposing the *student's* inadequacy: a student who feels a need for explicit training is not a suitable person to qualify as an anthropologist. Although the majority of our informants felt that qualitative ethnographic methods in anthropology were unteachable, a clear contrast was drawn with quantitative methods:

> The participant observation is not, I would say, a research method which can be taught in the classroom and then applied in the field, whereas statistical methods can be taught in the classroom and applied in the field. But of course participant observation is hardly a method, I think it's the *sine qua non*. It's something you can only learn by doing it.
> (Dr Trevithick, Southersham)

Such contrastive rhetoric, juxtaposing explicit teaching in quantitative research skills and tacit competence in participant observation, is characteristic of how anthropologists explained to Odette, an outsider, the defining aspect of their research. While specific skills can be taught formally, the central aspect of research experience remains grounded in personal appren-

Fieldwork

ticeship and tacit acquisition. Personal commitment to anthropological fieldwork is seen as especially important:

> In many ways somebody who says 'I want to do anthropology, I want to do fieldwork, I think I can take it on', in many cases that person is capable, because it's not a decision you take lightly. There are problems of a nature that are not academic. I tell my methodology students, you have to be able to get on with people at a very basic level. You have to be able to cope with loneliness. And although loneliness has never been a major problem, anyone who's done fieldwork knows that loneliness is there. You also have to be very confident, because there are many times when you work and you don't see the results of that work – and you have the confidence that one day everything will make sense. But there are times when you worry about the quality of what you collect. When people are confident they should be good fieldworkers. But you also have to be inward looking.
>
> (Dr D'Urfey, Kingford)

None of the anthropology departments that we visited provided their students with training in participant observation. This reflected the general feeling that it is unteachable, unlike quantitative research techniques:

> I do feel that a lot of people who take on anthropology felt defeated by numbers in school and are rather anti-numerate, and slightly resent having to use numerical techniques. It can be that a technique rather than an idea can inspire them, they might be in the field and suddenly see the relevance of a [quantitative] research technique we've taught them.
>
> (Dr Drummock, Kingford)

Even when academics welcomed the introduction of research training, and contrasted such provision with their own experiences as graduate students, they reserved commendation for training in research methods other than qualitative, participant observation: 'If they can be given training on things like survey techniques and questionnaires, and become computer literate, that's to the good. They're picking up skills I wasn't given twenty years ago' (Dr Geodrake, Masonbridge).

Because of the reservations expressed about the teachability of participant observation, the pre-fieldwork preparation available in the departments we visited was of a discursive and experiential kind, rather than grounded in specific research techniques and skills:

> You're sending people to completely different places in completely different contexts and circumstances, with the different problems that

they face there. I think it's very important to give students some kind of chance for discussion of problems they're likely to face before they go, but it has to be done in a very specific, very sensitive way. And I can't imagine any pre-thought-out syllabus that would cater for the needs of particular students.

(Dr Throstle, Southersham)

In contrast to the scepticism expressed concerning training for fieldwork by the established academics, there was greater enthusiasm for more pre-fieldwork training among some of our student respondents, particularly if fieldwork difficulties had been experienced. They again reflected the lack of emphasis on specific training, and attributed problems in data collection to a lack of preparation. For instance, students said:

But definitely research methods would be very good. I mean basically for me it was very hit and miss in terms of how you interview people, how you collect information, it's all learning by experience in the field.

(Emily Coughlin, Kingford)

My reservation is that you have to take in too much on courses, but I think I could have been better prepared. I suppose what you need is a kind of ... to know what you're going to do and have more help looking at the methodology of what you're going to be doing. So a sort of blanket course which goes over research methods wouldn't be tremendously helpful. But more help would be.

(Nina Yeager, Kingford)

There are some things I think would be extremely useful to people preparing to go to the field. Specialized things that some universities are good at providing, and others aren't. So for instance, courses on linguistics would be useful – not language courses – and quantitative methods, to teach people how to survey and do statistical collection would also be useful. Because, again, some people can't. I'd learnt to survey at eleven at primary school, and had vague memories of this, and had a compass and a tape measure. And it wasn't until I was in Somalia that I tried to survey again, and found it was bloody difficult. I wished someone had demonstrated it to me more recently. When I was eleven was a long time ago and I wasn't sure which bearing was which. And the same with surveys and statistics and stuff. In sociology it's quite common to do surveys but I'd never been taught anything about problems with questionnaires – my own fault perhaps for not having read anything about it. It wouldn't be a bad thing to have courses like that on the basis that you could take them or leave them.

(Douglas Travers, Southersham)

Fieldwork

It is, once again, noticeable that here the student speaks somewhat wistfully about training in research methods, but only about methods such as field surveying and questionnaire-based surveys.

Training in participant observation is not part of the discourse. It is noteworthy that a fellow student who had not yet conducted fieldwork spoke in very similar terms about the sorts of research preparation she felt she might need. She began by explaining that her fieldwork would be carried out mainly among the Mountain Cheremis. (The Moutain Cheremis live in northern Russia and speak two dialects related to Finnish.)

> Mountain Cheremis is an oral language: it isn't used for writing there, they mostly work in Russian. It's a very difficult language to learn, you don't pick it up very easily. It's incredibly context bound, so I'll learn it quicker by speaking there. With the language, I feel that's something in which I'm not so well prepared. I did some undergraduate work in linguistics: this was in a different area – not, for example, in how to pick up a language, or phonetics. This is a general problem of the first year before you go into the field, and it's a problem of time in the end, I guess. And I feel some basic linguistic training in picking up a language would help me. And also some training in research methods. And there I really mean things like I will have to measure a garden yield, I will have to do surveys, and I've never been taught how to do that. And the problem with anthropological research is that whenever I want to – I think this would be a very straightforward matter to teach, which isn't dull. And of course, it isn't the most important thing – because these data, this information, will only be used as supporting evidence. It's not the main thing I'm going to do. I'm very much aware that as information it's useless: it has to be interpreted and the terms of the interpretation have to come from somewhere else.
>
> (Louisa Montoya, Southersham)

Again, the student identifies areas in which research methods training might be useful. But the data so collected are not valued. The real understanding comes from 'elsewhere', and escapes specific preparation. It derives from the ineffable, indeterminate experience of participant observation through fieldwork. The majority of the students we talked to subscribed to this anthropological 'orthodoxy'. The majority firmly believed that participant observation skills could not readily be taught or learnt prior to immersion in the field.

The emphasis on fieldwork as a personal accomplishment is, perhaps, a particularly British phenomenon. One of our informants was able to contrast British anthropology with their own experience in the USA:

Fieldwork

> There's a problem which I think is peculiarly British, and that is the skills that you would take for granted, that students in the States have, that they've done some undergraduate statistics or maths, or that they've done a few courses in sociology, and if they're majoring in anthropology that they've done some writing courses, learnt to work with word-processors in some way. And you can't take that for granted at all, given the undergraduate system in the UK, where there's three years of doing the same thing straight through. And I think that becomes a problem when there's four years' money, one year's fieldwork, and somewhere along the line they're supposed to acquire these skills, which if they're American-trained they would have tucked away somewhere. And I'm a bit worried – the ESRC want us to come up with some sort of programme we can give these students in the first year, because I think it's too much, along with reading and before going into the field, learning a language, and on top of that to learn how to do statistics or how to do fieldwork – that's a tough one – in the States you might have done some mini fieldwork in an undergraduate course.
>
> (Dr Feste, Kingford)

At the time Dr Feste was interviewed, the ESRC, the British government's funding source for PhD students, was preparing to publish its Postgraduate Training Guidelines (ESRC, 1991, 1996) for the first time. These include mandatory UK-wide training in generic and subject-specific skills.

In cognate disciplines, in which fieldwork is undertaken nearer to home than most anthropological research, preliminary fieldwork and preparation may be more feasible, and more in keeping with the discipline's ethos. Evan Cooper, a geography student at Hernchester, was advised by his supervisor to carry out preliminary work, as a result of which he was confident that his fieldwork could be successfully completed:

> June and July was a preliminary survey – to see if I could get the sort of information I wanted from the directors of personnel companies. If I couldn't get it, it was a good time to decide I'd have to do it another way.

As Evan Cooper describes, inside information from somebody 'in the know' can be a useful way to proceed in the field:

> Obviously my supervisor gave me some advice and encouragement on how to approach organizations – but also there was a research assistant employed on the large ESRC project I was linked to and he was also dealing with large financial institutions, but for another reason. And I

Fieldwork

did talk to him and that was the person who really helped me with my research.

The personal and intellectual commitment to fieldwork in anthropology means that there can be a fine line between independence, isolation and disorientation. The research student 'in the field' needs to be able to work independently of the supervisor. Dr Teague from Southersham described the student's overseas research as if it were a private matter:

> I don't feel that one should be poking one's nose into a student's fieldwork. It's very much an independent business and it can be awkward, embarrassing and annoying for a research student who's coping with all the delicacies of the field ... to have to worry all the time about keeping their supervisor satisfied.

The supervisor does not, therefore, intrude on the intensely personal conduct of field research. Dr Drummock talked in comparable terms about the proper place of supervision in the process:

> My own personal feeling is that the student has got to be independent enough to form their own judgement and make their own decisions because the supervisor's not going to be around the corner to make that decision. And that might mean, when they're in the field, an enormous shift of interest. They might go out wanting to study land tenure in relation to some aspect of kinship, because the literature suggests this is rather important. Then when they get out there they might suddenly find they've got some kind of witch-finding cult. They might think they're not interested in that, but it might be related to what they wanted to study, and they have to make a decision. And I think it's very important for the student to be able to say 'what is my problem?' because if they can't say that they probably won't be collecting the right data. This to me is the crucial part of research – you go out with one set of problems and the problems change. As an anthropologist you have to deal with that and decide when to act on it at the right time. So it seems to me that supervising in the field – corresponding – it's not a matter of saying 'you should do this', and making the decision for them, but helping them to step back and say 'is this what I really want to do – is this what I'm prepared to live with when I'm writing up?'.
>
> (Dr Drummock, Kingford)

Dr Drummock highlights the importance of data collection when he suggests that graduate students should try asking themselves whether or not they will be happy with what they have collected when they come to write it

91

Fieldwork

up. We return more specifically to the special demands of 'writing up' later in this chapter.

Social anthropology students themselves are aware of the importance attached to such independence in the field, over and above the independence necessary for them to operate successfully in isolation from the academy. It is certainly a matter of concern for students who feel inappropriately prepared that they find themselves caught up in playing a game, the rules of which (if they do exist) are not available to them:

> I felt that I was certainly being tested somehow. There was a feeling that I was going through this thing, and that you have to come out in the right shape, and then once you're back there's a much more positive response, you're treated more like a man.
>
> (Colin Ives, Kingford)

The fact that social anthropology training is still characterized to a large extent as an initiation affects not only students travelling to far corners of the earth but also has implications for the minority who stay close to home to carry out fieldwork. Some anthropology graduate students who do their fieldwork 'down the road' from the academy see their supervisors as infrequently or even less frequently than those working in distant societies. In this way fieldwork 'at home' is conducted in such a way as to replicate the most characteristic feature of more traditional fieldwork. Nina Yeager, a Kingford student, describes how in retrospect the 'traditional' approach to anthropology fieldwork may not have served her best interests. She was after all, unlike many of her peers, in a position to receive regular supervision during the data collection period:

> Then during fieldwork, because I was in Glasgow, I could have seen them [her supervisors] more often. But it was a case of 'You're on your fieldwork now', and looking back that was a mistake. I think I should have seen them more regularly.

Another student who was about to begin fieldwork in a European country (of which she was a national) expressed the separation between 'department' and 'field' in terms of an explicit injunction: 'You're not allowed to visit the department when you're in the field. Because you're supposed to be in the field' (Beulah Wyston, Southersham). Janet Lundgren, from Southersham, summarized the experience graphically: 'Although I did my fieldwork here, I feel I've been abroad for a year – out of touch.' In a sense, students doing anthropological fieldwork 'at home' or 'near at hand' are *supposed* to feel as though they have been abroad for a year. Only then does their research approximate to and share the legitimacy of proper overseas fieldwork.

In some cases the passage between dependence and independence is not a

Fieldwork

smooth one: the process is clumsy and unsatisfactory to either one or both parties concerned. Two of the most common characteristics of situations which go wrong are supervisors who will not let go and students who refuse to let go. When the student is dependent upon close supervision and where this is either physically impossible or unavailable then problems will inevitably arise. Again we cite social anthropology as a discipline where this is most likely to occur. Here Dr Fitton is describing a PhD student, completing her fieldwork abroad, who needed more supervision than the situation allowed, and who he felt may not have been equipped with the necessary prerequisites in the first place:

> She spent a couple of years doing fieldwork and eventually sent back one fieldwork report on the geology of the place and all sorts of things, and it was not clear if it had been written in the village or not. She kept writing to say she was floundering and I kept writing to her to suggest angles of approach and she didn't seem to take them on. She was really a weak student who needed her report written for her, but couldn't provide enough raw data for us to do that, if we'd wanted to.
> (Dr Fitton, Kingford)

The *rite de passage* that is fieldwork may be described as a form of biographical disruption. Graduate students describe going 'away' and into 'the field' in terms of disorientation. They do not know how to proceed. For instance, one student expressed the experience in this way:

> That's another thing I think about anthropology. There's an idea that you just get out there and do it, and that from reading anthropology you should have ideas about what you're interested in, and that everybody had to find their own way of doing it – so why should they tell you? You'd find your own way of doing it anyway. ... I had no idea what I was supposed to be doing when I arrived. It was like 'Where the hell do you start?' I started off doing obvious things, like collecting genealogies, and doing household surveys and stuff like this, which seemed very practically based. But at the same time, you know, a lot of the work involves sitting around chatting to people. The practice is described as participant observation, and that's really what it is: you just get in there and participate in the social life of the place as much as possible, and observe. So, really I didn't feel I had any idea of what I was supposed to be doing out there. I wasn't prepared for what I was going to find in Somalia. One of the problems there was I hadn't spoken to many people who'd been there recently. I don't think Professor Tenderton's been there since the seventies. So I was not really prepared for Somalia or the fieldwork experience. The place I was in hadn't been worked in by an anthropologist before and it's renowned for being quite a violent place.

Fieldwork

And one of my research interests was into gang warfare and tribal fighting. So I was a bit concerned about personal security and what was going on there. So in that sense I really felt I was going into the void. It was inevitable because of the place I chose, and the way I wanted to do my work.

(Douglas Travers, Southersham)

Writing Up

Fieldwork is not an end in itself, however central it is to the apprenticeship of the anthropologist. The work of writing is crucial to the task of transforming fieldwork – with all its complexity and indeterminacy – into a text. 'The ethnography' is both the process of research and the text that embodies its outcome. All research students face issues of 'writing up', and the particular requirements of writing, such as the appropriate style and format of a thesis, are aspects of disciplinary culture and subculture. The writing of a PhD thesis is integral to the entire research process. It is a significant stage in the process of academic apprenticeship. For anthropologists and others undertaking field research it is an especially significant aspect. The transmutation of a complex, often messy, collection of data into a coherent text is a major task in itself. For those who are successful, the thesis will eventually be transformed into the published monograph – another major act of writing – and is thus a major component of the anthropologist's 'cultural capital'. By no means all graduate students find themselves up to the task.

Following fieldwork, students' doubts and insecurities about their ability to meet requirements and standards during data collection are transferred to writing. Our student informants in anthropology could be broadly divided into those who were managing to write up and those who were not. For those who were not managing, or at least felt that they were not, the experience could be one of acute misery:

I had very bad problems when I got back [from the field] because I found it very difficult to write. I'd got very close to the people I was with out there, I had writer's block. I was being forced into writing a chapter every two or three weeks, and I couldn't write anything that made any sense, and I hadn't got a structure ... and my first draft was way off course, there was no way I could do it like that.

(Elizabeth Bettman, Kingford)

Writing up appeared to constitute a further initiation test for students, which would reveal their competence, or lack of it, as fieldworkers. Students who were struggling with the process accounted for problems in personal terms, rather than as matters of specific skills or their lack. Hence, post-fieldwork problems were not interpreted as deficiencies in writing skills but were seen

Fieldwork

largely as personal. Eunice Lester, a geographer at Tolleshurst University, who was within sight of submitting her thesis said of the process of writing up: 'It has been a lonely process. There are ups and downs. There are times when I am sick and tired of reading my own prose, I don't want to do it any more.'

Some of our respondents drew our attention to the recent changes in attitudes towards the way in which ethnographic fieldwork is written up. In recent years anthropology and human geography have been the intellectual sites of considerable debate, innovation and dispute concerning their textual practices. In some quarters this has been seen as essentially liberating, in others as constituting a major epistemological crisis. Professor Hurrell (Masonbridge) felt that postmodernism had made PhD students too narcissistic. Dr Galley, his colleague, summarized the debate:

> In recent years of course there's been a revolution in the way we look at the data we come away with. It's recognized much more now as far more attached to the objective viewing and particular circumstances of immersion.

These changes, namely the growing self-consciousness of scholars surrounding text construction (Clifford and Marcus, 1986; Spencer, 1989; Atkinson, 1990, 1992; Behar and Gordon, 1995; James et al., 1997), have made the task of writing up harder for some students. The critical inspection of other texts in the discipline can be stultifying and can hinder students in the task of writing their own thesis: 'They teach you how to criticize and deconstruct other texts, but it doesn't help you at all when you go to the field because it's a completely different way of writing' (Elizabeth Bettman, Kingford).

Dr Fustian, whom we quoted earlier (p. 77), commented on the same discrepancy – between, on the one hand, theoretical sophistication and, on the other, a relative lack of attention to students' own writing, which, like participant observation, was believed to be unteachable.

Some students were aware of the changing nature of anthropological writing, however, and did feel that it had implications for their own theses:

> Basically anthropology is going through a bit of a changing period at the moment, and people are expecting PhDs to be something quite other than they used to be. To the extent that there's no longer this empirical thing, where you write your introduction then there's the main part which is based on statistical work that you did in the field etc., then a neat conclusion saying this is how people are. It's much more experiential at the moment. People are trying to bring in the experiential aspect of doing fieldwork – what it means to the actual researcher – which is quite a dislocating thing. It's more reflexive in approach, but at the same

Fieldwork

time not 'the researcher on the couch' sort of thing. It's a midway sort of thing. People are trying to find a path through the mess that's been going on in anthropology. And as far as I'm concerned it's made doubly difficult in that Georgia has undergone huge turmoil. There's been a lot of killing, unrest, injustice, really. So theoretical ideas about power – interpersonal power and agencies – have become no longer just a semantic thing about how people use rhetoric to get power. In the Georgia situation it's also about barrel-of-the-gun power. So for me it's an opportunity to match those things that have gone on before with the postmodern move towards making everything about words rather than the actual physical reality.

(Emily Coughlin, Kingford)

Acquiring the Habitus

Although our research has shown that anthropology students find some difficulties with the isolation of doing PhD work in anthropology, we found that research students internalized the ethos of the subject. Many of them explicitly endorsed the view that success in anthropology – especially in the intellectually and personally crucial phase of 'fieldwork' – rested upon *personal* qualities. They shared the view, widely articulated among academic staff, that the making of an anthropologist was dependent more upon the student's personal capacities than on the acquisition of specific skills and competences. 'Socialization' into this disciplinary ethos is so successful that even students who had 'failed' in anthropology endorsed it. Our informants included a number of research students whose anthropological work was – in their own eyes as well as others' – unsuccessful. (This was not dependent upon the failure of a submitted thesis: it was usually a problem of 'inadequate' fieldwork or inability to 'write up' satisfactorily.) These unsuccessful research students were likely to explain their problems in terms of their own personal failure to 'match up' to the personal qualities needed by a successful anthropologist. Their accounts were couched in terms suggesting that they 'didn't have what it takes' to become an anthropologist. This is well illustrated by the case of a respondent who 'totally' regretted their choice of topic, because they were 'persuaded into it', that 'it had never really interested' them, that they 'couldn't get the kind of information' they wanted and that they 'had really bad problems trying to write up', both because they had brought home inappropriate data and they 'had writers' block'. In the case of this student, the grant had expired several years before, their financial position was difficult, self-esteem was low, but loyalty to the discipline was still absolute: 'It's marvellous – I love anthropology.'

Indeed, among the subjects we studied anthropology stands out as one where the graduate students internalized the habitus of the discipline. Their accounts of themselves and their work were remarkably consistent. While they were far from uncritical of their departments and their supervisors, their accounts of success and failure were couched in terms of the dominant culture of the discipline. We have already seen how graduate students themselves articulate the role of fieldwork in their socialization process in ways that directly parallel the accounts of their mentors. It is clear that anthropology is especially successful in promoting a strong sense of disciplinary identity among its 'converts'. Many of the research students themselves explicitly endorsed the view that success in anthropology – especially in the personally and intellectually crucial phase of fieldwork – rests on personal qualities. They share the view that was widely articulated by the academic staff: that the making of an anthropologist is dependent more on the student's personal capacities than on the acquisition of specific skills and competences. Success involves having, or acquiring, the 'right stuff'. Those succeeding at the game – like Nancy Enright, who did a PhD at Kingford and was appointed to a lectureship at Latchendon – come through and win the respect of the academic community.

The process of fieldwork, then, is an especially important part of the apprenticeship of the novice anthropologist. It helps to create a specific personal and academic identity. Even when students are working within a clearly identifiable tradition – such as a regional specialism, a theoretical perspective or a departmentally defined 'school' of thought – the experience of fieldwork defines a unique intellectual biography. The successful completion of fieldwork and the successful transformation of that experience into a thesis (and later a monograph) is the essential prerequisite to membership of a relatively small, exclusive academic community of anthropologists. The process of initiation through fieldwork is the hallmark of the fully-fledged anthropologist. All doctoral research is, implicitly, predicated on a paradox: in order to acquire the professional licence to profess the discipline at large, one must become expert in one very small domain. In anthropology that paradox is more starkly apparent than in most other disciplines. The unique understanding of a particular society, culture or group determines the anthropology student to become a mature member of the discipline. The majority of anthropologists recognize this aspect of their own academic culture. By no means all endorse it with equal enthusiasm, even while acknowledging its existence and its symbolic significance. For instance, one established anthropologist stated:

> The debate over the fieldwork experience, the way knowledge is constructed out of observation, interaction between the informant and the investigator – the general reflexivity of the process – is very much the stuff of the training before going into the field. ... There remains a certain mystique about [it]. Yes, in order to do the *rite de passage* properly, you've got to do it by yourself, and not have a partner or a team. I'm not so happy about this myself. I've done fieldwork by myself, and

Fieldwork

> with my wife, and with my family, and I've seen the advantages and disadvantages of all ways of doing it, and I don't think one is superior to the other. I think the notion that to be a proper anthropologist you've got to be there on your own, and to do it to achieve the *rite de passage*, is a little bit mystical.
>
> (Dr Dorroway, Kingford)

Dr Fustian offered a mystical analogy as well:

> Ultimately there's only one rule. They have to pursue what they're interested in, and that applies to everyone in the academic world. What you're interested in you have to regard as the Holy Grail, and you have to follow that as a light. Otherwise you'll never get anywhere.

Conclusion

As we have illustrated, fieldwork is not confined to anthropological research. In the disciplines we studied, it is also a feature of graduate research in development studies, urban studies and town planning. In some respects there are similarities with the experiences of academics and students in anthropology. To some extent, all our informants who talked about field research commented on the unpredictability of such research and of the emergent nature of research problems. There are, however, differences of emphasis and habitus between the disciplines. They do not all place the same stress on fieldwork as a unique, defining characteristic of their discipline. While anthropologists articulate the belief that fieldwork is special to their discipline and implicitly deny the place of such research methods in other social sciences, others do not invest it with the same symbolic and personal value.

We do not claim, therefore, that our data and our analysis are applicable to all disciplines and to all areas of research in which field research is conducted. We stress, rather, that in those disciplines and departments that we have documented fieldwork is invested with particular significance. It is used to convey the role of personal and tacit knowledge not only in the practical conduct of research, but also – more fundamentally – in the construction of academic identities. In undertaking fieldwork the novice anthropologist in particular undergoes a rite of passage that, if successfully accomplished, warrants his or her admission to the professional ranks. The PhD is the public recognition of a successful outcome. But that PhD should be the outcome of field research, and thus a recapitulation of the socialization undergone by the preceding generations. Fieldwork is thus far more than a mode of research. It is in itself a powerful symbolic mechanism of reproduction. The young researcher is thus committed to a double process of intellectual and personal 'immersion': first, there is the immersion in the field and, second, the immersion in the disciplinary culture. Such personal and intellectual commitment is by no means confined to field disciplines. Indeed, throughout this book we explore the different expressions of faith that make possible doctoral research. Likewise, we find expressions of the unpredictability of research and the need for doctoral students to cope with uncertainty in a wide variety of academic contexts. It is, however, striking that in anthropology and – to a lesser extent – in human geography such contingencies are seen as essential features of academic socialization.

6 Modelling Realities

> Mobilising all available scientific expertise in an attempt to objectify our social milieu.
>
> (Bourdieu, 1988: 5)

In the past two chapters we have explored two major ways in which graduate students learn to produce particular kinds of knowledge. The disciplines we have discussed in detail – social anthropology, human geography and biochemistry – are defined in large measure by those distinctive research orientations. Their defining characteristics include these major types of research practice: for the social anthropologist or human geographer, field research defines the paramount reality of the subject, while the biochemist relies implicitly on the work of laboratory experiment. For each, knowledge production is defined in terms of a method and a site – 'the field' and 'the bench', respectively. In this chapter we turn to a third mode of organizing knowledge. We examine the work of computing, in two rather different disciplinary contexts – physical geography and artificial intelligence. The specific contents of these subjects are different, but their common features depend on the use of computer science to create models. (All scientists produce models and representations of the natural or social world, of course: here we are referring to the specific means and ends of the research process.) The bench scientist's primary concern seems to be 'Can I get my experiment to run?' and the field researcher's concern is 'Can I survive and can I make sense of all this?'. The computer scientist's interest is 'Will this program run?' and 'Will this model yield the right predictions?'. While their programs and models do ultimately aim to reflect an independent reality, these scientists are strongly focused on the internal coherence of their computational work, and are often working at some remove from observations and data in the 'real world'.

This chapter therefore examines the experiences of students and supervisors from specialist areas within physical geography and artificial intelligence. We explore how graduate students and their supervisors use computer-based methods in order to accomplish a number of related

Modelling Realities

research objectives: modelling physical phenomena in order to predict future outcomes; instructing machines to accomplish specific tasks routinely carried out by human beings; replicating human thought processes; and representing the knowledge of experts in order to provide intelligent advice. Although these may seem like diverse tasks they share a common purpose. As we shall see, whether students program robots, design knowledge systems, or model aspects of physical phenomena in their endeavours, they all share the common goal of mapping and representing reality. They experience uncertainties which accompany any attempt to translate aspects of the 'real world' into computer systems or models, and in addressing these problems they seek practical solutions in the approach to and organization of their work.

The aspirations of Dr de Manuelos, a physical geographer at Ottercombe, captures the kind of intellectual desire that is characteristic of this kind of work:

> Hopefully we'll end up with an all-singing, all-dancing mathematical model that will predict what's going to happen to a river if you divert water out of it, add water to it, if you engineer it by flood control ...

Of course, all the research students and other academics we were dealing with were engaged in tasks of simplification and representation – the scientific experiment and the anthropological monograph are just different ways of accomplishing similar analytic goals. The construction of a computer program or computational model is not totally different. It is, however, another way of representing or constructing reality, and a different embodiment of a discipline's collective identity. Experts in artificial intelligence or specialists in certain sorts of physical geography – together with others – find the expression of their individual and collective identity in the computer-based composition of models. Their *raison d'être* is a computer program that 'runs' and a model that is adequately predictive.

Mapping Physical Reality

In order to map reality Dr Pilgrim, who is a computer modeller at Illington, describes how it is first necessary to determine the crucial parameters of the physical phenomena to be represented. He is concerned with a readily recognizable form of computer modelling and the creation of images:

> [Just as] an engineering drawing will typically have different views of the same object – taking one from the top, the front and side – we [in artificial intelligence] are looking at gluing these together, these things that

Modelling Realities

had already been seen and identified, into a three-dimensional representation which we could then store in a model.

Physical geography PhD student Aaron Boatman, who was member of a research group at Hernchester working on computer modelling techniques, described what he was doing as 'testing physical laws in a computer simulation [where] you try to bring about the conceptual understanding of an area with the actual computability of that conception'.

Aaron's supervisor was Professor Barsington, who is director of two research groups in physical geography at Hernchester, which together comprise six research students and one research assistant. At the time of our research the two current project areas were landslide predicting and flood forecasting. The groups are organized so that at any one time there is a minimum of three people working on each project. There is thus a 'critical mass' that needs to be maintained in order to ensure a division of labour among members of the group, and the desired continuity of research problems and solutions from generation to generation. The combination of research costs and funding constraints demand that continuity is maintained between the two different research groups and over time. The two groups are not discrete bodies existing in a delimited time frame; they develop and changed over time as some members leave and new ones join. There is also an overlap between the groups, which allows for a six- to nine-month familiarizing period for new recruits. The continuity of the group allows ideas and interests to develop and be sustained through the work in which the group is involved. Central to this group continuity is the simulation model, which Professor Barsington describes vividly, suggesting that it is like

> a baton in a relay race passed on to the next one and knowledge is encoded in the computer code. That is why the overlap is so critical. When there's no overlap we can say here's the code, but what does it mean? To maintain knowledge you have to have an overlap. This overlap business is very serious.

He thus stresses the significance of pedagogic continuity being 'encoded' in the dense interrelationships between students' research projects and the work of the group as a whole. This is an intense *group* orientation towards knowledge production. Responsibility for the knowledge is both collective and personal. It reflects the collective as much as the personal commitment of the individual researchers.

Professor Barsington's research students routinely experience this approach to research work. Peg Conroy, for instance, neither expected nor wanted to construct or invent her own unique project, but wanted to contribute to the development of a model with which group members were already familiar: 'The model [developed here] gets handed down through the group. Two or three of us are quite keen because its a model that's already been through several people.'

However, just because the model had been developed by others does not make it easy to use. PhD students must initially familiarize themselves with the model and, as Peg explained, although it was well known to others in the department, the model she was using had 'never been documented particularly well – it's a bit of a nightmare to get to know'. Part of the socialization that students must negotiate successfully, then, requires them to gain an 'inside' view of the research group's taken-for-granted stock of knowledge and assumptions. The fact that the models depend on the precise description of phenomena, and to that extent depend on explication, does not mean that the assumptions underlying the model and its applications are also subject to thorough explication. In contributing to the collective research effort, therefore, the graduate students acquire the tacit knowledge that is the common property of the research group. The transmission of that knowledge from generation to generation is as much a feature of such collective research enterprise as is formal or explicit knowledge.

Computer modelling is problem-oriented, aiming to address particular defined needs. In the words of Professor Barsington, it is constructed to yield 'visible, ultimate conclusive applications. It's scientific problem-driven research – so the focus is the problem you're trying to solve. What's the problem, the scientific problem and how will the knowledge base expand?' Professor Avril, at Hernchester, describes how problems that arise outside the academy translate into research questions. He explains, for example, how he might be approached by a third-world government whose members have 'an interest in road building and don't know the best way to design things, and you formulate together a research project with an application spin-off'. That the work is often commissioned by government agencies and other non-academic organizations puts university research departments in direct competition with research laboratories. Research laboratories differ from university research groups in two ways. First, they are established and well equipped. Second, they have a pool of permanent staff on which to draw for different project work.

The research students we observed and talked to had major responsibilities for developing and carrying out modelling research. Professor Avril, at Hernchester, is aware that because his modelling research depends upon research students there are problems in both the structuring and funding of this work:

> It's difficult to sustain multiple projects at once. It is vital that everything to do with the project research must be parameterized: that is, funds, the research group, time, etc. Research students are important to the department. [However] there are major problems if there are too few students, in terms of the technical support, supervision and money ...

Modelling Realities

studentships are awarded against approved projects. It's not menu driven. These are NERC [Natural Environmental Research Council] studentships, and supervisors apply to NERC and for project money and are assessed on the quality of that supervisor.

The constraints within the academy in turn affect the way in which group members interact, and consequently how work is carried out. Typically this is characterized by arrangements described by Professor Avril:

For the research assistants [and] doctoral students there are various levels of interaction. [There are] contemporaries working on the same project or in a common area ... second- and third-year [doctoral] students working on other projects and technical support.

Supervisory work relations are similar to those we experienced in the biochemistry laboratories. That is, Professor Avril's advice to his students is:

'See me when you like' – they'll knock at the door; it's an open door policy for direction. 'Don't see me for day-to-day direction [or] technical computer problems.' They can talk to each other, staff members or technicians for that.

Self-evidently, data are necessary in order to model reality. In a discipline such as physical geography, the structure and duration of groups means that participating members have different levels of interaction with the original physical phenomena. Among Avril's research group, for instance, most had little experience of data collection and others had none. Those involved in the initial stages of a project have most experience of data collection and those further down the line, have least. Peg Conroy at Hernchester did collect some data in the course of her research, but she explained:

Quite a lot of data collection had already been done – like the rainfall and the discharge from the catchment – so I went out there and was sampling fields. In the first three months I was basically trying to get to know the models and from that to get ideas about how to do the fieldwork.

Others, like Aaron Boatman from the same department, have a different experience. Aaron describes his PhD work as 'very computer based. I mean there's been a lot of fieldwork done, but I think the emphasis is moving away from that'. Aaron's work revolves around refining models that represent physical phenomena, and this entails:

Modelling Realities

> Taking two models that were already there, combining them and then developing another model. ... The problem tends to be some sort of computing problem, and I tend to sit down all day trying to solve that problem. That involves working at the screen and running programs and then maybe spending some time thinking about it.

In other words, although research projects are ultimately grounded in data, for many of the research group members – including graduate students – their computer-based models and simulations are primarily self-referential. Their work in modelling is tested against the group's developing models, rather than being tied directly to data collection or data production, as it would be in the field for the anthropologist, or in the laboratory for the biochemist.

Students derive support from other members of the research group who have either worked on their model or who are modelling another aspect of the same overall research problem, but their day-to-day programming routine can be very isolating. Wilma Ross, a PhD student at Illington, told us that the room in which her workstation is located had a

> terrible atmosphere. I mean because people are working in it so if you start talking to anybody, or just saying 'hello' you get glares and all sorts of things go round in the machine about people talking too loudly. But a lot of them who work there just use the machine until they have rooms where they can study and talk and whatever but we work there and use the machines there and that's the only place we can be, sort of thing. So it's very isolated.

Other sources of data for modelling, as in for example the study of robotics, include observation of behaviour. Dr Waite from Illington bases his work on the study of animal behaviour. He described the process of deriving measurements from observations in the following terms:

> I started by looking at biology and what really happens in small animals. They only have a few things they do and they scuttle about on the floor, but basically they can't climb trees or dig holes, they just scuttle around the floor. This sort of correlates quite well with what our robots can do.

Dr Waite's work, however, is not based upon his own observations about animal behaviour, but derived from secondary sources:

> I don't actually study the animals I just read most fairly introductory books about you know generally what animals do, what they're capable of, how their neurones work. Most models are developed for a specific

Modelling Realities

species but I want something a bit more general than that because my robot is not going to be like any particular species I can think of. I've got a model for a general vertebrate which was developed by an ethnologist who did most of her work on fish but is supposed to have generalized and I've made a program to simulate that model.

There are a number of problems routinely encountered by those modelling aspects of the real world. For robotics students those problems include the translation from real world phenomena to computerized representations of those phenomena. They in turn have practical implications in the difficulties that students encounter in controlling the physical environment which their machines encounter. In robotics, unlike 'pure' modelling, students' representations may engage directly with a real world. Robots' competence in dealing with an environment provides a direct test of the adequacy of students' ability to mimic behaviour. In this respect, Dr Pilgrim at Illington describes how

assembly robots have always suffered from the difficulty of dealing with uncertainty, the difficulty of bringing sensors into the robot architecture and a difficulty of connecting a robot in the real world with the kind of ideal, abstract planning system.

The functioning of the robot provides a direct check on the researcher's success in modelling reality.

When the environment cannot be fully controlled the problems intensify. For example, research student Celeste Mallory, at Illington, explained:

When you have a factory robot you might think that telling it what to do is fairly simple ... but as soon as you get a mobile robot, or in fact as soon as you get a real robot in a real factory, where you don't have ideal conditions then you find the part is not quite right in the place ... what do you do then? So you can try adding sensors so it can see but what if the part's wrong? ... Programming robots got very complicated because you had to foresee everything. Now what happens if the cleaner comes along and knocks the wire?

Ideas, Programs and Knowledge

We have described engagements with real environments but not all computing and modelling is so closely wedded to such real world phenomena. Research can become justified primarily in terms of computational and representational issues rather than their direct referential values. Those working in artificial intelligence who try to model intelligent human behaviour through computer programming, distance their work from

Modelling Realities

programmers by talking about underlying ideas. For example, Dr Passington, at Illington's artificial intelligence department distinguishes between

> people who are good at programming and people who are good at ideas, and I have become one of the ideas people. If a certain problem has to be solved and usually when this happens I or someone like me looks at different ways of solving it and knock up a rough implementation of the solution of a program, and if that works then the other guys who are programmers will take it over and neaten it up.

Central to this work is representation, and since symbolic AI emerged in the 1970s, partly as a critical departure from behaviourism, the focus of this representation turned from external observable phenomena towards inner mental states. For those working in symbolic AI, mental activity became understood as a kind of computational activity which could be captured in terms of symbols and symbolic manipulation (Adam, 1995a, 1995b). From this position advocates of the new cognitive approach argued that intelligence could be represented symbolically on a computer (Newell, 1990) with the strongest voices asserting the equivalence between a digital computer and a human mind (Pylyshyn, 1984).

Adherents of this position, such as Dr Subonadier at Yowford, argue that it is possible to map human thought processes. They see the human brain as a sophisticated computer and understand neural networks as

> a set of mathematical models of computation in which you have a bunch of variables which change according to certain rules and those rules are governed by certain parameters analogous to a program ... except the way that it's set up is very different from a normal computer.

One area of AI which endeavours to map cognitive activity in detail is connectionism. This attempts to model knowledge through a system which mirrors the neuron firings of the brain. This approach is described by PhD student Russ Martins at Yowford as the application of neural networks to

> building cognitive models. The idea being that the traditional cognitive models are essentially black-box approaches where you label theoretical constructs such as short-term memory, long-term memory, and you draw arrows between these boxes, which constitutes an exploratory theory. [Connectionists] would argue that more brain-like models are better candidates for more general theories of cognitive activity.

However, given the incompleteness of our knowledge about how the human, or animal, mind actually works, for Russ, what connectionism 'ends up

Modelling Realities

doing in fact is just creating many little boxes with their kind of drawn circles in them, with loads of little arrows instead of a few'. The very endeavour of attempting to map and represent intelligence raises philosophical questions about the nature of thought, which are taken on board by Dr Harme, from Illington, when he makes the link between robotics and AI. Dr Harme describes the aim of robotics as

> actually giving the machine ideas, or if you like putting a mind into the machine. [My interests are] philosophy of mind because if you're trying to do something like make a machine think, you've obviously got to have some ideas about what's involved in thinking and you know what parts to put into a machine.

In order to do this, certain assumptions must be made in respect of the constituents necessary for thinking. Dr Harme suggests that some of the prerequisites for anything beyond the most basic thinking may be beyond current understanding. Hence he notes:

> Artificial intelligence seems to be quite happy that you can do at least a considerable amount of thinking without having any emotions. Now, this may as a matter of fact not ultimately be true; it may in the end require emotions to do the furthest and highest kinds of thinking but if we had to have emotions in our machines we haven't a clue how to do that. ... We can make our machines think without emotions, so we've all made that presumption, so that's a certain model of mentality in the first place to say that at least up to a certain level those two things can be separated without loss.

Even were it possible to compute accurately all the dimensions and parameters of thinking, the implications for robotics are impractical. Dr Waite, from Illington, who bases his work in robotics on the study of animal behaviour argues:

> Of course nobody really knows [how an animal's brain works] and in the end I've got to have something that you can compute, that you can put on a robot – I can't have ten neurons in my robot's brain because there isn't the computational space. I can't even have one.

Furthermore, the problems of first understanding and then representing physiological phenomena are intensified by the boundaries which define disciplinary work and which hinder cross-disciplinary dialogue. For Christine Helsgood, a PhD student at Yowford, disciplinary relationships have crucial implications for the task of representation. In her own research she experiences 'an enormous problem with talking to biologists about biological neural networks. Because they use a different language for everything.'

One area of application in AI which endeavours to represent ways of thinking focuses upon the development of knowledge-based systems. Knowledge-based systems, which are more commonly known as expert systems, are based on the principle of constructing software systems to represent knowledge acquired from 'experts' in any chosen field. The purpose of ideal systems, as Collins (1990) observes, is to replace an expert in the chosen area, possibly making him or her redundant. Dr Hackington at Illington describes how expert systems are constructed:

> You try for some small part of the problem-solving capability of some expert in a particular domain and try and represent that as a computer program. So then you can replicate what that behaviour was, and there are standard ways of doing that that have been developed over a large number of years.

Dr Hackington describes the utility of expert systems as their potential

> to represent the management decisions people take in those local areas in their normal day-to-day business and then to take that representation across to the UK, supplemented with the sort of information that experts typically supply, but here you're supplementing explicitly what the management decision has been said to be. Take that back and then the idea is that that will give people also a low cost version of the expert information and will also put it more into context.

Helen Nagle, PhD candidate at Illington, explains the practical potential of an expert system which she is developing:

> my interest in this idea [is] maintenance of systems for developing countries. I wanted to build a tool which would assist in that. What I wanted to build was something that local experts could use themselves to build medical expert systems right from scratch themselves so there would be no involvement with the first-world engineer.

Expert systems should not only faithfully represent appropriate options but must also be user-friendly. Dr Hatchett from Illington points out that it does not matter how 'expert' a system is, if professionals will not use it. Referring to his medical diagnostic model, Dr Hatchett explains:

> Medical technology is generally unacceptable to medical practitioners unless it's extremely simple to use, [the] user interface is much more important than what it's actually doing. So a lot of the technology is a

Modelling Realities

very basic fact, but wrapped up in a very glitzy package to make it easier to use – so whether it can be made acceptable, whether it can be reliable – which is important of course and really the question about how we actually even access these qualities.

Helen Nagle recognizes the importance of bringing users on board when she discusses the way in which she intends to evaluate the program that she is developing:

> I'm going to have independent evaluation which is of the concept itself. I'm going to talk to them [potential users] about the whole idea of having a knowledge acquisition system for medicine and also the particular type of implementation that I've done, the way I've done it. To find out whether they think it's a good idea, whether they understand the idea and whether they can actually use the idea. And after that I'm going to ask them to use the system and again ask the same types of questions; whether they understand the way the system's working, whether they find it useful or not, whether they can actually do anything with it. ... I'm concerned what is much more important is the concept underlying the piece of software. I mean, I'll be equally happy if my evaluation shows that the software is rubbish but the idea is fine.

Underlying the concept of expert systems is the epistemological claim that it is the knowledge of experts which is going to be put into such systems and that this knowledge will be in the form of hard scientific facts (Adam, 1995a). This position assumes both a certain amount of agreement between experts and also a lay consensus in the way the content of these systems will be perceived and acted upon. PhD student Julie Kylie, at Illington, explains how advice and information which models impart may not be universally received. In her work she attempts to resolve differences in points of view:

> When you're collecting knowledge from different people the norm is that you try and get a consensus before you actually implement that in the computer and I'm actually interested in actually implementing different points of view. And then trying to build reasoning mechanisms within the system to recognize the differences in the points of view and to look for possible ways of resolving conflicts between them.

Julie's model is based upon data which she has collected:

> where I'm getting my data is from getting people to talk about the greenhouse effect and what their opinions are about that. My contention is that it is possible to give a logical analysis of different points of view, justification of those points of view in terms of whole

Modelling Realities

argument structures, and resolution of those and the coming to consensus.

She understands that the success of her program for resolving differences will be the extent to which it measures up to how real people

> do actually talk about things and formulate arguments and then disagree with one another and the way that people are prepared to say 'Right, OK, if we drop the stuff that we've heard on the telly and assume that that's rubbish, I still think that there's sound reasons for me believing that ...' and that sort of thing.

Underlying Julie's approach is the assumption that there is a universal understanding or consensus opinion to be reached. This is one of the most significant components of the disciplinary culture here. In order to embark on any system of simplification and representation, it is necessary to ground that work in a number of fundamental assumptions. Here the assumptions concern the nature of knowledge itself. The construction of expert systems like Julie Kylie's is dependent on an assumption of consensus among experts. This in itself is a contested notion. As Collins (1994: 502) suggests, there is little reason to expect scientific experts to agree with each other: 'reasonable people are always disagreeing: the most highly trained and most intelligent experts, of the highest integrity are always disagreeing with one another'. Yet the kind of representational work attempted by students and academics who construct such systems depends on suspending such radical doubts. The faith of the programmer here rests on a willing suspension of disbelief.

Furthermore, the disciplinary culture rests on an under-socialized view of knowledge. This contrasts sharply with the perspectives of sociologists of scientific knowledge such as Collins. Collins (1996) describes how the roots of the sociology of scientific knowledge (SSK) lie in academic questions about the universality of knowledge. Collins (1995) recognizes that AI and SSK both have knowledge as the object of their study, and as such notes that findings of the AI community are of interest to those working in the knowledge field. At the same time, he acknowledges his own disagreement with fundamental claims of AI because his own work emanates from an alternative epistemological position, which locates scientific knowledge within scientific communities and not as the property of individuals. The existence of intelligent machines contradicts a basic premise of knowledge science because a machine cannot be a community or a member of society (Collins 1990). It is, Collins (1990: 6) argues, 'at the wrong end of the reductionist telescope', because it is made not out of social groups but little bits of information. This way of thinking about knowledge has implications for the potential of intelligent computers. That is, a computer with specialist

Modelling Realities

instructions is not the same as a socialized human being, because knowing how to do something and actually doing it are often inseparable. For the purposes of AI this separation is crucial. The underlying assumption of symbolic AI is that human knowledge and intelligence can be expressed as a set of rules, the principal organizing feature of which is logic. Dr Passington from Illington describes how this works:

> You start off with a natural language process and then move quickly into logic. Having got something to play with, you then make deductions from your understanding and feed back those deductions in that natural language back to the computer.

However, any approach that depends entirely upon systems of logic denies legitimacy to the contexts in which things occur, or the circumstances in which something is said (Nye, 1990). The emphasis of AI on propositional knowledge, or in other words on knowledge which is represented in the form of logical propositions or rules, has attracted criticism from a phenomenological position (Dreyfus, 1979, 1992) because of its failure to recognize the importance of common-sense knowledge and skills. As one of its greatest critics, Dreyfus and Dreyfus (1986) highlight the impossibility of AI representing all the know-how, interests, feelings, motivations and bodily capacities which together make up human beings.

There is then something of a paradox concerning this particular aspect of knowledge-production. The young scholar working in a subject such as AI becomes enculturated into a particular disciplinary culture. For many, their own initiation into the field had been something of a 'conversion' experience (see Chapter 3 above). Their style of work is closely dependent on the social and intellectual organization of a research group. Yet the models of knowledge that they seek to implement and reproduce are themselves dependent on the idealization of essentially individualistic representations of expert knowledge.

Conclusion

This chapter has highlighted some of the issues faced by academics and students who do computer modelling. These manifest themselves as practical problems, such as those encountered by Celeste Mallory at Illington when trying to program a computer for environments that cannot be controlled. The practical problems overlie philosophical doubts about what is intelligence and whether or not it is possible to construct intelligent machines. These doubts are not unknown to the modelling community, but, rather than dwelling upon the philosophical issues and depending upon their research areas, students learn to come to terms with the practicalities of mapping either external physical phenomena or internal mental processes.

Modelling Realities

As we have seen, modelling is a problem-oriented activity driven by research questions that often arise outside of the academy. The practical application element leaves little room for philosophical doubt in the research student community.

In many cases the structure of group work means that most of the mapping of phenomena has already been accomplished, leaving students to resolve problems of representation. To this end, logic is deployed to construct systems which mirror (either external or internal) reality. Systems, or models, are handed down through the research group with individuals taking up and carrying forward the work of predecessors. That is not to say that these models are user friendly. From Peg Conroy at Hernchester we learnt how students inherit the shortcomings of models, as well as about difficulties they initially encounter in getting the model to work. The structure of working which characterizes modelling research, provides a supportive environment for PhD students (at the various stages of their research), research fellows (who may have previously completed their PhD research using the model) and technicians. Group directors or supervisors characteristically use the 'lab' model of working: that is, students see them for direction and guidance but routinely rely upon other group members for problems which arise on a day-to-day basis.

Because modelling, whether in AI or physical geography, is largely a computer-based activity it can be a lonely, isolating business. Those students who do not need to collect data spend practically their whole period of study in front of a monitor screen at a computer workstation. Here they deal with algorithmic models in which knowledge is stable and transferable in recipe form. It is at the workstation where logic is deployed to address the problems which arise – problems which constitute the hard edge of systems development. Students learn their modelling skills in a different way, through more informal social contact in the research group. This is the group in which the model perhaps first emerged and has been subsequently developed and refined. Each time the model is transferred, it is more used, more known and more user friendly. At each point of hand-over, however, it must be rediscovered or learnt anew. The fact that others have grasped and used it makes the prospect less daunting for new graduate students than it would be if it were completely novel.

In the construction of knowledge-based models or 'expert systems', because these systems respond to an identified need, students confront the relevance which their model has for users. On the one hand, choices must be made about what constitutes 'expert knowledge'. For students constructing these systems, the practical problem may be identifying and harnessing appropriate expertise. There are, however, underlying and often unacknowledged epistemological issues about the construction of knowledge. In AI the epistemological position is that characterized by the natural sciences and by positivistic research paradigms. From this position the object of study (that

Modelling Realities

to be mapped and represented) exists quite separately from the agents and tools of research, and resists inadequate or false methods. This is a realist position in which knowledge (which is universal) becomes the property of the neutral observer. An alternative view, not popularly held by those building expert systems, is that knowledge is not to be found, but discovered in the knowledge communities which construct it. This view does not assume universality of knowledge, quite the reverse. It sees knowledge as partial and subjective, and the outcome of social interaction. We found that some of these ideas were taken on board by those who did not assume that information imparted by expert systems would be received consensually by user groups. For example, some students were attempting to build reasoning devices into their systems in order to resolve different user viewpoints. Ultimately, however, PhD modelling work must *assume* an element of social consensus, both lay and expert, in order for systems actually to work.

In dealing with modelling and programming in this chapter we have not meant to imply that they are modes of knowledge creation that are totally self-contained or *sui generis*, any more than we implied that this was the case for geographers' or anthropologists' fieldwork, or for biochemists' laboratory experiments. We have acknowledged that all research involves some element of simplification and modelling reality. Indeed, each disciplinary culture is predicated on *particular* ways of establishing conventional representations and simplifications. The social anthropologist is engaged in the reconstruction of a given culture, group or society, and the laboratory scientist's experiments deploy selective and conventional ways of constructing natural phenomena. They clearly have different ways of accomplishing their work. The intellectual and practical processes involved contrast. The disciplinary regimes that regulate such work also contrast. Each discipline is based on its own characteristic ways of constructing and reconstructing knowledge.

Each disciplinary culture rests on what we might call articles of faith, and the work of the doctoral student is dependent on a personal faith that mirrors that discipline. The young anthropologist's venture into the field, and his or her attempts to 'write up' that fieldwork reflect an implicit belief that it is, in principle, possible for a young scholar to encompass 'the field' and to make sense of it through the reconstructive work involved in writing a thesis or a monograph. He or she must acquire a good deal of tacit disciplinary knowledge, in addition to any explicit theory or methodology, in order to carry out that reconstruction. In a parallel but different vein, the young laboratory scientist must maintain a belief that even in the face of failure and difficulty his or her experiments will 'work' in the end. Hence the belief must be maintained that the natural world is tractable through the particular representations of laboratory experiments. In a similar fashion, the student working on computer models and programming must maintain a fundamental faith that a computer model will eventually 'run', or that real world phenomena such as expert knowledge can be reproduced adequately through a computer model.

The specific content of disciplinary faith differs. The mechanisms used to investigate and reproduce the social or natural world also differ. The disciplines embody real cultural differences and intellectual resources. Each student's project creates a sort of microcosm of the discipline. Each discipline functions in ways akin to what Kuhn and others describe as a paradigm: it prescribes certain sorts of problems and methods. Each discipline shapes what will count as a 'doable' project – one that embodies reasonable hopes and expectations of outcomes. In some ways, however, the role of faith is common across the disciplines. All researchers, whatever their specific methods and modes of representation, rely on the shared belief system of their discipline. That belief system defines what sociologists of science have called the 'epistemic community' of disciplinary membership (Knorr-Cetina, 1999). Such faith is reproduced at the individual level. Each separate researcher, especially the postgraduate student, needs a bedrock of tacit faith that the discipline into which he or she is being inducted will furnish the kinds of problems that have solutions, provided that conventional methods of knowledge creation are adhered to. Each postgraduate student thus recapitulates the system of beliefs and methods that constitutes the discipline itself.

7 Genealogies and Generations

> Recruitment was a form of anticipated co-optation whereby the elders chose not subordinates destined for subaltern careers ... but their potential peers.
> (Bourdieu, 1988: 152)

Time and Generation

The social organization of academic socialization depends on the intergenerational transmission and inheritance of knowledge, skills and orientations: in short, of the academic habitus. As we stressed throughout the preceding chapters, there are significant cultural differences between different academic disciplines in the organization and construction of such transmission. Indeed, 'generation' itself is subject to different constructions in different cultural contexts. The nature of academic generations, and the character of transmission between them is subject to contrasting disciplinary definitions. In the course of this chapter we examine how disciplinary identities and loyalties are reproduced through the generations; how academics and their graduate students construct generations and the relations between them; and the implications these have for the reproduction of academic knowledge.

It is easy to assume that the cycles of renewal and recruitment operate more or less equally across all aspects of the academy. Indeed, many of the time frames and cycles are common across the university system (though subject to wide variation between different national systems). Academics themselves are accustomed to working with essentially common, arbitrary, schedules. The annual calendrical cycle of terms or semesters, undergraduate degree schemes that last three or four years, annual dates for student recruitment, the *rites de passage* of degree ceremonies; these are all part of the taken-for-granted organization of the university system. In themselves they are anthropologically interesting. Times and rhythms of academic life are so familiar that few academics inside the system are explicitly aware of their culture-specific nature, or of the arbitrariness – even absurdity – of such systems. Curricula are never predicated on a calculation of how long it will take the average student to reach a particular standard in a given discipline. In England and Wales, the default value for a bachelor's degree in, say, physics (three years) is precisely the same as the time to be devoted to a first degree in English, or Classics. In Scotland, those subjects also have the same timespan – but it is four years for an honours degree. (There are good historical reasons for the difference between the two university systems, of course, and we do not ignore those.) Equally, at postgraduate level, universities calculate the 'tariff' in terms of standardized periods of registration. Although there were variations between different universities in terms of detailed regulations, most of the postgraduate students we studied were subject to common patterns of time. The patterns of registration for Masters and PhD degrees, the pressures for completion, the funding of studentship funding and so on – these were broadly common across the system.

Such uniformity in the university system, however, overlies disciplinary differences. The social cycles of renewal and of generations differ in significant ways between disciplines. Not only is the nature of the 'relay' between generations different, the social organization of generations themselves is also different. Moreover, the cultural arrangements between the generations is subject-specific. The reproduction of university disciplines is not just a matter of individual students working in isolation. Even when the research process itself is relatively solitary, even when the number of researchers and students is small, there are matters of local tradition, schools of thought, and departmental traditions that colour the process. When graduate research is grounded in research groups and major research departments, with large groups of active researchers, then collective traditions and loyalties may be even more pronounced.

Different academic disciplines operate with rather different principles of transmission. One can paraphrase standard anthropological terminology for the analysis of kinship in suggesting that disciplines operate with their own distinctive *descent systems*. Patterns of descent in laboratory science contribute to long-term change with short-term continuity – a stable equilibrium. In anthropology there is a *longue durée* of disciplinary stability coupled with strong inter-generational pressures for radical discontinuity. Science has long-term revolutions while anthropology has short-term rebellions combined with family feuds within and between descent groups.

Part of the socialization process for academics, and also constitutive of academics' cultural capital, is the acquisition and expression of disciplinary *pedigrees*; that is, the ability to place oneself socially and intellectually in appropriate lines of descent. These include one's immediate mentors, but also – where appropriate – longer lineages of major figures, local schools and traditions, and extended networks of significant others. Such individuals and their descent systems are among the reference groups (Shibutani, 1967) through which identities are created, maintained and claimed.

Genealogies and Generations

Our work suggests that there are some key differences between major academic disciplines (or families of disciplines) in the construction and use of generations and genealogies. The very notion of a generation itself is a cultural construct. Generations are not naturally occurring phenomena, any more than classifications of time and persons. As Mannheim pointed out, the very idea of a generation is a cultural imposition, and the identification of particular generations and generational differences is an essentially arbitrary construction. The processes of biological and social reproduction are not given in terms of neatly demarcated cohorts and generations. Certainly, academic generations are not naturally given. Like the genealogies we describe, the sense of succession and generation is dependent on the cultural norms of disciplines.

Biographies, Genealogies and Pedigrees

This chapter begins with accounts from the supervisors of PhD students. It goes on to consider narratives from some of the graduate students. For obvious reasons, established academics are in a position to produce genealogical accounts in a way that few doctoral students can. What is striking, however, is that there are clear disciplinary differences in the form and content of such autobiographical descriptions. We begin to explore this phenomenon by examining some of the academics' own autobiographical accounts. Our interviews included a request for informants to summarize their academic careers to date. They were illuminating from a number of perspectives, not least for some of their formal narrative properties (Coffey and Atkinson, 1996). Before we turn to consider in detail the construction of genealogies and descent systems, we shall examine some more general features of academics' biographical accounts, as manifested in our interview data. Consider, for instance, the following account from a social anthropologist, Dr Talisman from Southersham University.

> My first degree was at Cambridge, 1975–8, in archaeology and anthropology, specializing in anthropology. After that I had a year off because I didn't know what I wanted to do, and then decided after a year that nothing interested me as much as carrying on in university and doing some research of my own. And in my year off before going up to Cambridge, I'd spent some time on a kibbutz in Israel. I very much liked the farming and the outdoor life, and the community of the kibbutz as well. I felt rather alone in Cambridge, and I liked the togetherness of the kibbutz, combining something academic with a style of life that I liked.
>
> So I decided to go to Manchester to do a PhD, because with Max Gluckman, the previous professor, there'd been a strong link with Israel, and lots of research projects started from Manchester. He was a South

African Jew, and when his family left South Africa, he was the only one who came to England, the others went to Israel, and I suppose he knew how to get money to do research in Israel. There was a man called Bernstein who funded a lot of projects, and Gluckman's links with Bernstein were such that he was able to fund a lot of research projects in Israel.

So I went there rather than stay in Cambridge or go somewhere else, and was really pleased to go there. It was a small department, very together, intimate, and I thrived. I really liked it. I really liked the anthropology there, it was more individualistic; less emphasis on social structure, more on the flux of social life, the creativeness of social life, really relating to my interests in the self and the individual. So I did my PhD there and I finished in February 1983, which was just over three years. Then I went to Australia, on a postdoctoral fellowship in Western Australia, and ended up spending two and a half years there altogether. It turned out that my first research wasn't in Israel: the professor who was in charge there at the time, Emrys Peters, was quite keen to alter the focus of the department. He was an arabist himself, worked in Libya and the Lebanon and convinced me that the kibbutz was old-fashioned to study, and I was also very interested in Europe, so I ended up doing my PhD on a small French farming village in Normandy, looking at communication, world view, perception, interaction, how the farmer saw the world.

In Western Australia, where I did my second piece of research, I looked at how people talk about violence or why people talk about violence so much – it sort of took the place of the weather in English conversational exchange – and wrote a book on the nature of urban interaction. I was doing fieldwork in the only real city in that part of Australia, and doing covert participant observation in the university itself, and in bars, and hospitals and courts of law. Anyway, after three and a half years there I'd had enough. I wanted to move back to England, but jobs were very scarce here still – that was in 1987 – so after a year here as a fellow here at Southersham, doing some work as a tutor, I got a lectureship in Israel in 1988, and went out to Israel. ... I was teaching there and also doing some research on a new town in the middle of the desert, looking at why the American immigrants who were there had come and whether what they'd come for they'd found. After a year there I managed to get a lectureship here in Southersham, and I started in October 1989.

This autobiographical account may be compared with one from a second anthropologist. The content is, of course, different, but it displays similar

Genealogies and Generations

features that we suggest are characteristic of the discipline as a whole, as reflected in the accounts we collected:

> I started in engineering in Ohio State University. At the end of the first year when I'd enjoyed myself very much I was asked to leave, because I hadn't done very well in my engineering exams. But we had to do courses outside, and I'd done English, and I'd done extremely well in English, and they thought that perhaps I was ill-suited to the course that I had chosen. Anyway I'd run through my money as well, so I transferred to another university, which was closer to home, so I could work and support myself, and I still continued with science subjects – I was doing physics and maths, and in the course of that I was in a programme where we were streamed and the upper 5 per cent of the university was put into what was called an honours college where we were taught by special members of staff, and the standard of teaching was much higher.
>
> And in doing that I was still doing science subjects and the head of the programme called me in one day and said 'why are you doing all this stuff?' And I said, 'Well that's what I want to do professionally.' And he said, 'This is probably the only chance in your life you'll have to try something else, so why don't you do something different?' I thought 'Why not?,' and said, 'What do you suggest?,' and he said, 'You could do some philosophy, or English, or anthropology.' So I thought, 'All right.' So I took a course in symbolic logic, thinking I wasn't risking very much, and I did a course in anthropology, and I thought they were fantastic. I loved them both.
>
> So I finished in that line, and by the time I graduated I was doing almost nothing in the physical sciences. I almost completely changed over to the arts and social sciences. By that time I'd decided I wanted to go on and do something in sociology and social anthropology so I applied to graduate schools in the States and I was given a Fellowship at Northeastern University in the African studies programme. And it was in the Department of Sociology and Anthropology, so I went there. When I first went to Northeastern, Paul and Laura Bohannon were both there on the African studies programme, and the first year I worked with Paul Bohannon, and was completely bowled over by British social anthropology which I was encountering for the first time. The clarity of vision and the way in which problems were phrased seemed quite strikingly different from American anthropology which I'd got acquainted with up to then. And I thought, 'Yes, that's what I want to do.'

Genealogies and Generations

Unfortunately the Bohannons left at the end of my first year, and there was virtually no one around to do anthropology. But because of an arrangement at Northeastern University I was able to go over to Harvard and I had two seminars, one with Tambiah on religion, and another with Darryl Ford who was visiting that year, on African religion, and that confirmed with Bohannon, that it was the kind of anthropology that I wanted to do. How all this relates to what I'm doing now – there is a connection, and that is that the head of my department at Northeastern was Gary Joplin, a sociologist who'd done fieldwork in Turkey, and he had a project in which he'd invited two Turkish scholars to come to Northeastern to do community study techniques, and they needed a dogsbody to work with the Turks and help them with their interviews and all their statistical apparatus, and as it happened I had the most experience in maths and statistics by far, most of the other students being innumerate, and I was given by Joplin to work with the Turks on the project, to teach them a little bit of statistics and do the results.

And as a result of that I was invited to go to Turkey at the end of this project and do some research when I got back home, and again they wanted someone to come and help them train interviewers and do the practical aspects of the data process. So I was invited to Turkey and spent the summer there, five months, working with the Turks – having had no interest or training in that part of the world previously. That was the summer of the Anatolian earthquake, and it was in Anatolia that I was working, and the earthquake put an end to that project, and I had to leave because of the earthquake. I was moving to the University of Lockport which had just started a little PhD programme in social anthropology. It was a complete unknown, I was going in as one of the first of their postgraduate students, but having looked around at other universities I decided that I preferred to do something that was unknown in social anthropology, rather than something that was more mainline American university anthropology. That wasn't what I wanted then, although it meant taking quite a gamble.

It turned out to be excellent, one of the few good choices I've made in my life. The programme was very well taught, an awful lot of energy went into the training of the students. I thought on the basis of my African studies experience in Northeastern that I wanted to do fieldwork in Africa. But that seemed to be increasingly unlikely because of political problems then between the US and Uganda where I was thinking of doing my fieldwork. A friend of mine from Northeastern days, working in Uganda, was sending back frantic letters about the difficulties he was having getting permission to do fieldwork. So the

Genealogies and Generations

head of my department at Northeastern said I should look around for some other place to do work. And I thought of going to Central Brazil to work with Lewis, but that seemed like hero stuff, and I didn't think I was quite up to that. Then there was the possibility of going back to Turkey, and it was really on the spur of the moment, after dithering for months, that the head of the department called me in and asked where I wanted to do my work and I said, 'It's very complex, because on the one hand ... on the other hand ...' and I outlined all the complexities, and he said, 'I know, but where do you want to work?' and I said, 'I can't answer that,' and he said, 'That's all right, you've got half an hour to make up your mind, I just want to know before you go out of that door.' And I blurted out, 'Turkey.'

That was the summer of '63. It was a five-month project, a sociology project. That was the first time. My own fieldwork was done from '67 to '68, I think. The dates are a bit hazy without having a CV to refer to. Then I was back again in 1970. So that's a long answer to how I got my training. ...

While I was a student at Lockport, Freddie Bailey was a member of staff for a year. Vic Turner, who was at Cornell, came to Lockport, for a term, and he gave the Morgan lectures. Max Gluckman was in the country and he came to Lockport for a time. I went to Cornell to attend a couple of his seminars. So the Manchester school, as it's known, was very much at the forefront of my consciousness, and I knew that it was a very interesting department. And then when I first started teaching, I was teaching in a small college in upstate New York, and one of my first undergraduate students went to Manchester as a postgrad. So I was aware of what was going on in the department through him. And I always fancied my chances of going there. And several years later I was at Carnegie Mellon University, working on a project that was coming to an end, so I was looking around for something else, and there was a job going there at Manchester, so I thought, 'If I don't put in for it I'll always wonder what might have happened.' So I decided to put in for it, and lo and behold I was offered it. It only lasted two years, though, while one of the permanent staff was away on fieldwork, so I came on here to Southersham.

This autobiographical chronicle displays a number of interesting features. The narrative here talks in terms of key anthropological figures, key turning points, the influence of particular academic departments. The balance between decisions and luck is also highlighted. Key anthropological influences feature – social actors like the Bohannons (a married couple of anglicized American anthropologists), Joplin, Bailey, Turner and Max

Genealogies and Generations

Gluckman again. (Although real figures from the world of anthropology appear here, we should stress once more that key aspects of the narrative have been fictionalized: it makes no sense at all, however, for us to invent entirely fictitious major figures from the history of the discipline.) The story is replete with turning points – doing poorly in engineering examinations, the interview with the head of department, the relationship at Northeastern, the invitation to Turkey. The tensions between planning and luck come over perhaps even more strongly in this material: running out of money, being a 'dogsbody' to visiting Turkish scholars, the earthquake, getting to know Manchester through coincidental contacts. These are all expressed in terms of chance, but all had an influential impact on the life course and career of the social actor. This extract is also replete with *contrastive rhetoric* (Hargreaves, 1984). (This is a term we explain in more detail in the following chapter.) Here we can note particularly how the respondent compares anthropology in the American and British traditions. We get a sense of the different approaches to anthropology, and different people and places associated with those approaches. The chronicle itself is a relatively 'elaborated' one. By that we mean not only that it has a certain degree of length and complexity, but more that it elaborates an individualized identity through a series of personal transformations, turning points and personal influences.

It is noticeable, for instance, that this personal chronicle traces a personal pedigree, and describes a series of personal influences. The personal chronicle constructs an academic career. It also constructs a particular kind of academic identity. Its contingencies are closely linked to the personal relationships of mentoring and influence. The intellectual odyssey is intimately connected to a personalized descent system. The interviews with social anthropologists were characterized in particular by these personally elaborated accounts. They constructed long pedigrees, in which key major figures played a prominent part. We are, of course, aware that such pedigrees are of significance in all disciplines. In the natural sciences there is ample evidence concerning the personal and academic significance of such genealogies. For instance, there are highly influential descent groups among leading scientists, within major research groups and laboratories. Membership of the group surrounding a Nobel laureate is itself a major predictor of winning a Nobel prize (Zuckerman, 1977). Likewise, membership of a 'core set' (Collins, 1985) is a key social element in establishing a scientist's identity and her or his relationship to disciplinary knowledge. Nevertheless, the natural scientists whom we interviewed did not characteristically produce accounts that were elaborated in terms of these autobiographical elaborations. Rather than the personalizing accounts we have just seen, they more characteristically gave us accounts that were much less developed or elaborated in terms of personal biography and the nuances of such influence and descent. The autobiographical accounts of anthropologists may therefore be compared

Genealogies and Generations

with those of natural scientists. Here, by way of introduction, is an account from a biochemist, Dr Duval, at Ribblethorpe:

> I did my first degree in biochemistry at Leeds 1969–72. Then I went to Leicester to do my PhD. I went there for a number of reasons. First, there were two of us – my wife and I wanted places to do a PhD. Second, Professor Kornberg was there and there were studentships available. We were there from '72 till 's75. Then we went to Switzerland where I did two years postdoc work. My PhD was on slime mould – molecular biology. Since then I became disillusioned with slime moulds and their lack of relevance to mammals. In 1972–85 I was at the Wedgewood Hospital working on mammary glands, lactation and breast cancer. Then I took the lectureship in Ribblethorpe. My wife doesn't work now. Well, I mean she's a housewife. We have children. At the Wedgewood I became interested in mammary genes and how these are hormonally regulated. For technical reasons I was limited to where to go from there. You see, we're constantly looking for new ideas in the same area. So I moved to the male reproductive tract because the techniques are similar. My interest is in trying to develop a test for male infertility. That's my main interest.

Consider too the following account from Dr Garnette, at Baynesholme University:

Dr G: I did my first degree in plant science. I actually did the first year at Birley University, but then my husband changed his job – I was a mature student, I was 25 – and I rang up Baynesholme in September and asked if they'd take me on for the second year of their plant science degree course, and they said yes. I did my final two years here. I finished in – must have been 1985. And I took auxiliary biochemistry with the degree, but my degree is actually single honours plant science.

OP: What made you decide to carry on and do a PhD? Did you do that straight away?

Dr G: I did it straight away. My daughter was born at the end of my second year of undergraduate study, and I decided, having done the first year – I decided I couldn't drop out between the second and third years, as there'd already been so much upheaval. There was no point taking another year off because I knew I wanted to do research. I knew that practically from when I started to do my degree. So I applied in Baynesholme, and Professor Gantry had some money for a research assistantship, which meant I actually got a salary. In fact that was the only offer I had in Baynesholme,

Genealogies and Generations

because my tutor in plant science offered me a studentship but he went to Thursby, so that was no longer a possibility.

In much the same vein, we find an extremely truncated response from Dr Quayne, from Forthampstead University:

> I did my first degree and PhD at the University of Leicester, so the first degree was in biological sciences, and as I say my PhD was in biochemistry. And then I went for five years to the University of Hadleigh. That was as a postdoctoral fellow, and from Hadleigh I then came here as a lecturer.

Now it would clearly be wrong to read too much into necessarily small extracts of accounts from relatively small numbers of academics. Nonetheless, the differences in self-presentation and autobiographical construction are quite marked. We have suggested that the accounts given by the social anthropologists can be described as 'elaborated' and 'personalizing'. They construct biographies that are highly developed in terms of narrative complexity, coupled with biographical density. They portray their biographical and academic development in terms of successions of personal influences. They trace out narratives of personal development, and of personal transformation. By contrast, the scientists' accounts are lacking in biographical richness. They do not embellish their accounts with personal epiphanies and transformations. The personalizing accounts are developed in terms of personal motives, responses, intentions and so on. In contrast, the scientists' accounts are more readily characterized as 'positional'. Their biographies are not developed through narratives of personal engagement. Rather, they seem to progress through predefined positions, in laboratories or departments that are minimally formed in terms of individuals.

That sense of 'positionality' reflects not only accounts of personal careers, but also the relationship between biography and research problems. We have already seen this phenomenon – approached from a different perspective – in previous chapters on the disciplinary construction of knowledge. The positionality of scientists' biographies is directly paralleled by the positionality of their research problems. Research topics are 'given', and are prescribed not in terms of personal commitment and interest, but in terms of research *group* commitments. For instance, consider how Dr Quayne's account continued:

Dr Q: I'm basically an enzymologist, so I was working on the structure and function of enzymes. I worked in a group which was about ten people strong, so we had a supervisor. There were postdoctoral students in the lab, and there were PhD students like myself. And it's very much how I now run my group in that really I would

Genealogies and Generations

discuss with my supervisor a set of experiments, I would go away and do the experiments, I would analyse the data, I would show him the data, we would try and formulate conclusions from that, and then from those conclusions we would design more experiments. And that is in a way how I think science works. The experimentation, analysis, design of new experiments, and so on. All the way along you are formulating models which explain data, and then you're designing new experiments to test that model or to refine the model. And I did it in three years.

OP: When you applied to do your PhD was the topic or area spelt out for you or did you come along with your own ideas?

Dr Q: No, it was very much spelt out for us. And again that's the way I work here in that it's the supervisor who is generating the subject and driving his or her own research and not letting the students drive it – at least the topic. But having said that once we've decided on a topic then I think the student will gradually put more and more into the project of his or her initiative. I mean it's not a doctorate of being a technician, it's a doctorate of philosophy. ... You're wanting them to come back with ideas, and indeed from then on guide the project in particular areas although I think the supervisor provides the overall broad direction.

While Dr Quayne acknowledges the creative contribution to be made by a doctoral student, he or she understands that within a tightly specified framework. The image of 'driving' the research helps to capture the strong sense of direction that is imparted by the senior scientist. The student's own contribution is thus to be circumscribed by the prescribed research agenda. This is not a matter of individual negotiation either: the postgraduate student and his or her research are equally defined by their junior position within the group. Identity is largely ascribed in terms of a collective identity and a collective orientation to knowledge. Dr Quayne's entire understanding of science is predicated on this collective and positional model of academic work and knowledge transmission.

Those autobiographical accounts were taken from established academics whom we interviewed primarily about their role and experience as supervisors of graduate students. It is instructive to compare them with the accounts offered by graduate students themselves. Obviously, their personal careers are shorter, and we would not expect to find many opportunities for autobiographical complexity in comparison with their older colleagues and mentors. Again, we begin with a graduate student in social anthropology, Wanda Soczewinski:

WS: I got married in 1960, and I went to live in Poland. My husband's Polish. And I suppose living in another country, and being

Genealogies and Generations

married to someone from a very different culture, and being married to someone from a very different background, you inevitably begin to question the way you behave, the way other people behave, what is right, and so on. Also there were things in anthropology that I'd always been interested in – customs and ritual and things like that – but of course when I began to study my interests developed in a different way. But I think I can say there's always been some kind of interest, and living abroad and being part of the Polish family accentuated it.

OP: And why did you decide to do it at Kingford?

WS: I waited until my children were at university, then I thought 'Why shouldn't I do something I want to do?' so I decided. By that time my husband had come to Kingford; we'd been parted for five years and didn't want to go on doing that, so it had to be Kingford.

OP: When you'd done your undergraduate degree and got a first, and decided to do a PhD, Kingford was a natural choice, then?

WS: I took a year off, for personal reasons, We'd moved, and there was a lot to do in the new house. Then I suppose like many others who were happy here I had withdrawal symptoms when I left, and since I'd been told if I wanted to come back to Kingford I would be welcome, I naturally came back.

The following graduate student in social anthropology is really unusual in having obtained a PhD some years previously, and then registering for an MA in social anthropology at Southersham. She displays a highly personalizing account:

I submitted [the PhD] in 1984, but how that came about was that my primary interest was dance, and at that time you couldn't study dance at degree level. I came out of school in 1972, and there was no way you could study dance at undergrad level at all, so what I wanted to do was to become a choreographer on the theatre side. So I went to the Institute of Choreography in London, and I realized that if you wanted to study dance you had to be able to write it down, and the Institute taught you how to do that. While I was there I came up against other kinds of dance other than Western European forms and I became very interested in them. But I also had an interest in British traditional culture, for want of a better word – I don't think I would have called it that then – and I knew I had to get a degree to be respectable, because I wanted to write about dance. So I did English as a degree after that, because there was an element of folklore in it, at the University of Maplestone. ... So I went there and stayed on to do my PhD which was on dance traditions in the south-west of Scotland. And what I was interested in was that all the literature said that folk dancing only happened in the countryside,

127

> and that didn't fit with what I'd studied at university. So I decided to look at the effects of industrialization and urbanization on traditional dancers. And I took one particular group and did an ethnographic study of that group. So that's it. ... Whilst I was at Maplestone I came across a lot of anthropological literature, and the problem with folklore as a discipline in this country is that it's only taught in one university – which is Sheffield – and it hasn't got a very high status. Dance hasn't got a very high status in this country: most dancers are only interested in theatre. And I was reading lots of anthropological books and thinking this was the same as folklore. So I wanted to know more about this literature more thoroughly and I'd been thinking for a number of years about the best way of doing it, so I signed on to do an MA here. I thought about that as soon as I'd finished my PhD, and got a place here. But I also changed jobs at the same time and spent a lot of time working on that, so I didn't take the place until last year.

It is by no means unusual for research students' commitment to anthropological work, and to particular research topics or areas of specialization, to be grounded in personal, biographical commitments or experiences. Equally, it is unremarkable for the relative complexity of the graduate student's personal and intellectual career.

As before, we can compare these accounts with those of graduate students in other disciplines. Here, by way of initial contrast, are accounts derived from our graduate students in biochemistry. Elissa Tyrone at Baynesholme described her career in these terms:

> I did my undergraduate course in biochemistry here in Baynesholme from 1989 to 1991. In the third year I did a drugs option. Actually it's called the toxicology option but it's known as the drugs option. And I did a third year project on the effect of putricine on detergents. I found the theory of this very interesting and the subject – but was bored with the techniques, which I'm very well used to because I've had this summer job in Ribblethorpe working for a pharmaceutical company who do some work at the university. Because of that the techniques were very familiar to me and I wasn't learning anything new. It was good experience for me because it gave me a real sense of bench work before starting the PhD. I've always wanted to do a PhD. I've always seen it as the next thing to do. Why stay here? Well I've got a lot of friends here and also somewhere good to live. I was keen to stay partly because it's less hassle. The project was offered too, and I was quite interested in the subject. I'm looking at an enzyme which is the first step in chlorophyll biosynthesis. It's part of the ALA compound. The reactive part of

chlorophyll is common but this enzyme is different in mammals and I'm trying to stop it, so to prevent chlorophyll synthesis.

While Elissa's account here includes some personalizing elements, she expresses them in terms of taking the line of least resistance when it came to the place of her doctoral research, the project that was 'offered' to her. Otherwise, her route to the PhD, in terms of topic and location, is characteristically restricted in form. Consider too the following account from Giles Perrin at Ribblethorpe University:

GP: In Dranllwyn [where he did his first degree] you do a two-term practical project – rather than in Ribblethorpe you just do a ten-week practical project, in Dranllwyn you do a two-term project, which was quite useful. We'd done twice as much research as other graduates. And that was in sort of genetics and biology.
OP: Genetics and biology?
GP: Cell biology. It was related. It was in a cell biology field but using molecular genetics.
OP: So then you decided that you were going to do a PhD, or had you decided already?
GP: I'd decided already. Well, that was the reason for taking the year out because it wasn't like a sandwich year, although it looks like a sandwich year – it was completely voluntary.

In this last example, it is noticeable that Odette Parry intervenes with the voice of the interviewer more than in previous examples. This kind of question and answer sequence, rather than an unbroken autobiographical account, is far more characteristic of the interviews with graduate students – and indeed with their supervisors – in the science disciplines. The biographical information has to be elicited rather than it being proffered in terms of an autobiographical narrative.

We have already seen how the distinctive patterns of work and knowledge-reproduction in different disciplines create the possibilities for different patterns of succession. We can make the point most clearly by contrasting social anthropology with the laboratory sciences once more. As we have seen, the laboratory scientists in biochemistry – and to a considerable extent, the physical geographers too – operate within a cultural system that cascades research problems and supervisory responsibilities across short generational steps. As we described in Chapter 4, research problems are often defined and passed on within tightly defined boundaries. The time frame is short. Successive postgraduate students may work systematically through a series of related projects that are closely linked and part of a wider research programme. There are direct lines of continuity between one graduate student and his or her immediate successor in the research group, and

129

between postdoctoral researchers and the graduate students. Day-to-day guidance and supervision is largely carried out within these close interpersonal relationships. Senior scientists may have ultimate responsibility for the research programme, but are often removed from the everyday practicalities of supervision. They are relatively distant figures.

Research Groups and Succession

Given the numbers of doctoral students per supervisor (which could be as many as ten at any one time among the groups we studied), it would not be feasible to take full responsibility for training graduate students. For instance, Dr Duval, a biochemist at Ribblethorpe, describing the lab he runs with Dr Dewry, said 'Most of the training of the PhDs is the responsibility of the postdocs. We couldn't do it otherwise; there could be up to twenty-five PhD students.' In other words, the research group or laboratory 'shop' provides a network of social relations through which responsibility for supervision is delegated and shared between the generations of researchers. The group leader has overall responsibility for the direction of the research effort, but the practical induction of students into the everyday work of the group and the solution of mundane problems is the responsibility of postdoctoral research staff, who are themselves not much older or – formally speaking – more senior than the doctoral candidates whom they mentor.

The supervisor provides guidance on the framework and direction of research while the experienced group members – such as postdoctoral researchers or doctoral candidates more advanced in their work – help the inexperienced PhD students on a day-to-day basis. Because of this, PhD supervision is seen as a collective responsibility:

> I work within a group ... a whole group of people, research associates, PhD students, and technical help and consultancy help. That makes about ten people. So for fieldwork problems or day-to-day things I don't have to go to my supervisor. There's all sorts of people to draw from who did similar PhDs, and who've come through here. So it's like a big supervisory group.
> (Jim Vorhees, physical geography doctoral student, Tolleshurst)

The burden of supervision falls upon postdoctoral researchers and is taken for granted as part of their work and their contribution to the functioning of the research group. A senior scientist, Professor Fardian, a geologist at Ottercombe, explains his understanding of his very different role:

> I would prefer to see students overlapping. I mean, if you've got one student who's been working for three years it's very nice to be able to

start the next one before the other one has finished. Because there's a lot of peer-group teaching, if they overlap they teach one another.

... I think the postdocs give day-to-day guidance. My role as head of the lab is a psychologist. Experiments don't always go well and I need to cheer them up. Especially the PhD students when nothing seems to be working.

(Professor Gantry, biochemistry supervisor)

Postdoctoral researchers themselves acknowledge their roles and responsibilities in this respect (Becher et al., 1994: 148). They recognize that the status passage from graduate student to postdoctoral researcher involves taking on the supervision of new PhD students. As one of them said:

Recently my role has changed. I'm now a research associate which means I'm a stepping-stone between PhD students and their supervisor. There's two PhDs working on the model. Here I am the direct line of unwritten responsibility.

(Steve McAlister, geography postdoctoral researcher)

Students tend to locate their own research by specifically linking it to previous work within the laboratory. For instance:

I've got a model ... which was developed by a biologist, an ethologist, who did most of her work on fish, and I've made a robot to simulate that model. I've found there are a number of problems with it, so I'm, constantly trying to work out what are the best ways of adapting the model to try and make it work better.

(Celestine Mallory, artificial intelligence postgraduate at Illington)

The majority of our science students described their projects as taking further the work of others: 'I think of my work as extending what other people have done, I think it has come out from a base and it's pushed out from there' (Aaron Boatman, physical geography postgraduate, Hernchester).

In many cases our graduate student and postdoctoral informants were able to cite the individual who had originated their work. That predecessor might be a postgraduate or postdoc or the supervisor:

Once you identify a structure there's a lot you can do with it. I have the structure from my boss, my ex-supervisor, and by looking at it and finding out what is important I take her work forward, using my own knowledge and methods.

(Dr Danberry)

Genealogies and Generations

> You can see the progress and how things are moving on. And results seem to have more of a major impact because I'm working with Pete's model and I'm extending it and seeing how its application can be valuable. That means Pete, and John who worked on the model before Pete, are very interested in my results.
>
> (Clay Batchelor, physical geography postgraduate)

The following postgraduate is also working on the model just mentioned: 'Pete was here then, working on a computing model. He was just finishing his PhD as I started mine. Pete got John's job when he finished' (Dean Caldwell).

There is direct continuity and succession as ideas, models, methods and apparatus are passed down from one graduate student to another, while the more senior researchers obtain their PhDs and move on, as postdocs, to supervise the new postgraduates. This pattern is not only recognized retrospectively but also provides a structure for the description of individual research trajectories:

> The idea is that Martha [postgraduate student] is doing a PhD and was going to take over from me when I finish. Also someone else is coming to be a PhD in October. By then I'll be the postdoc on the project.
>
> (Sheridan Ireland)

Often individuals who have been working in the same project – whether it be the development of an enzyme or of a modelling programme – have different funding sources. Their work concatenates into a succession of problems and solutions:

> Tim has a joint SERC and industry grant. He was also funded to do his PhD on this enzyme. There was a person working on the enzyme before him. That was Connor. Connor started off by trying to purify the enzyme and he came quite close. Then a year later Tim started and actually purified the enzyme and started working on it. Now I shall be taking that work a little bit further. Maybe if they get another award they'll be someone carrying on my work in the same way.
>
> (Elissa Tyrone, biochemistry PhD student, Baynesholme)

Reliance upon pre-established knowledge in scientific work can itself be problematic. Hacking (1992) highlights how the process of passing down old skills and equipment means the production of 'new' science then depends to some extent upon the mastery and reproduction of older, even outmoded, equipment and techniques. The personal recapitulation of earlier approaches and techniques is not always straightforward, however. Despite the fact that many of our PhD students, especially those in the early stages of their doctoral work, were reproducing models or experiments that were

Genealogies and Generations

inherited, the majority of supervisors we encountered were responsible for setting up projects for PhD work, attracting funding and inviting applicants. Although many of our PhD respondents claimed to have a reasonable amount of freedom in their everyday work, such as following their own leads, ultimately most were aware of having a fairly tight research brief from the outset. Constructing a realizable topic was seldom a responsibility of the student (See Becher et al., 1994).

Doctoral students were equally aware of the necessity of producing results within the allotted time, and reported being prepared to structure their own research work accordingly. This may entail the manipulation of an original project: 'You have to take your idea in hand and engineer it to fit in with the rest of the system' (AI doctoral student). It may also mean simply recognizing when to give up if results are not forthcoming: 'You have to (a) pick the right experiments and (b) know when to give up' (Dr Danberry, biochemistry postdoctoral researcher, Ribblethorpe).

Whereas the natural, laboratory sciences operate with short-span generational links, mediated through collaborative research groupings, disciplines such as social anthropology are transmitted on quite different principles. The inter-generational links are based primarily on individualized links between supervisors and students, without intermediate steps, such as post-doctoral fellows, senior research assistants or technicians. The steps between them may be of virtually any chronological length, as supervisors may be very senior figures in the field, or relatively junior academics not much (if at all) older than the graduate student.

We have also seen from previous chapters that the personalizing mode of anthropology, contrasted with the more impersonal, less autobiographically elaborated, mode of the sciences, positions the student and supervisor(s) rather differently, while implying different stances vis-à-vis the reproduction of disciplinary knowledge. The junior anthropologist is faced, implicitly, with the heroic enactment of a unique intellectual odyssey. The student is not one of a research group, but takes his or her place in a series of unique supervisory relationships with a supervisor. The relationship between supervisor and student is a very special one, and is part of the highly personal pedigree of the developing scholar. The junior scientist, on the other hand, constructs a career as part of a collective commitment.

We explore some of these themes in more detail in the two chapters that follow, both of which are concerned with the inter-generational transmission and re-creation of disciplinary knowledge. In Chapter 8 we explore narratives of supervision and discuss the 'essential tension' between supervisors' control and students' autonomy in the reproduction of academic knowledge; this draws primarily on supervisors' accounts. In Chapter 9 we return to and consider students' accounts of their relative social position in departments and research groups. There we develop further the themes of *positional* and *personal* identities in comparing students' accounts across different disciplines.

8 Supervisors' Narratives
Creating a Delicate Balance

> I need only mention the astonishment of a certain young American visitor ... to whom I had to explain that all his intellectual heroes ... held marginal positions in the university system which often disqualified them from officially directing research (in several cases, they had not themselves written a thesis ... and were not allowed to direct one).
>
> (Bourdieu, 1988: xviii)

Collecting Academics' Accounts

The title of this chapter comes from Dr Crupiner, a geographer from Tolleshurst University, who told us: 'It's caused a lot of angst to me creating a delicate balance between letting them do something which is their own and giving them a good topic.' This was the most succinct statement of a dilemma facing the social science and natural science supervisors. This chapter outlines how social science and natural science faculty members talked about one of their dilemmas – the 'delicate balance' of the title – and contrasted their own experiences as doctoral students with their supervisory practices today.

There has been far too little qualitative research on doctoral students, their work and training. Many features of these important aspects of higher education remain stubbornly invisible. To some extent, this reflects the relative neglect of the field, but it also reflects the fact that many of the key social processes are treated as 'private' by academics themselves. Processes of supervision and training remain especially invisible. Notwithstanding some of the recent research in the UK, we have only indirect evidence on how postgraduate supervision is conducted. The research literature documents doctoral students', supervisors' and some others' accounts from interview data. There is, however, a continuing lack of observational data on actual conduct of the most private supervisory relationships. The data that are available, and that have been reported in recent years, consist almost exclusively of accounts, collected under the auspices of qualitative interview studies.

134

Supervisors' Narratives

The social science research on doctoral candidates and supervision has never included prolonged and systematic observation of supervision actually happening. In the natural sciences the supervision of postgraduate and postdoctoral work has been observed *de facto* in the course of more general 'laboratory studies', because it can happen in the semi-public laboratory while others in a team are present. Sociologists of science conducting ethnographies of laboratories and research groups (e.g. Traweek, 1988; Latour and Woolgar, 1986; Lynch, 1985) have seen doctoral supervisions, but have never written them up specifically from the perspective of academic socialization (Delamont,1987; Ashmore et al., 1995). For all practical purposes, therefore, we have only supervisors' narratives for natural science too. Researchers have relied on students' and supervisors' accounts of the relationship and the processes. The studies reported in McAleese and Welsh (1983), Wakeford (1985), Scott (1985), Young et al. (1987), Wright (1992), Becher et al. (1994), Burgess (1994) and Hockey (1994) are all based on interviews. Such interviews only provide data on what supervisors think they do and are prepared to rehearse in front of researchers.

The status of accounts and narratives gathered through research interviews can be problematic. Some authors are willing to take interview accounts as evidence – albeit partial and perspectival – of how individuals and groups organize their everyday work and activities. More analysts are willing to use interview data as evidence of respondents' personal experiences and subjective evaluations of them. Yet others, more radically, insist on analysis of accounts *as* action and not *about* action. Gilbert and Mulkay's (1984) analysis of scientists' talk is a classic exemplar. Such an analytic perspective does not render interview accounts unusable as data. Rather, it implies a very particular perspective on those data. Gilbert and Mulkay place their emphasis on close analyses of the accounting devices used by scientists in the construction of their talk. They examine how scientists' accounts are accomplished. The talk itself accomplishes particular kinds of social action, for instance in reconciling potentially incommensurable frames of reference in accounting for scientific discoveries and evaluating the work of other scientists.

Our position is not the most radically sceptical. We believe that interview data *can* be used to illuminate cultures and settings, while recognizing their recurrent limitations and imperfections, and the attendant methodological problems that have now been so thoroughly aired. Equally, we recognize the extent to which narrative accounts (whether derived from interviews or from 'naturally occurring' spoken interaction) may – indeed, should – be inspected for their formal properties (Cortazzi, 1993; Riessman, 1993). Irrespective of whether we believe that interview accounts can have referential value beyond themselves or whether we believe that they must be treated *sui generis*, it is equally important to attend to the organization of those accounts. Narratives and other kinds of accounts are a pervasive feature of social life, and are fundamental to everyday practical action. They have their own organizational features and regularities. We certainly cannot treat them as 'transparent'. As a pervasive medium of personal and interpersonal expression, narrative accounts deserve attention in their own right. We should therefore inspect accounts and narratives for the rhetorical devices that are employed and deployed in their construction. Analysis needs to pay due attention to the structures of narrative discourse. One may undertake such without assuming that accounts have no referential value beyond themselves. Indeed, one can examine the structure and the rhetoric of accounts without strong assumptions about reference one way or the other (Coffey and Atkinson, 1996).

In presenting an analysis of academics' accounts of their experiences of doctoral supervision we do not assume that such narratives give us direct access to the actual practices of academic supervision, and the patterns of social interaction between academics and their doctoral students. Rather than examining them from such a perspective, we document the themes, images, metaphors and accounting devices used by supervisors to talk to fellow academics (their interviewers) about this important but relatively invisible aspect of their professional work. We regard these narratives and their characteristic accounting devices as part of the occupational culture of the academics we studied, not therefore as idiosyncratic or private experiences, nor as situated actions of no relevance at all beyond the interview context itself.

Our analysis documents recurrent motifs and rhetorical forms in the corpus of accounts collected in the course of our research. In the analysis that follows, therefore, we emphasize rhetorical and accounting devices that are shared by academics across a number of disciplines in the natural and social sciences. In doing so, we recognize that there is a danger of appearing to construct an ideal-typical speaker, blurring important differences between individuals and under-emphasizing potential differences between different academic disciplines, sectors of higher education and so on. But it is not our intention to construct ideal-type social scientists, or to imply that they all share a common culture of rhetorical devices and narrative themes. A preliminary mapping of common accounting devices is a useful preliminary to any more detailed understanding of patterned difference.

As we have indicated, our data were collected by means of open-ended interviews, and do not derive from naturally occurring organizational and collegial talk between members of the same department or discipline. There is no reason a priori to assume that the interview accounts are radically different from those accounts that might be produced in other social contexts, even though we were explicitly soliciting them for our research purposes. Since the interviewer was a fellow member of the profession, there is also no reason to assume that the interview represented a radically

Supervisors' Narratives

different context for talk about academic work than other more 'naturally' occurring occasions for talk between colleagues.

Supervisors were asked what their aims were in supervising doctoral candidates, and how they tried to achieve them; they were invited to tell us about particular (anonymous) case histories of successful and failed relationships. We also asked for their academic biography, and for their accounts of their supervisory careers. We collected accounts of how they had worked with graduate students in the past, and about their current practices. We were interested in doctoral students of all kinds, part-time as well as full-time. In the event, most of our informants had little experience of part-time doctoral students, and therefore the accounts excerpted in this paper refer to full-time students. Accounts of work with overseas students are included as well as accounts of work with UK 'home' students.

It was striking that most staff thought they had been poorly supervised, and were motivated to do better themselves. As one geography lecturer from Tolleshurst, Dr Kenway, said, 'I decided I'd keep a very close eye on graduate students because I felt remarkably scarred by my own experience.' Dr Kenway stated that, 'when I was a graduate student I didn't have any supervision at all', so now, he said, 'I do feel strongly about care and attention'.

The analysis of our interview data shows a number of disciplinary differences in the nature of those supervisory narratives. In this chapter, however, we concentrate on the similarities that may be identified across the disciplines. There are recurrent motifs and patterns in the narratives that supervisors produced. One of these similarities was the use of contrasts drawn between the way staff had been supervised during their own doctorates compared to their aims and practices as a supervisor. Many of the respondents told us stories similar to Dr Kenway's, from which we have just quoted. Dr Kenway draws a moral about supervision and his own goals as a supervisor by drawing out a contrast with his own past experiences as a student. In the corpus of interview data, therefore, one may identify recurrent uses of 'contrastive rhetoric'. Hargreaves (1984) used the term 'contrastive rhetoric' to describe a common feature of teachers' talk in school staffrooms, where staff draw rhetorical contrasts between sensible, realistic schools and teachers who operate with real children in real time under real pressures, and 'others' who are ridiculously 'progressive' or ridiculously 'old fashioned' or full of airy-fairy ideas. More generally, one may identify the use of contrastive rhetoric in many social settings, in which participants create accounts based on distinctions between us and them, past and present, here and there. It is a feature of such rhetorical accounting devices that they are used to establish justifications of what the speaker(s) do and believe, and to distance them from the errors committed in other institutions or in a discredited past.

As we shall show, the supervisors used contrastive accounts to compare their experiences as students, or their experiences as inexperienced supervi-

Supervisors' Narratives

sors (or both) with their current practices. They often did so in order to capture and illustrate another tension, contrast or dilemma. They reflected on the balance to be achieved between interventionist supervision and the research student's autonomy; between the imposition of control and the granting of licence to their students; between the establishment of tight frameworks and timescales, and the students' need for freedom of manoeuvre. In the following section we exemplify and discuss supervisors' expressions of this 'delicate balance'; we then go on to present the specific contrasts of past and present that the academics often used as an accounting device.

The Balancing Acts

Supervisors' accounts were constructed in terms of various themes of tension and balance. At the beginning of this chapter we quoted a geographer, Dr Crupiner, who talked of his 'angst' about creating a delicate balance between letting doctoral students pursue work that is their own and 'giving' them a research topic. This dilemma captures one of the dimensions in terms of which contrasts were drawn throughout these accounts. Other academics constructed their accounts in terms of similar tensions and dilemmas. They described tensions and balances at every critical stage of the research process: not only topic choice, but also research design, data collection, analysis and text production. At all stages supervisors expressed a pull between tight control and non-interventionist supervision. In these rhetorical devices the academic staff variously express the tensions and contradictions between the imposition of supervisory control on the one hand, and the granting of licence to students to pursue their own ideas on the other.

Dr Nuddington, a social scientist at Boarbridge, said he was much less directive than some of his colleagues:

> I have colleagues who will lay out a very clear-cut routine for the student to stick to – I'm a little bit more casual than that. I don't really believe in regimenting the students too much, because if I do that I'll impose my will on them too strongly – it's supposed to be their PhD not mine. But I would hope to see the students on a regular basis – 'regular monthly meetings'.

For the natural scientists, who were more likely to have teams of doctoral students and postdoctoral researchers working on closely related problems around a funded project, there was a tension between the individual thesis topics and the overall research programme. Professor Nankivell, a natural scientist at Ottercombe, explained to us:

In my mind I constantly try and weigh up the balance of supervision that is required and I've come to the conclusion that it depends on the individual, especially with my experience with the MSc person who needs his hand held all the time. Now I could have been really blunt with him and kicked him out but that wouldn't have benefited him, but it would have benefited me because I would have got the research done that I had hoped, so I'm always balancing my own intentions, research in hand and trying to develop the individual's research skills and I find it a difficult balance to strike.

Dr Rennie, a social scientist at Rushberry, highlighted the importance of the managerial side of the supervisory task. In doing so he identified one of the particular dilemmas of supervision; that is, the extent to which the doctoral student may experience a lack of independence if the thesis topic is close to the supervisor's area of expertise. Dr Rennie expresses a solution to the dilemma by stressing positively the role of the supervisor in 'managing' the student rather than intervening too directly in the subject-matter of the research:

The main thing, in my point of view, is to know what the job is, to manage the student. To be a good supervisor I don't happen to believe you need to know an awful lot about the substantive field the student is doing. A good student will already have become more expert in the substantive field than the supervisor. There may be problems if there's too much overlap, when the student feels he hasn't broken away from the knowledge area of the supervisor.

Dr Netley, a social scientist at Boarbridge, told us, 'It's very difficult to get the right balance between how much you teach them and how much you let them get on with it.' His colleague, Dr Munsey, expressed a similar tension:

If I feel the student wants to be hand-fed, i.e. he wants me to do half the work, that's not on. I look for the independence of personality in addition to motivation. They should be academically capable and physically capable of doing the data collection and analysis, with some guidance obviously, but I'm not prepared to give up more than 10 per cent, or 15 per cent of my time to a study if I find they keep knocking on my door every day, asking me to provide them with information and data.

These accounts of the supervisory relationship draw on contrasts of dependence and independence on the part of the research student. Dr Coltness, of Tolleshurst, was adamant that 'supervising is extremely difficult, let me say that. I think it's the most difficult part of my work. It's the part I enjoy least because I feel I don't do it well enough.' Central to Dr Coltness's doubts was the delicate balance:

> How much should you be spoon-feeding? Should they be doing it themselves? Should I be in the library sussing out things? How much re-writing? Do you go through it with a toothcomb? ... There are no guidelines at all. So I find it very problematic. How much to help the weaker ones, how much to try to keep up with the brighter ones? They are so different, they're not off-the-peg.

Many of the academic supervisors framed their accounts in terms of changing funding policies and the changing policy context of doctoral work in the UK (Becher et al., 1994). Sanctions policies (government funding being withheld from departments in which students took too long to submit their theses) were leading some of our respondents to report that they had altered their supervisory pattern. One such was Dr Crupiner, a social scientist at Tolleshurst:

> Sometimes a PhD student doesn't want to see you because they want this to be their own stuff and there's always a dilemma about saying to a student 'This is a great topic, this is what you should do', and I'm more inclined to do that these days because of the time limit, whereas in the past I'd avoid it. It's caused a lot of angst.

Similar views on the increasing pressure from ESRC and the difficulties of the delicate balance can be seen in the interview with Dr Wishart, a social scientist at Latchendon:

> The PhD programme should really be a marriage of your interests and the student's interests. You develop together. Now I'm conscious of the pressures that are coming from the ESRC to churn over PhDs in terms of three or four years, but I perceive the PhD as something that is essentially your starting point in a long career. ... As a supervisor I'm not saying 'You must produce Chapter 1 in four weeks, get them all done in ten months.' I much prefer to allow people to choose their own pace and in a sense to me that's a part of the learning process of being a PhD student. I think it's a lonely existence for many but I think they have to push at the limits, they have to engage the supervisor. I can push them to a certain extent, I can say 'OK, what have you been doing for the last two or three weeks?', but in the end I'm going to put barriers in their way and they're going to have to jump over those barriers. I'm not necessarily going to demonstrate how to jump over those barriers. Some are smarter than others in terms of how they proceed with the problems

of jumping over these hoops. Others are less certain and need more direction, more of a helping hand.

Dr Danson, a natural scientist at Forthhamstead, described this process:

> Once we've decided on a topic and an area of work then I think the student will gradually put more and more into the project of his or her initiative. I mean it's not a doctorate of being a technician, it's a doctorate of philosophy.

Dr Danson claimed that growing intellectual autonomy was particularly important in a laboratory discipline. Successful researchers have to become independent:

> Therefore you're not actually wanting someone to do something and then tell them to do something else and something else. You're wanting them to come back with ideas, and indeed, from then on guide the project in particular areas.

As our data show, this concern is not in fact restricted to the laboratory-based disciplines. Social scientists claimed to value growing intellectual autonomy in their research students just as highly. Dr Shannon, a social scientist at Chelmsworth, gave us a particularly detailed account of how the student's growing scholarly independence affects supervision. She emphasized how the delicate balance can change over the student's registration period:

> I do think it's quite a difficult process for both parties, supervisor and student. And it changes over time. It's a very personal thing. To begin with the supervisor's in quite a strong position in defining and directing students, and they're relatively subordinate at the beginning, willing to accept your advice and direction.

For Dr Shannon, the student needs to outgrow that early phase, so:

> as the student gets more and more into the subject, that relationship begins to change, because they develop an expertise which the supervisor is no longer sharing. Also, they develop a view about their intellectual property which is separate from their supervisor. And it's a bit like a growing-up process, an intellectual growing-up, and it leads to conflicts at a certain point in time, as the student develops that independence.

Supervisors' Narratives

Dr Shannon compared the time when the balance begins to shift to the stormy relationships of adolescence:

> I've always found there's this period in the middle where there is that conflict, like my relationship with my daughter, where there is a change occurring, and it's quite difficult as a supervisor to begin to 'let go' almost. You feel they're not ready for it, they're not in control, and that leads to a degree of conflict which can be overt, or could be not overt. Sometimes people will avoid seeing you – it's like that.

Dr Shannon said she had observed this period of conflict between colleagues and students, especially

> where people don't seem to be able to complete, and I think it might need to be overtly addressed. And I think the most successful candidates are when you can be relatively open about that, get through it and then move to completion. But otherwise you can get stuck in that phase where the supervisor still tries to over-direct, over-control, and the student tries to pull away and develop their own interests. And if you're not careful you can get bogged down – the student doesn't know how to progress and you're not giving them the sort of advice they need to get through. I don't know if other supervisors have felt this, but I do think there's this shifting relationship which is actually quite difficult to cope with.

Several of our informants focused their account of the delicate balance on the production of the text of the dissertation. These supervisors described their difficulties in balancing intervention and non-intervention in the students' writing. One particular supervisor found it particularly difficult not to do the students' writing for them. Professor Brande, a social scientist at Hernchester, recognized that he was in danger of being too interventionist a supervisor. He told us:

> I think also I'm too anxious to do the work for them or with them. I can't bear to see them do something which I could do slightly better. ... I tend to be too closely involved ... it gets to be my dissertation rather than their dissertation and that's not fair on them. It's even worse with word-processors because they bring in their text on a disk and you sit at the keyboard together.

Professor Brande was not alone in raising the supervisor's role in the production of the text. A social scientist, Professor Woodrose of Latchendon, also suggested that this was an area where the delicate balance has to be struck. He told us that 'You can't drive them any faster than they can write – the papers, the literature reviews, the definitional papers which take them on to the next stage.'

Dr Godlee, from Gossingham, was eloquent about the supervisor's role in text production.

> You get a first draft which consists of probably some interesting sets of ideas, but not very effectively linked together. And most students I've supervised seem to have a lot of difficulty in establishing a clear line of argument which runs through the thesis as a whole. My job as a supervisor is to try to discuss with the student the different stories that can be told with the material that has been assembled and then to execute the option which is selected as professionally as possible.

In various ways, then, the supervisors' accounts of their work described and justified a number of balancing acts. They are described in terms of the degree of intervention or control that may be appropriate in the supervisory relationship. The supervisors' accounts were particular sensitive to such issues, which featured repeatedly in the interviews. In constructing those accounts, the academics used contrastive rhetoric. In particular, they used contrasts between past and present: they compared their current approach to supervision with their experiences as graduate students; some also compared their current practice with their initial efforts as novice supervisors. All who used such rhetorical devices did so in order to justify what they described as more systematic and regular supervision. We turn now to a more detailed consideration of such contrastive accounting devices.

Past and Present

Drawing exaggerated contrasts is a useful way to emphasise differences, and the doctoral supervisors frequently told us horror stories about how they had been neglected by their own supervisors in the bad old days. These enabled the supervisor to contrast his or her own supervisory behaviour. Take, for example, these extracts from our interview with Dr Mincing, a natural scientist at Ottercombe. First, he describes his own experience as a student:

> My supervisor ... hadn't had any experience of PhD students before and he took on four at the same time. And we all sat there in this room for the first year virtually doing nothing, twiddling our thumbs and accomplishing very little indeed.

Dr Mincing then pointed out that, because they were novices, he and his fellow students did not know what to expect from their supervisor, and so did not protest or attempt to change his behaviour:

Supervisors' Narratives

> I had no idea what a supervisor was supposed to do. As far as I was concerned that was what a PhD was about. You sat about in a room until something came to you with very little direction and very little help.

Now he is himself a supervisor, he behaves differently:

> I certainly give them very much more supervision than my supervisor gave me because, I guess, I appreciate that people coming from a first degree don't know what's expected of them, and shouldn't really be expected to know that. It's PhD *training* – training means supervision.

Dr Mincing is a male natural scientist, but his contrastive story is very similar to that of Dr Challoner at Tolleshurst, a woman at the qualitative end of social science:

> When I started my PhD my head of department at Snipehurst decided he was going to supervise all the first-year postgraduate students. Now there were eleven of us, and he took us all on and then had absolutely nothing to say to any of us! So in my three years as a research student I saw my supervisor, officially, twice. Not only that, he imposed a ban, so if we went to see other members of staff they got letters from him saying 'How dare you talk to my students!' I found that a searing experience, because I had no idea how to do things, what to do. We got some support from each other but it cost me a lot of time and a huge amount of confidence. He was regarded in the department as being difficult. ... So my PhD was on urban ecology, and the first talk I had with him, 'Of course,' he said, 'we don't really know what reality is.' And the last session he said the same thing. So I did everything by trial and error. OK, I learned a hell of a lot through doing it, but I think it cost me an enormous amount in terms of the PhD and my confidence, and in my subsequent career, because I never had any of the kinds of advice that you normally give to graduate students – where to publish and so on. The learning was very ad hoc and there was none of the old boy network that works with other academics.

Exactly like Dr Kenway and Dr Mincing, Dr Challoner drew a contrast between that experience and her own supervisory style: 'I have vowed and declared that will never happen with my graduate students.'

Dr Challoner described in detail her approaches to supervision:

> I've just started to act as joint supervisor with a lad – he's come to work with Phil Coltness primarily, but he's away at the moment so I've started Julius off and I think the way I've done that is characteristic of the way

I work with students. I see him once a week for a supervisory session of about an hour. We have a cup of coffee, mull over what he's been reading, talk about his ideas – basically to embed him in the department and give him a sense of belonging. That's crucial for what we're doing. I keep my students to very tight timetables in terms of reading, writing and research. I think it's essential to get them writing quickly. ... So the aim all the time is to keep them focused in terms of what the product will be at the end and how they can put into operation their ideas.

Dr Challoner felt that her students were completing in reasonable time: 'And the fact that they've got through is a validation of my method. That's why I do it the way I do.'

In describing and advocating her preferred style of supervision, Dr Challoner was drawing on the contrast between her present aims as a supervisor and her own experiences as a graduate student in the past. As can be seen in the extracts quoted above, she contrasted: the frequency and regularity of meetings (twice in three years when she was a student, weekly now she is a supervisor); embedding the students in the department with student isolation; tight timetables with time-wasting; keeping the students focused with learning by trial and error in an ad hoc way. By implication, she has a great deal to say to her graduate students, whereas her supervisor had nothing to say to her. This list of oppositions displays what we mean by contrastive rhetoric.

Many other supervisors drew contrasts of a similar nature. Dr Coltness, also of Tolleshurst, said he thought that graduate supervision now was 'much better in all sorts of ways'. He went on:

As a graduate at Reddingdale I was left to my own devices and told to get on with it. There was one weekly seminar which was a trial by fire, a performance kind of thing, which wasn't very helpful. There was a computing course outside the department, and that was it. It was basically 'do the research, write it up, you're on your own'.

He contrasts such a past with his own practice in the present:

I have an open-door policy. I'm here five days a week from early till late, and I have the door propped open so people can come in whenever they want to, undergraduates and graduates. ... In terms of more formal meetings, for a new student, I'd see them for at least an hour a week to begin with. After that, about once a fortnight when they're in their second or third year, and towards the end when they're writing up they'd be giving me their work, I'd read it, make comments, return it to them, then they'd come and see me to discuss the general issues raised. But you'd also see them at the seminars – the Tuesday one on human geography, the Thursday one – and graduate students become friends in the course of a PhD.

Dr Meade, a member of staff at Boarbridge, claimed that when she had done her doctorate there several years before,

> it was very much being thrown in at the deep end ... it was a big jump from undergraduate work. I started off with one supervisor here – excellent academically but in fact just let me carry on in my own sweet way.

Her story contained a twist, in that her first supervisor left and 'I was taken on by another lecturer who turned out to be absolutely superb, gave me very good advice, really became involved.'

Dr Pilgrim, a natural scientist at Illington, talked about his days as a PhD student at Tinworth:

> I was very isolated, it was a much smaller department than this is ... the project I was working on was being supervised by the head of department whose other activities were getting busier and busier so he didn't really have time to supervise.

Dr Pilgrim felt that his supervisor was 'not very close technically to the work I was doing ... so I probably knew more about what I was doing than they did'.

We are not claiming that these negative stories are true in any absolute sense, nor do we dismiss them as fictional. They have validity for the academics who told them, but their significance is not to be found in a naive reliance on their face value. Rather, they are best understood as rhetorical devices designed to show that the speaker's current practice, and often that of his or her colleagues as a whole, is better organized and more supportive. Compare Dr Pilgrim's story of an over-committed supervisor with the following material from his colleague at Illington, Dr Panthing. Having worked overseas, he based his contrast on a lack of knowledge of what a British doctorate should be:

> I would say also I did not have a clear idea of what a PhD was. ... I had not read enough of them ... I never had a clear – I don't think I had a clearly focused problem. I was always sort of exploring a lot of things, and I didn't have a clear question in mind that I was attempting to find the answer to. I think in effect I probably had about enough work for two PhDs.

Supervisors' Narratives

He juxtaposed that past lack of understanding with the experience he has today. Now as a supervisor Dr Panthing says of his work with doctoral students:

> I try and help them firmly identify a problem, explain to them that their research field is a life-time occupation, but the PhD is just a milestone and should be focused. Get it done, get it over with, and move on.

This is a typical contrast between the lecturer's own past biography, when no proper guidance was provided, and his own supervisory role offering proper advice and support. Most supervisors preferred their current role and institutional framework to that available to them as students in the past (and often in different institutions). A typical contrast is that drawn by Dr d'Hiver, from Gossingham, a social scientist with a PhD from Hadleigh:

> I must say from my experience at Hadleigh I think the level of supervision that we provide is much higher than what I got in Hadleigh. Particularly in terms of quantity. I mean there if you were clever you were left to get on with things on your own. It also depended on your supervisor.

Dr d'Hiver's original supervisor got a chair elsewhere and left Hadleigh:

> The second one I had was much less interested in my work. I don't think he even read what I wrote, although he was a very nice person. So I was left very much on my own. My impression here is that you're given more support than at Hadleigh, though perhaps at Hadleigh it has changed.

Here Dr d'Hiver is constructing her biographical account in terms of various dimensions of contrast. She compares her past experience with her current role. More specifically she also draws comparisons about the institutional structure and support networks available in the past and now in her department at Gossingham. The underlying rhetorical device is consistently that of contrastive rhetoric. Like others among our respondents, Dr d'Hiver bases her contrastive biographical account on a series of autobiographical and institutional themes. They include reference to networks and mechanisms designed specifically for the support of the doctoral student. Her colleague, Professor Hakapopoulos, drew a vivid caricature of the British PhD in order to contrast it with prevailing arrangements at Gossingham:

> One still has the vague idea that this chap got a first in whatever field he's in, he has an intellectually oriented mind, he has an interesting idea that he wants to pursue, he can sit down in the library and occasionally

Supervisors' Narratives

> chat to members of the senior common room and lo! a thesis will appear.

Here Professor Hakapopoulos identifies an important dimension of contrast. The point of reference is an image of the PhD in the past: something based on the personal qualities of individuals, with little or no structure, highly dependent on implicit criteria. In Professor Hakapopoulos' account it carries overtones of a leisured and privileged academic world, contrasting implicitly with contemporary realities that are based on more explicitly structured requirements.

Dr Barnabas, a social scientist at Hernchester, drew a similar contrast between his time as a PhD student at Hadleigh and his current teaching at Hernchester:

> when I did my own PhD I got very little supervision help. I guess that was more the pattern then ... it was very much 'go away and produce a PhD'. In fact after my first year my supervisor never read another word. I didn't feel I got much support at the time.

By contrast, his account of his own practices portrays a supervisory style in which he is far more directive with his students: 'I've always been keen on seeing graduate students roughly once a week, in some cases more than that, but certainly having a meeting once a week, and of getting them to write things regularly once a month.'

In contrastive accounts such as these, our informants consistently described a past characterized by little direct supervision, in which students were forced to make do with their own resources, and in which the PhD was a largely personal matter. This was juxtaposed with accounts of policy and practice in which supervision is closer and more directive, and in which the PhD is more overtly grounded in explicit mechanisms of oversight. Such a collection of themes can be detected in the descriptions provided by Dr Palinode, now lecturing at Portminster in an applied social science. He described his own PhD experience at Boarbridge: 'I know supervision is always problematic, it's a problematic relationship, but the quality of supervision I had at Boarbridge I didn't think was very good at all.' Dr Palinode's use of 'quality' here did not seem to depend on special connotations of quality assurance and the like. It seemed to reflect more the lack of attention and lack of direction he had experienced as a doctoral student. His emphasis was on himself as lost and isolated, especially in the early days of his doctoral experience:

> I think you need to be able to talk to a breadth of people who are not necessarily close to your subject but understand generally, and can give information that can help, rather than being in the lost position I was.

Supervisors' Narratives

... But the first day you arrive, there you are with a blank desk and you think 'what do I do now?' And I spent the first six months deciding what I was going to do. ... I think it's quite important to be settled in, and for people to help you early on. I think the doctoral programme, although you can't see it at the time, is quite useful – it depends – it could be argued that you should do a year's research, understand the processes of doing it and then do a research methodology programme, and then do the PhD.

Dr Palinode has not yet had any successful doctoral students himself, but when he was asked if his experience would make him a better supervisor, he replied: 'I would hope so ... I think it would make me a better supervisor, but that sounds quite arrogant really.' Dr Palinode's retrospective account partly blamed the particular supervisor he had: 'the guy who was supervising me was ... ready to retire, a cynical old bugger. He was a very negative person.'. Dr Palinode expressed the hope that he would have learnt from this how to be a better supervisor himself. Perhaps the most striking feature of Dr Palinode's contrast is that he began his PhD in 1987, not 1957, or 1967, like many of our respondents. The contrastive rhetoric that compares one's experience as a student with one's aspirations for the present generation of students does not need to refer to a chronologically distant past.

A number of our informants used the contrast of past and present to reflect not only on their experiences as doctoral students, but also on their recollected performance as younger and inexperienced PhD supervisors. For instance, Dr Jelf, a social scientist at Eastchester, described how he had changed his behaviour: 'It was a learning process for me. In the early years in the '70s I was far too soft, not directive enough, thinking I'd give them a few hints but they should learn from their mistakes.' By the 1990s however, Dr Jelf described himself as much more directive, imposing a more overt framework on the work and emphasizing regular production: 'I try to get them writing very early on. I insist on that. It's essential. They don't solve half the problems they come across until they try to write them down.'

Dr Jelf attributes his changed style of supervision to the fact that he now believes that students need 'a clear idea of the constraints from an early stage'. Dr Morrow, a social scientist at Boarbridge, also contrasted her early inexperience ('so six months after I'd arrived I was supervising three people which I found deeply terrifying') with her current expertise. By the time of her interview she was much more confident in her supervisory skills:

> when the student starts they feel very lost and lonely ... poor student with a desk and a filing cabinet, and they were sitting there looking at it and what were they supposed to do next? So I'd always try to give them something to do – read certain articles, review them in written form. And that's something I know about myself, I'm not very good at

commenting on verbal discussions – I need something in writing, however scrappy. Then having got some flavour of how they work and where they were at, I would try to set various projects for a term's duration.

In this way, Dr Morrow aims to respond to the individual student, but also to set up a framework. Supervisors such as Dr Jelf and Dr Morrow describe themselves as being more firmly directive with students now than they had been earlier in their careers.

The precise contents of these comparisons vary, although the basic *form* of the accounts is consistent. A less than perfect experience as a graduate student is used as a bench-mark, in order to project one's own goals and values as a supervisor in the present. Various dimensions of contrast have been noted in the data extracts reproduced here. They do not constitute different forms of contrastive rhetoric *per se*. They do, however, suggest that the accounts are composed in terms of certain recurrent motifs or vocabularies. As we have seen, the past is constructed in terms of: a lack of help and a lack of supervisory direction; a lack of system; a lack of research focus; an undue reliance on the informal and the personal rather than institutional frameworks. The contrasts thus reflect various facets of an implied shift from the implicit and the personal in the past, to present arrangements based on the explicit and the organizational.

Conclusion

We have made three points in this chapter. First, we have stressed the fact that research on supervision is based on interviews rather than direct observations. We have suggested that there is thus a need for care in interpreting such interview data. In the absence of direct observational evidence, interview materials need to be dealt with appropriately. We do not necessarily treat them at face value, assuming that they reflect precisely what students and their supervisors actually do. On the other hand, it is not necessary to discard them altogether. We can inspect them in order to detect the recurrent themes in such accounts, and to note how they are constructed.

Second, therefore, we deploy the concept of contrastive rhetoric to explore supervisors' accounts, most of which compare their own (negative) experiences as doctoral students with their practice as supervisors today. We thus explore how the academic supervisors describe and justify their contemporary practices through such a rhetorical device. Their accounts are not characterized by myths of a lost golden age. The experience of graduate work – in these respects at least – is remembered in terms of poor help from their supervisors and the departments in which they found themselves. The past is described in terms of implicit and personalized (often individualized) working relationships; the present is described in terms of more explicitly structured and institutionally organized arrangements.

Third, we show how thoughtfully supervisors reflect on the difficulties of creating the delicate balance of the paper's title. As they describe it, their current practices are based on a perceived tension – between the need to guide and structure doctoral work on the one hand, and the desire to preserve the doctoral student's autonomy on the other. The more tightly framed arrangements that they describe in contrast to past practices create new tensions and dilemmas.

There is no reason to assume that accounts such as these are restricted only to the academics we studied, or that they have no general relevance for our understanding of academics' work and lives. The recurrent motifs of these supervisory accounts reflect wider concerns and tensions within the academy. Academic staff repeatedly find themselves juggling various 'delicate balances', between autonomy and accountability, between professionalism and managerialism, between research productivity and creativity. The accounts of doctoral supervision we have presented here are part of a wider occupational culture in which academics attempt to account for change and to reconcile such tensions.

9 Pedagogic Continuities

> The thesis for the state doctorate is, as we have seen, what enables the professors to exercise a lasting control over those aspiring to their succession.
>
> (Bourdieu, 1988: 154)

In the last chapter we used supervisors' accounts to explore the theme of 'balance' – the tension between a supervisor's intervention and the original, individual efforts of the doctoral student. We showed that such a tension reflects issues that are pervasive in the supervision of doctoral students, in turn reflecting the 'essential tension' in scientific discovery and scholarly research generally – between originality and continuity, and between collective and individual responsibility for a research student's contribution to knowledge. In this chapter we move explicitly to research students' accounts – although we include relevant material from members of academic staff as well. Here we explore similar themes to those of the previous chapter in accounts of the social and intellectual status of the research student. Again, issues of collective and individual responsibility are prominent, and we once more explore key differences between academic disciplines.

We examine these differences in terms of a key dimension of contrast – the distinction between *positional* and *personal* modes of socialization and sources of identity. That contrast derives from the work of Bernstein (1977) who used it to characterize modalities of socialization, with particular reference to families. We extend the usage to capture key aspects of academic disciplines and departments as agencies of apprenticeship. In the positional family – and by extension, the positional discipline – social roles are primarily *ascribed*. One's identity is determined primarily in relation to a closed set of roles and relationships. Such roles are explicit, and reflect clear distinctions of generation and hierarchy. The group (the family or the research group) has clear external boundaries round it; there are clear lines of demarcation within it. The personalizing mode of socialization, on the other hand, is predicated on *achieved* identities and a more open-ended set of relationships. Boundaries and roles within the socializing group are much more fluid, and there are weaker external boundaries too. The individual's

Pedagogic Continuities

position is not based, then, on ascribed positions, and identities are matters of negotiation rather than reflecting strong hierarchical or generational divisions.

We use Bernstein's distinction between personal and positional families because Bernstein is particularly concerned with modes of control, socialization and identity formation. In his positional family the lines of social control are clear – age, sex and position define an explicit distribution of authority. In the personalizing family, on the other hand, there is still social control, but it is based on more implicit social relations. Positional authority is more coercive; personal authority is grounded in negotiation and persuasion. In all disciplines and departments control is exercised, as Bourdieu points out, by the established academics over their successors. In both science and social science senior academics exercise authority, but in the natural sciences, control is more clearly hierarchical and overtly structured. In the social sciences the system of control is more implicit, more negotiable, more based on an individual's personal qualities than on seniority or leadership of a research group. This is not a novel point about science. It is the explicit, positional control that irks those who dislike being *taught* science (e.g. Tobias, 1990; Downey and Lucena, 1997) and it is central to the mechanisms of pedagogic continuity (see Chapter 4). Here we focus primarily on the social relations that are experienced by the students themselves, how they view their place in the discipline, and how they place themselves in relation to the knowledge they are creating.

Where academic socialization is essentially positional, then we would expect to find a clear division of labour within the department or research group: the student would occupy a clearly defined junior role. The division of labour for research, and indeed for the supervision of research, would be established, with clear boundaries and allocation of responsibilities. Equally, we would expect the research student to be *incorporated* within the group's boundaries, with strong collective mechanisms to mobilize loyalty. The process of socialization is explicit, and in that sense the students 'know their place'. It is not necessarily a deferential system, but it is certainly a hierarchical one. Likewise, when the mode of academic socialization is essentially personalizing, the culture will stress individual achievement. The student's own status will be less explicit; it will be derived from individual negotiations with significant others – the supervisor especially. Working relationships will not be determined or mediated by positions of seniority or inferiority within a bounded group. Equally, mechanisms for the cultivation of loyalty will not be based on membership of a collectivity.

This analysis will be concerned with students' accounts of identity and status, which are couched primarily in terms of their relative standing. These are accounts of academic identity that are structured in terms of two polar extremes – from the position of underling to that of professional colleague. The contrast, or tension, is by no means confined to the self-perceptions and identities of doctoral students. They recapitulate similar tensions that have been identified for many years in programmes of professional training. For instance, in the late 1950s there were two classic studies of the occupational socialization of American medical students called *The Student Physician* (Merton et al., 1958) and *Boys in White* (Becker et al., 1961). In their choice of titles the two sociological teams stressed contrasting ideas about medical students: were they 'Boys' (sic) or were they junior colleagues? Using our data we argue that all PhD students feel themselves to be junior colleagues in some ways, and very much as powerless dependants in others, but that there are marked disciplinary differences in the roles available to them. This is not a surprise: all the research evidence (Becher et al., 1994; Burgess, 1994; Clark, 1993; Hockey, 1991; Parry et al., 1994a, 1994b; Winfield, 1987) supports the view that disciplinary identities are so strong and the experience of doctoral study so different between disciplines (even *across* national boundaries) that generalizing about research student identities across them produces only confusion.

The existence of strong disciplinary cultures, into which successful academics have been socialized, has encouraged the growth of myths surrounding the ways in which different disciplines carry out doctoral research. During the course of our research several of the respondents (science and social science PhD students and supervisors) evoked these 'myths' when they compared ways of doing doctoral work in the social sciences with the natural sciences. Whereas the social science PhD was seen typically as the product of an individualized relationship between student and supervisor, the science PhD was seen as the product of a laboratory-based research group or stable, based on the concept of 'team work' (Becher, 1989).

The personal or positional structures that produce research students' identities reflect powerful organizing principles of disciplinary work. Contrasts between lone scholars and team members is a recurrent motif in the production of symbolic boundaries round and between disciplinary fields. For instance, as Professor Nankivell, an environmental scientist at Ottercombe, expressed it: 'The difference between us and social science is that we tend to do PhDs through team work. ... I think social scientists are loners.'

Our findings go some way to support these myths, in that doctoral students in the relevant disciplines do indeed produce accounts of their work and experiences in such terms. Whilst we have distinguished a number of ways in which PhD work is organized, it is possible to identify two quite distinct models or 'ideal types' of PhD work in the students' accounts. These two 'ideal type' models of PhD work are explored below. We contrast single-discipline science departments with single-discipline social science departments, and both with multidisciplinary settings. The student experience in multidisciplinary settings – such as departments of town planning, development studies, area studies and artificial intelligence – is more complex than that of their contemporaries in single-discipline departments, and may be complicated further by the different expectations about social status by various staff.

Our use of Bernstein's distinction between personal and positional modes of control over research students is not intended to be evaluative. As social scientists we are more used to personal rather than positional relationships with research students, but we claim no general superiority for such a mode of socialization. The science student has a clearly defined place in a team. It may not be an exalted position, it may be circumscribed, but it is relatively secure. If the students fulfils his or her role, then completion of a PhD should follow. The social scientist is not in a more comfortable position: taking personal responsibility for one's work readily implies an almost competitive relationship with one's supervisor and other more senior academics. In that sense, the research studentship can be a lonely social position to occupy if one is expected to make one's own way. The social scientist may have superficially more egalitarian social and working relationships, and in one sense the personalizing mode of academic socialization is predicated on an egalitarian ethos. But the academic 'equal' is likely to find himself or herself without a fixed position, with all the uncertainties and isolation that can ensue. The individualistic mode of socialization is by no means a comfortable one.

The social and intellectual identities of the science and social science PhD students are different. The social organization of knowledge production and reproduction constructs different selves for academics and for doctoral students. The differences in social and intellectual roles make the everyday life of the graduate student very different. In the course of this chapter we explore the disciplinary cultures as they impinge on the students, and, in particular, we examine the 'isolation' expressed by many students, as well as sources of social integration in some disciplines (such as student participation in learned societies).

The science doctoral student is socialized into a positional group. The funding for the studentship and the nature of the research are often prescribed by the research grants that keep the research group in business. The thesis topic is chosen by the supervisor or research group leader or lab head, and assigned to each student. The theoretical paradigm into which the thesis topic 'fits' is chosen by the supervisor and/or the head of the lab. The experimental paradigm is determined by the lab group to which the student belongs. The experimental equipment is predetermined by the supervisor. The experimental design is predetermined by the supervisor. Moreover, as we showed in Chapter 7, the work is ephemeral – it produces the PhD degree and two or three papers for conferences and publication, and is quickly superseded. It is an important topic for a very short season: it is quickly overtaken by new research (see, for example, Atkinson et al., 1998 on the

Pedagogic Continuities

immediate aftermath of a scientific discovery claim). The science PhD is not meant to be the life work; rather, the next degree – the DSc – is the recognition of lifetime achievement.

Simultaneously, however, the science PhD student has a clear job: to do a set of experiments that move forward the research group's work. It may be a relatively menial job, but it is well-defined. He or she sees the supervisor and other team members regularly – often every day – in the lab, and socially outside the lab as well (so long as the student is male, drinks alcohol, and is sports loving or clubbable). The science PhD student publishes with senior colleagues, and attends conferences with the research group. The science PhD hears the findings of the group discussed formally and informally, and so is included in the debates about the specialism. Because he or she is part of the group, he or she is treated as a junior colleague.

If the science student gains security from a well-defined role in a group, the social scientist is by contrast an isolated individual. Social science PhD students may never interact with their supervisor outside supervisions, and may rarely even see their supervisor. Certainly they do not experience the supervisor or other senior staff actually doing social science alongside them. They rarely see the supervisor working directly on research. In social science there is no tradition of the whole research group from professor down to the first-year PhD socializing regularly. There is no tradition of publishing as a group with all the names on the paper. There is no tradition of regular conference attendance as a team, and no regular weekly discussion of a group's findings at colloquia. Indeed *no group exists* for many social scientists, so there are no colleagues across ranks to be collegial with.

The social science PhD student, however, is treated as a potential intellectual equal. Students choose their own topics for their theses, they choose their own theories for their theses; they choose their own methods for their theses. The thesis is seen as an individualized project, which is a one-off, and even the candidate's lifework (as in the case of Anthropology – see Chapter 7). The thesis should be the piece of intellectual work which the successful person 'lives off' for years. It should produce material for a book and articles for a long time to come. This is particularly true for anthropology, but is also the case in the other social sciences. In sociology of education, for example, Ball (1981) is best known for his doctoral ethnography of *Beachside Comprehensive*, Burgess (1983) for his study of Bishop McGregor School, and Lacey (1970) for *Hightown Grammar*. In practice, the supervisor may be controlling the student's topic and its execution, but it is not experienced in that way. The supervisors quoted in the previous chapter had not recognized any such personal authority exercised over them, and many of our research student informants did not seem aware of such control either. They reported being 'free' – sometimes too free – to make their own mistakes.

The Science Research Group

The positional research group or team model of the PhD, traditionally associated with the natural sciences, is strongest in experimental disciplines. Where a research group exists, its structure typically revolves around one or two supervisors or research directors, with doctoral students and postdoctoral researchers working alongside each other on topics that are to some extent related. In this context, a specific set of research related patterns emerge which inform the habitus of the group.

We have discussed the pedagogic continuity engendered by the research group in laboratory science in Chapter 4 and Chapter 7; here we focus on the consequences of this pedagogic continuity for the student. To researchers coming from outside science, it is striking that science PhD students do not complain of either social or intellectual isolation, as social scientists frequently do (see Eggleston and Delamont, 1981). They may experience routine drudgery in their scientific work, but they are members (albeit the most junior members) of a group. One American graduate student in physics interviewed by Gumport (1993: 265) even described himself as having bad days when he felt like a 'peon' – a derogatory term for a menial labourer.

For a social scientist, one of the clearest ways in which the science PhD student appears to be constrained and to lack freedom is the choice of thesis topic. Science students may choose which team and supervisor to join, especially if they are geographically mobile and have good credentials. Once they are committed to a particular laboratory, however, science students do not choose their topic: it is assigned to them as part of pedagogic continuity. For example, Antonia Viera at Forthamstead told us, 'The topic was given to me,' and when Odette asked her to expand on this she went on: 'It was a definite topic. The research project was fairly set out when I arrived and it had an outline to it and how it was theoretically supposed to go.' The project had not proceeded according to plan, partly, Antonia suggested, because, 'I'd come from America and had very little lab experience'. Many of the students' accounts of their work in the laboratory sciences are couched in terms of problems and projects being determined for them. They construct research problems that arise from the laboratory, the research group or the group leader. They are not derived initially from a personal commitment or personal relationship with the topic of their research. Karl Gunderson, a biochemist from Baynesholme, for instance, describes a research topic that was not originally grounded in his own intellectual commitments in biochemistry: 'My PhD is on lipid biosynthesis [in olives]. It wasn't an area I was interested in before but I'm very interested in it now.' Karl's current commitment to, and interest in, his doctoral topic has grown while he worked on it. That is how, in a positional system, intellectual enthusiasm should come. The more senior scientist has the right to assign the problem. The novice, if a promising scientist, will learn with experience what a good

Pedagogic Continuities

problem it is or can be made to be. Mitchell Scovil, a student at Forthamstead, also illustrated this point:

OP: Was the actual topic set out for you?
MS: Yes. It was really. I was taking over from someone else's work, who'd just finished her PhD and I was to follow on with her work.

Antonia Viera at Forthamstead, drawing on her US experience, related the need for PhD students as pairs of hands to the lack of control over topic choice: 'PhD students in America are pretty much treated like – slaves is probably a bit strong – but dogsbodies. They're not really allowed to follow their own line.' The sense of 'dogsbody' work is amplified by the experience of routine drudgery in practical laboratory activity, marked by routine and repetition. As Dr Garnette told us: 'The bits I really dislike about biochemistry are the nasty, routine, boring bits – once you've done an experiment and you know you've got to do the same experiment over and over again – it's really tedious.' The PhD students and postdocs provide vital labour to keep the research agenda going. As Dr Dewry told us:

> The PhD is really another pair of hands; if you get a postdoc with reasonable money then the two can run in parallel. We need PhDs because we need the hands, the people to do the work. The PhD is not all spade work, but at the same time if you want the PhD to be wholly novel you'll be in danger of nothing working.

This observation also reinforces the tension between the needs of the research group and the risks of 'novelty', with the attendant dangers of failure. The strong orientation towards group, collective effort outweighs individual originality.

This does not mean that graduate students in such natural science environments remain entirely alienated from their doctoral research. Students can and do become interested in and feel ownership of the project even when they did not choose it. But the relationship between the student and his or her research remains a very particular one: it reflects the positional ascription of status and research problem within the research group.

The way in which the research group is organized affects the roles which respective members adopt. Because supervisors or research directors tend to have several PhD students at any one time, they often take a back seat in regard to practical day-to-day supervision of students. As we have shown already, responsibility for graduate students is a collective one, delegated among the different generations within the group. The PhD students describe the research group as a mutually supportive environment in which ideas and materials are shared on an everyday basis. Even where members of the group work on different research problems, there are overlaps in the materials, equipment and techniques which they use:

> We're all working on the same sort of areas, we use a lot of the same assays and substances ... a lot of the substances I make will be used by other people as well. If I invent a method to make something easier then they'll use it as well.
> (Alma Stottle, a biochemistry doctoral student at Ribblethorpe)

At its most extreme, one of the PhD students in Professor Gantry's laboratory at Baynesholme, described his everyday work in the team: 'Professor Gantry tells me what experiments to do, and other people in the lab show me how to do them.' This is a succinct statement of the role of the PhD student in a positional discipline.

This environment can be especially supportive for new postgraduates joining the group. Less experienced members of the group are able to rely upon the more experienced members while they learn the ropes. New postgraduates who were surprised and disheartened when their experiments repeatedly failed turned to other members of the laboratory as sources of support and assistance at times such as these: 'If things keep going wrong, then usually someone who gets it right will sort of go through the experiment one day with you' (Ian Angelworth, a biochemistry doctoral student at Baynesholme). The work of supervisors is expressed in terms of providing guidance on the framework and direction of research while experienced group members such as postdoctoral researchers and doctoral candidates, more advanced in their work, help the inexperienced PhD students.

The distinctive position of the research student in the physical sciences is reflected in their accounts of their colleagues. The doctoral students we talked to in science departments described the expectations they held of the different members in their research groups. In the following quotations physical geography doctoral students from Hernchester describe the role of their supervisor, Professor Barsington: 'I use my supervisor to sort out my structure and any individual problems only when I feel it is appropriate and when I can't get it from [a postdoc] or someone else.' Here the supervisor is seen as above the day-to-day functioning of the research group members and not as an appropriate group member to approach for problems which arise out of 'run of the mill', everyday laboratory work. 'I think we have a really healthy research environment. We don't always, or often even, take our problems to our supervisors. We're a well established group working along the same lines.' Just as research topics are owned and distributed among the research group's generations and individual members, so too is the responsibility for supervision and problem-solving.

Doctoral supervision is therefore understood as a shared responsibility, by far the largest share of which falls to the postdocs. Postdoctoral

Pedagogic Continuities

researchers often take on this role as a matter of course because they themselves were supervised largely by postdocs during PhD research. The attitude of the postdocs we talked to was acquiescent – 'after all, it was the way I was trained' – and they also recognized their qualifications for the role: 'One thing you do get as a postdoc is troubleshooting other people's problems and you do generate a feeling for what is likely to make the difference between something working and not working' (Dr Fonteaux, biochemistry postdoctoral researcher at Baynesholme).

As also acknowledged by the geography postdoc, the change in role from being a doctoral student to a postdoc brings with it automatic supervisory responsibilities: 'Recently my role has changed. I'm now a research associate which means I'm a stepping stone between PhD students and their supervisor' (Bill Staley, geography postdoctoral researcher at Hernchester). Although it is accepted practice for postdoctoral researchers to supervise PhD students on a day-to-day basis it is nevertheless an unofficial line of responsibility: 'There's two PhDs working on the model. Here I am the direct line of unwritten responsibility. It's not in my contract and I don't really see it as my role. But I help them and sort it out' (Steve McAlister, geography postdoctoral researcher at Hernchester). These research relationships ideally provide a supportive environment in which PhD students work. On occasion, where the relationship between student and supervisor breaks down, the collective support of group members can rescue the PhD. We have already quoted the testimony of Earl Mohr, a biochemistry postdoc, who described how his research group effectively rescued his doctoral study after the collapse of cordial relationships with his supervisor (see Chapters 5 and 7).

The type of PhD organization described above is only possible where certain conditions prevail. We found two features crucial for the model of group research to operate. First was group size: only where there are sufficient numbers, or a critical mass (Delamont et al., 1997b), of postgraduates (at different stages of research) and postdocs can the team or group model of supervision function. Second, the group or team structure depends upon a continuity of funding that allows for several individuals (students and postdocs) working in the same area both simultaneously and in succession. Under these conditions, topics or projects can logically follow on from each other, with new PhD students developing the work of previous students (cf. Walford, 1981). In this way, a pedagogic continuity operates as skills and equipment are handed down through the research group. Third, group research work is more congruent with disciplines that have a discrete subject area and identity, with shared theoretical approaches and methods. In other words, a collective orientation is easier to sustain within the boundaries of relatively 'pure' subject areas. Some group research does take place in the multidisciplinary fields, but it is much rarer. Within the strong boundaries of pure science, established academics and their junior colleagues are placed

Pedagogic Continuities

within a relatively fixed set of social relationships, with clear divisions of labour between the generations and between individuals. The cascade of research methods and problems, which we have discussed already, reflects the social relations of scientific production within the essentially 'positional' research group or laboratory. This contrast with the essentially 'personal' approach of the lone scholar, and the individualistic mode of supervision more characteristic of the social sciences – and, of course, the humanities, which lie beyond the scope of this monograph.

Individualized Doctoral Research

In contrast to the natural science model, doctoral work in the social sciences depends on a more individualized relationship between a student and his or her supervisor (or panel of supervisors in some cases). In many social science departments the supervisory relationship may form the main, if not the only, source of support for the doctoral student. Under these circumstances, described by Professor Caldecot of Tolleshurst, the risk of isolation for the postgraduate increases:

> The PhD system which we have is very individualistic and very dependent upon the attitude of the supervisor. I think it worked very well when it was all less pressured and postgraduate communities were much larger. Now you've got very few people doing it, it's isolated, which is a real problem.

The social scientists reported both social isolation – being lonely – and intellectual isolation – working alone on their topic. Isolation of both types is a function of the mode of socialization. Students are socially isolated because there are relatively few of them and they are often uninvolved in the social circuit of conferences, colloquia and so on. They are intellectually isolated because they are treated as individual scholars in their own right, each responsible for his or her own project. The risks of isolation are exacerbated by a fragmentation of research interests within social science departments. We found no examples of flourishing social science research groups supporting postgraduate and postdoc communities at the sites we visited. Where there is no community of postgraduates and researchers the onus is thrown almost entirely upon the supervisory relationship. That supervisors are not able, or in some cases willing, to devote extensive time to their postgraduates was a source of grievance and frustration to some respondents. Hence, students' accounts of work and supervision often emphasize the unpredictability or sparseness of supervision. There is no equivalent to the position of the postdoc in these accounts to provide the daily overseeing of work or resolution of problems. (Because much of what follows consists of students expressing overt dissatisfaction we have left their comments entirely

161

unattributed.) For instance, in the following account an anthropology doctoral student describes the level of supervisory contact:

> I haven't seen him [supervisor] very often at all. When we initially started perhaps every two or three weeks I saw him. But after that, certainly one term I didn't see him for a whole term. Though I tried to see him he seemed to be extremely busy. He has been very much involved in interviewing people who are coming in. He does a lot of that sort of thing.

In descriptions of this sort the research interests and work commitments seem to drive student and supervisor in opposite directions. Within the laboratory research group, the commitments of the senior, junior and student members are part of a collective enterprise. There is no ultimate conflict between their research commitments. For the lone supervisor and the lone student, on the other hand, the individualized, personal commitments of the busy supervisor can manifest themselves as detracting from the individualized, personal interests of the graduate student.

We found that although supervisors exercised a range of supervisory styles, the 'hands-off' style was most common. Although students accepted this as the normal process of doing a PhD in anthropology, they repeatedly referred to problems arising from hands-off supervision: 'It's a kind of do it yourself. You don't even have the opportunity to evaluate your teacher. You do it yourself. The course outlines are perfect but you're under constant stress' (PhD student).

Isolation is a problem to which postgraduates in most disciplines are susceptible (Eggleston and Delamont, 1983) but especially, it seems, in anthropology. Whereas pre-fieldwork students derived some support and companionship from their postgraduate peers, post-fieldwork students tended to be much more isolated from their contemporaries. This is partly a consequence of the fact that PhD students progress through their research and writing at different paces. They enter and return from the field at different times, and so levels of contact with their fellow students are reduced. Paradoxically, the shared experience of fieldwork – a mark of collective identity within the discipline – reduces opportunities for collegial relationships between research students. The departments we visited offered few facilities or social networks for students at the writing-up stage, and this was reflected in accounts given by the postgraduates themselves:

> maybe you don't see it directly, working by yourself and writing a thesis up, but it is quite a stressful experience, and I think there's more to be

Pedagogic Continuities

done in terms of encouraging people to get together or to meet other people who are not doing the same thing and talk over problems.

Isolation is reported with particular urgency in the early stages of doctoral study, when students report wanting more contact with supervisors than they actually received. The following account is provided by a doctoral student in human geography:

> In the first year I was pretty much left alone and it was considered that I was capable and I could get on with it. Whereas in fact at that time I think I needed not help, but someone else's views. And things tended to come back to me with 'seems OK to me' and 'she's coping, she'll be fine'. In fact then was the time that I think I needed more advice.

The role of the graduate student in the personal discipline, with all the responsibility of intellectual autonomy, is daunting. The importance of the supervisory relationship in social science doctoral research was probably nowhere more apparent than among the anthropologists. Many anthropology students completed fieldwork abroad and during this period supervision was maintained through postal contact, as we described in Chapter 5. Generally, the supervisors we talked to in anthropology were aware of the critical importance attached to maintaining some contact with students abroad:

> I think fieldwork is tremendously difficult. It's the responsibility of the supervisor to make sure that contact is maintained, to make sure reports, notes and whatever are sent back, and it's quite possible to keep contact, although of a different kind. The student is obviously more directly responsible for what they're doing than in many other disciplines, but I think good supervisors make sure before people go that contact will be maintained, and most students respond to that because it's so important when you're terribly isolated to feel that you are in contact with someone.

Note that this supervisor is stressing the individualized nature of the fieldwork – the student is 'directly responsible for what they're doing' – and the fact that the only contact between student and department is a personal one between candidate and supervisor.

Once the students have returned 'home' to produce the thesis, they are still personally responsible for their own destiny: they must produce a text which satisfies a supervisor. The individualized role is starkly apparent to the students themselves. Probably the most bitter complaints against supervisors that we encountered during the course of our research came from those anthropology doctoral students who had returned from the field and felt they had not been supervised 'properly' for that period. Although the physical and social isolation of fieldwork away from home is a major feature of students' autobiographical accounts, the intellectual isolation of the lone student is recounted with equal, if not greater, force. For instance:

> I developed a motto for myself in the field, 'never trust an anthropology supervisor', and everything I was writing back would get these responses which I found to be cryptic. Perhaps I was being paranoid, but I felt that I was being pushed to try and write something else, or if I got an encouraging letter it wasn't because it was good, but because they thought I was on the verge of doing something else which might be good.

The main complaints about a perceived lack of supervisory support or guidance while in the field were accentuated for students who discovered on their return that their data were not adequate for them to produce the thesis they and/or their supervisors wanted. Poor communication with the supervisor during data collection created problems for students when they returned home with their data. For the relatively isolated anthropology student, then, the return 'home' from fieldwork elsewhere is no guaranteed escape from isolation. The task is still individualized, inchoate and apparently endlessly negotiable, to be managed in a relationship with the supervisor which is itself individualized, inchoate and endlessly negotiable. It is not really negotiable, of course, because the power rests with the supervisor, who will approve or reject the emergent text – but it can appear negotiable to the student. The student who is 'writing up' after completing fieldwork does not necessarily establish a close working relationship or academic collaboration with the supervisor:

> He [the supervisor] wasn't very helpful at all. He gave no guidance; all I really got from him was spelling mistakes, and I had very bad problems when I got back because I found it very difficult to write. I got very close to the people I was with out there, and I had writer's block, and he just couldn't deal with my problems.

Some of the problems which bedevilled the student-supervisor relationship could be alleviated through joint supervision. Having more than one supervisor (and in some cases a panel of them) can solve some of the problems of the postgraduate student. The following anthropology student gives a positive account of joint supervision:

> It's different with the three of them. The actual structure is the same. I prepare a piece of work, they read it and comment on it, and we generally discuss it. Different approaches come from different supervisors. It

was in [the first supervisor's] field of theoretical interests, it fitted in with his own work, he would draw out strands that interested him and I would write on them. So it would be sort of collaboration. With [the second supervisor] he's just interested in it, it's not part of his work or connected with it. He's really excellent in going through really thoroughly and picking out small points and discussing it in very great detail. Whereas [the third supervisor] is more cavalier in her approach. She's just interested in it and she draws out things she finds interesting and talks about it. I prepare the same work for [all of] them.

Although joint supervision or supervisory panels can dilute the intensity of the 'one-to-one' relationship, we found that many students who were jointly supervised relied specifically upon one supervisor at a time, depending upon the student's particular interests at that time. The dangers of joint supervision are that students may receive inconsistent advice or, alternatively, fall through the net through not really being supervised by anyone. The following account of such an experience is given by a human geography supervisor describing a particular postgraduate student:

And I thought fine, OK, I'll take a back seat here, [the second supervisor] will probably be dealing with this very well. But I think what happened was [that the second supervisor] thought I was dealing with some of the problems, and although we were good friends we didn't communicate very well on this. And [the second supervisor] took a very *laissez faire* attitude to PhD students, saying if people didn't want to do it to let them go. And this student needed more support and fell between us.

Whatever the benefits or complications of joint supervision, the personal nature of social science departments means that the relationships between student and supervisors, and relationships within the staff team, have to be negotiated individually, on the basis of personal qualities and interests, not formal roles or ascribed criteria such as age or formal seniority.

In some departments regular meetings (either staff- or student-led) were held between postgraduates and were usually very popular with the doctoral students. Despite few overlaps in the content of their work doctoral students appreciated the opportunity to discuss methodological and theoretical ideas, and have a forum in which they could present their own work to others. One anthropology postgraduate described the way in which she found group meetings beneficial:

Oh yes, it was very helpful because they're all students and we all face the same problems although we work in different areas, we all have the same problems and it's nice because they suggest things for your work,

Pedagogic Continuities

which you haven't thought of which helps a lot. They look at your work from a different perspective. So this is very useful. And because it's a group of people, not just one person like your supervisor, it works like a workshop.

We found that these group meetings, which were well attended by PhD students, provided a measure of the support which characterized science doctoral work, as described earlier:

It's very nice. Because it is there that anyone can make a contribution, and if there's any area where you need to strengthen your emphasis you'll be advised how to do so, and if you have any difficulties you can express them and there will be somebody who can help you.

(Town planning PhD student)

Note here, however, that such seminars are not, like the science colloquia, part of the ongoing shared research mission of a group in which the PhD student has a clear role. These are gatherings of individuals whose work has little in common, who participate out of friendship, or curiosity, or loneliness, who bring their individual qualities to the meetings.

Doctoral students themselves regretted the absence of peers within their departments and the following account, provided by an anthropology PhD student, is also interesting for its comment upon the increased number of postgraduate-taught courses:

I would certainly appreciate it if there were more people here. A peer group. There are so many MAs here but they are not so committed or dedicated to their work in anthropology. But there are not so many PhDs and I think that would help a lot. Also exchanging experiences on how others work with their supervisors, I could have more of that.

Generally the lack of 'critical mass' was blamed upon current funding policies which effectively deplete the number of doctoral students and prohibit the formation of postgraduate cultures within departments:

The thing that concerns me is there isn't a large enough concentration of graduate students and I wish policy would allow this to change. We're just probably there at the moment, there's just enough – but even so it would be nice to have seven or eight because that's when you've got enough for groups to form without people being left out and I think that's really important. They can start their own networks.

(Human geography supervisor)

Pedagogic Continuities

Under the conditions which at present characterize PhD work in the social sciences, the positional roles and Hacking's 'rope' analogy, which we described earlier in the context of laboratory science, are inappropriate on two counts. First, the mutual interdependence of research interests, skills and materials is absent. Individuals tend to work upon isolated topics with little overlap with the work of others. Second, there is less continuity in that research funding for PhD students tends to apply to the interests of individuals rather than the development of ongoing research topics or projects. Once a PhD student has finished his or her research it is unlikely that the completed work will be carried on by a successor. The social science department is a personal one, in which the student negotiates an individualized set of relationships – intellectually, personally and emotionally.

Beyond the Department

The intellectual lives of students, as apprentices in disciplines, is not confined by the boundaries of their department. Their discipline is also embodied in learned societies. One of the ways in which students may be inducted into their discipline is through the conferences, journals and networking associated with its professional bodies. We found that many of the geographers and biochemists were reinforced in their disciplinary identities through membership of the Institute of British Geographers (IBG) and the Biochemical Society. If a learned society, such as the IBG or the Royal Economic Society, allows or encourages PhD students into membership, and if it has a postgraduate 'section' with conferences, newsletters and Internet mailing lists, a PhD student can use that to find colleagues. Many of the geography PhD students belonged to the IBG. Patsy Schroeder, one of only three full-time PhD students in geography at Wellferry (and the only female), used the IBG in this way. The IBG has a strong postgraduate section, which meant that, as Patsy Schroeder explained 'To me the IBG is great!' But she felt this was partly because 'I've been involved'. She had been an active IBG postgraduate since her first year as a PhD student, and spoke highly of its newsletter, the conferences and also the networking functions. Patsy and her friends believed that 'If you want to be a professional geographer you have to get into the circuit early.' Bryan Faul, at Hernchester, agreed: 'The IBG seems more academic – it organizes a postgraduate forum which is quite useful.'

Several of our biochemistry respondents were especially enthusiastic about 'their' learned society as a vehicle for meeting fellow students and leading scholars. For example, Suzanne Deladier, from Baynesholme, talked about her recent involvement: 'I went to a postgraduate meeting in Dranllwyn which was a meeting of the Biochemical Society, and it's supposed to be for second-year PhD students, but I went along.' Hal Tatley (also from Baynesholme) was a member as well: 'I'm a member of the

167

Pedagogic Continuities

Biochemistry Society: for ten pounds it's worth it. Free travel to conferences makes it definitely worth it. I went to a conference in Essex with students from other universities, we all went.' Giles Perrin, from Ribblethorpe, had been to an international conference with funding from the Biochemistry Society:

> I've just come back from Virginia, we had five days in Virginia. I learned an awful lot there, and it was good to put names to faces that you see in the journals. You sit down to have breakfast with somebody or dinner and then you realize you're talking to someone who's a major part of that field, and you see them in their real light. ... I want to find out about people to work with next.

Some advantages carried on beyond the PhD, as Dr Garnette, a postdoc also from Baynesholme, explained:

> I belong to the Biochemists' Society. There's big advantages to belonging to the Biochemical Society because they will often provide funding for international meetings. The only proviso is you have to participate in the meeting – i.e. take a poster or give a talk.

While few social science PhD students could look to a learned society for direct financial help, the geographers looked to the IBG for its communal academic functions, often contrasting it with the Royal Geographical Society (RGS), which had a wider and less scholarly membership. (The two have since joined forces, although the IBG annual conference is still the main scholarly event.) In fact, most of the students had not joined the other two geographical organizations: the RGS and the Geographical Association (GA). The RGS had a rather old-fashioned image, as Bryan Faul explained:

> My own perception of it is that it seems to have gone very much towards exploration, hacking through the jungles and showing slides about it. The IBG seems more academic, it organizes a postgraduate forum which is quite useful.

Nick Menakis described the IBG as 'the body purely for professional geographers – academics and postgraduates only', and he characterized the postgraduate forum as 'our lobby group'. Nick felt the RGS would be good to join 'for psychological reasons, because it's nice to feel part of a community'. Julian Perrini described joining the IBG as 'the natural choice – and it's cheap to join and it's meant to be very good'.

While the biochemists and geographers reinforced their disciplinary identities via their learned societies, the anthropologists were not able to use the equivalent society, the Association of Social Anthropologists (ASA). It is only open to people with a PhD, and therefore has no postgraduate section. There was no space for postgraduates to get 'into the circuit', or meet other students working on similar topics. The lack of access to the learned society increased the isolation of graduate students in social anthropology.

Multidisciplinary Work

To reiterate, we have presented two models of PhD research. The first – the positional 'group model' – has been described as characteristic of the natural sciences, whereas the second – the personal, individualized model – characterizes the social sciences. Earlier we made the disclaimer that there are not just two, but several, ways of carrying out doctoral research. In this section we will consider the experiences of postgraduate research in what, in Bernstein's terms, we are calling sites of secondary knowledge production (Bernstein 1990). By sites of secondary knowledge production we mean those or departments or research centres that comprise several subject specialisms and are described by their members as either interdisciplinary or multidisciplinary. The multidisciplinary departments that we looked at were in artificial intelligence, environmental sciences, development studies, area studies, urban studies and town planning.

Our tentative conclusion from these multidisciplinary departments is that in them the generic difficulties faced by research students can be compounded. As well as the complications of working in a department without one strong discipline, there was clearly a lack of a well-defined group structure characteristic of the traditional science department. The intellectual interests of staff members were fragmented, with each scholar working from within his or her own 'original' subject specialism. In the following account a town planning doctoral student describes how PhD work can be an isolating experience. In this case the student is the only geographer in the department:

> It's isolating within this department. I'm basically the only person interested in my area. My supervisor is the second most interested, but he knows less than I do about it. I still consider myself a geographer I must admit. You start to explain geographical information systems and you see their eyes start to glaze over. It's too technical a subject for them, I think. So I do feel isolation within the department.

Individuals tended to describe themselves in terms of their discipline of origin (or the discipline in which they trained) rather than their discipline of destination (their current discipline). Therefore we found that members of AI departments described themselves, for example, as mathematicians, engineers and computer scientists. Within environmental sciences members described themselves, for example, as geologists, hydrologists and chemists.

Pedagogic Continuities

The same phenomenon was observable in the social science multidisciplinary settings. Town planners, for example, described themselves as geographers, sociologists and architects; members of development studies departments described themselves as anthropologists, sociologists and economists.

Academic staff and doctoral students in the multidisciplinary settings therefore tend to remain loyal to their primary discipline and maintain the boundaries which define the constituent subject areas. This ensures that, as one informant explained, 'the demarcation lines between disciplines remain pretty tightly drawn'. The level of commitment to the discipline of origin stemmed from strong early socialization. As explained by a staff member in development studies, 'The paradox is while we're in an interdisciplinary setting we've all actually come from single disciplines and we've all come as doctoral students or whatever, and come to an interdisciplinary setting through a single-discipline route.' Madge Anderson, an American doing a PhD in Development Studies at Gossingham:

> In this system you don't get much support, you get very isolated – it's like being trained for the priesthood, it's a very long gauntlet you have to run. And you have to pull almost entirely on your own personal and financial resources – you're one person battling against the odds.

While this could be read as the familiar cry of the isolated social scientist, we found that there were more complaints of this sort from multidisciplinary settings than from single-discipline areas.

Within multidisciplinary departments, staff and students tended to work from within a single-discipline base. This was not thought to be a problem for the majority of PhD students because most of them emanated from primary disciplines and issues such as research topic, theoretical allegiance, choice of supervisor and methodology were treated accordingly. PhD candidates who had received their undergraduate training in a multidisciplinary context, and saw themselves as essentially multidisciplinary, posed more of a problem even within their own departments because, as outlined by a PhD supervisor in development studies, they could not easily relate to any particular disciplinary body of knowledge:

> The more I do this job the less I believe there is any such thing as multidisciplinary development studies. And you have to come to this subject with a strong disciplinary base and then you can make the connections out. Far too many people come with either no disciplinary base – as a result of which they're too far from the frontier of any of these disciplines to make any serious contribution – or they come with one

disciplinary base but wanting to pursue another one in the same situation. They're too far away from the frontier to say anything sensible.

Similar scepticism about multi and interdisciplinary PhDs was voiced by members of interdisciplinary science departments. In the following account a member of staff from environmental sciences describes the difficulties of interdisciplinary PhD work:

> I definitely believe the PhD is unsuited to interdisciplinary work because it is most often single-disciplinary. It has to be set in context. With interdisciplinary research you still only have one external examiner and you're open to judgement from their base. [The PhD candidate] I told you about had to rewrite his thesis in the single discipline of the external. After they've got a PhD then they can move on to interdisciplinary research. I think a PhD is very necessary in this field. For three years in a single discipline it's a good foundation. There are very few examples of interdisciplinary PhDs.

Although the multidisciplinary departments housed experts from a range of disciplines, we found that there were, typically, some clusters of specialists who shared a disciplinary background and attracted more funding and more research students than their colleagues with different disciplinary origins. Departmental members whose interests lay outside those dominant groups tended to attract fewer students. 'Group' PhD work was most apparent in departments with strong sub-disciplinary areas that had emerged through the shared interests and/or backgrounds of several individuals: for example, the study of robotics within AI. Although individuals had diverse disciplinary interests, they identified themselves with the robotics research. We also found, albeit to a limited extent, some evidence of research groups within environmental sciences:

> There's a subculture among the chemists – you know they feel rooted to some extent in chemistry, they all know about the process of analysis so they can take that as given, so when they see one another there's a sort of mutual aside sort of stuck to the board that says I know about chemistry and I can talk to you, we share the same language.

Conclusion

We began this chapter with Bourdieu emphasizing the control exercised by the professoriat over its successors. We have gone on to outline two contrasting modalities of social control and reproduction – personal and positional – and shown how the former is characteristic of the social sciences, while the laboratory disciplines are characterized by positional

Pedagogic Continuities

modes. Throughout the chapter we have emphasized the views of those two systems from the vantage point of the graduate student. Most PhD students have a secure disciplinary identity, and have internalized the mode of social control that reproduces it. However, we ended the chapter by paying particular attention to the work and social identities of students who are enrolled in multidisciplinary settings. Such settings recontextualize and apply knowledge originally identified with more 'pure' disciplinary research groups or departments. In that sense, therefore, they may be thought of as sites of secondary knowledge production. Graduate students in such contexts seem to have more difficulty in establishing an identity and in seeing themselves as successors or inheritors in the intellectual field. Admittedly, our research contained few settings and few students in inter or multidiscplinary settings; it would be unwise to make too much of our observation here. Nonetheless, it does suggest that contemporary emphases on research and research training that is interdisciplinary need careful evaluation in terms of the kinds of identities and loyalties that are fostered, and the kinds of intellectual apprenticeship that are enacted under such conditions.

10 Disciplines and the Doctorate

> Social science cannot break with common criteria and classifications and disentangle itself from the struggles of which they are end and means, unless it takes them explicitly as its object.
>
> (Bourdieu, 1988: 13)

In the course of this book we have not attempted to offer a comprehensive study of all aspects of academic socialization, even in the academic disciplines we studied. In contrast to some comparable works, for instance, we have not provided a systematic review of student culture in the graduate school; nor have we concentrated on how graduate students survive and learn the ropes in the early weeks and months of their postgraduate study. Rather, we have tried to concentrate on a more sustained discussion of how postgraduate study, and the work of doctoral students and their supervisors reproduce specific and distinctive forms of knowledge. We do not regard academic disciplines and their boundaries as 'given'. We acknowledge that the reverse is true: disciplines, research fields and their boundaries are inherently arbitrary. The natural and social worlds do not present themselves pre-packaged as the subject-matter for social anthropology, development studies, biochemistry, artificial intelligence or geography. In the most general sense, such academic divisions are arbitrary. We do, however, recognize that these distinctions and discriminations have considerable weight as social phenomena, and have equal, if not greater, significance in furnishing the social frameworks for knowledge production.

Academic disciplines and their subject-matter are mutually constitutive. A discipline furnishes its members with definitions – often tacit – of what is 'thinkable', with appropriate assumptions as to what 'counts' as research problems, suitable research methods, definitions of research programmes and the approved modes of graduate student research. It is not necessary to subscribe to Kuhn's notion of a *paradigm* in the natural sciences in order to recognize the general force of his argument, especially when related to differences between socially demarcated disciplines rather than mechanisms of change within such collectivities. A discipline, like a paradigm, offers

Disciplines and the Doctorate

experienced and novice researchers alike the resources to identify, accomplish and justify particular lines of thought and action. It defines a range of problem types and types of solution. It furnishes classic exemplars of research practice.

A broadly structuralist anthropology of culture thus helps us to understand the social conditions under which specialist knowledge is produced and reproduced. Our research has been consistently informed by the respective contributions of authors such as Basil Bernstein and Pierre Bourdieu. Without for a moment suggesting that these influential authors have said 'the same thing' about symbolic domains and divisions of knowledge, together they provide powerfully suggestive ways of approaching the social reproduction of scientific and academic knowledge. Disciplines are socially defined in terms of symbolic boundaries that demarcate the intellectual fields of research programmes and academic departments. They reflect the classificatory principles underlying the division of labour in the academy. Not all research and knowledge is defined entirely within those boundaries, of course, but even interdisciplinary or multidisciplinary work is – by definition – understood in relation to those symbolic boundaries. We do not mean to suggest that those boundaries are immutable. While research is conducted in accordance with disciplinary knowledge, it simultaneously affirms and transforms the frameworks of the disciplines themselves. The 'originality' of postgraduate research is always defined in terms of the essential tension between accepted prior knowledge and new discoveries or ideas.

It is for these reasons that we have repeatedly tried to maintain a sense of the specificity of disciplinary socialization throughout this book. There are some generic themes that run through our discussion of academic socialization, and we shall draw out several of those below. Nevertheless, there are very specific features of academic life and work that reflect the subcultures of the disciplines. It would be very easy to assimilate these research findings to single, over-arching analytic themes – concentrating on the single problem of academic socialization, or on the nature of supervision in the graduate school. To have done so, without regard for the considerable differences between academic subjects, would be to risk recapitulating the characteristic weakness of several major studies of student culture and socialization in higher education and professional training; that is, the lack of *content*. As we have seen, young scholars are not just preoccupied with survival or success as generic academics, or even as 'scientists'. They work with particular orientations to knowledge, operate within distinctive departmental and disciplinary traditions, and share characteristic subcultures and tacit assumptions. To lose all sense of those contrasting perspectives and practices would be to rob the analysis of its force.

We have, for example, identified and described three very different ways of conducting research, and some of their consequences for graduate students and their supervisors. We described the distinctive approach of 'fieldwork' that is especially characteristic of social anthropology. In that case, the approach to research is not merely a choice of 'research method' – a matter of matching one method among many to a particular research topic. The successful conduct of field research is absolutely fundamental to the enculturation of the young scholar into the mysteries of the craft. Indeed, the approach to research is seen as far more than a method – but a necessary and sufficient condition for membership. In a similar vein, the conduct of bench experiments is a taken-for-granted aspect of socialization into laboratory science. Again, experimentation is not merely a choice of method among many; it is an absolute requirement of competent membership of the disciplinary culture. In their very different ways, field research and bench science have parallel consequences. They both imply a particular kind of intellectual and personal commitment: to ways of working, to the disciplines of time and place, to embodied practices and skills. Both are predicated on 'extra-ordinary' ways of understanding the world, through commitment to a particular form of life. The laboratory and the field are not just neutral places in which to work. They are constructed as special places to work. Even when the anthropologist works in mundane settings 'at home', the field is likely to be treated as 'sacred' through a social mechanism of displacement and separation. Our third mode of knowledge creation is different again. We have described some of the social and intellectual features of research groups, such as experts in AI, who do not depend primarily on either field observations or laboratory experimentation. The construction of computer models and simulations provides an additional way in which academics commit themselves to particular kinds of work.

Each way of knowing does more than just solve particular kinds of puzzles. Each helps to define a particular kind of identity for students and established academics alike. In the course of doing doctoral research the postgraduate student is not merely acquiring specific skills. Students do acquire and use skills, of course. The bench scientist does need to hone his or her technical competence – calibrating and using equipment, making measurements. The field researcher needs to acquire survival skills in order to cope with the contingencies of the field. Computer scientists and those who program models in physical geography need to sharpen their programming and problem-solving skills in order to get their programs to operate and their models to run. But there is clearly much more to it than that. The cultural competence of the academic or the scientist goes beyond the mere learning of recipe-like techniques.

In the first place, even the 'skills' we have just referred to depend on shared, tacit knowledge. The craft skills of the bench scientist cannot be equated with mechanistic recipes for action. We have seen that there is a good deal of personal knowledge and personal experience that goes into the process too. There are indeterminate components of craft knowledge. These affect whether something 'works' or not. There is a great deal of learning by trial and error, as well as from the personal example of others. The bench scientist acquires a 'feel' for or a 'knack' for using the equipment. Such competence comes with doing. It is not transmitted by textbook knowledge or explicit didactic training alone (if at all). In just the same way, the social and intellectual skills of the anthropologist in the field are not dependent on formal training courses and explicit research methods. They are acquired (insofar as they are acquired at all) *in situ*; they are experiential in nature. This is not unique to the disciplines we have just mentioned. The mathematician or computer scientist does not depend solely on algorithms that are learned and deployed in a routine fashion. He or she also operates with powerful, and largely tacit, assumptions concerning aesthetic criteria such as 'elegance'. Indeed, one of the many 'essential tensions' that characterize academic socialization – the tension between explicit training and implicit enculturation – is a very important one.

That tension is paralleled by the tension we have touched on in a number of previous chapters: that is, the extent to which the graduate student is, or should be, treated as an independent, autonomous member of the community, or whether he or she is to be placed within a subordinate position; whether doctoral students are 'peons or colleagues', junior members of the profession or subordinate novices. At the same time, the academic supervisor is caught in a similar kind of tension or dilemma – how to achieve the right kind of balance between allowing the student sufficient autonomy and maintaining surveillance and control over the research.

This in turn is related to the recurrent theme of *isolation* among research students – a mixture of social and intellectual isolation. The relative isolation of the graduate student has been discussed extensively elsewhere, and we have identified its various manifestations in earlier chapters; we do not intend to cover the same ground again in detail. We stress, however, that isolation has two complementary aspects. Doctoral research is in many ways a *liminal* experience. The students stand on the threshold of their academic career. Many are poised between the collective experience of undergraduate education and full incorporation into the academic profession. They are anomalous beings within the classificatory system of the academy. The research student may feel socially isolated if there are few groups or networks of which he or she can be a member, and the social relations of the laboratory and the research group can clearly mitigate social isolation. But the intellectual isolation of the graduate student is of even greater significance. Even the laboratory scientist who is part of a supportive group experiences the loneliness and frustration of finding that his or her equipment will not function, experiments will not work, calculations will not come out or programs will not run. For the research student in a more individualized discipline, the responsibility for success or failure is even more personally felt. The natural scientist whose experiment fails is likely to treat this – and experience it being treated by more senior scientists – as a matter merely of technical failure. For the research student in a discipline like social anthropology whose fieldwork does not yield the right kind of material, or who does not come up with a way of understanding the culture in question, such problems are likely to be treated as personal or moral failure. Bosk (1979) draws a similar distinction between the types of mistake made by trainee surgeons. (A scientist who failed to do the experimental work, or who fudged the results would, of course, be treated as a moral failure, but we have no examples of such activity in our data.) There is, therefore, a constant tension between the individual responsibility of the student and the collective responsibility of the department, the group or the discipline. In that sense, then, postgraduate research is not just isolating, it is also a *risky* undertaking.

For students and their supervisors alike, there is a strong component of *faith* in undertaking doctoral research. That faith represents a strong personal commitment in the face of uncertainties and difficulties. Few of the students and academics we interviewed reported entirely trouble-free research experiences. Indeed, everything we know about the processes of research and discovery across all subjects suggests that its realities are more messy and less controlled than the formal published accounts would suggest. The specific, concrete manifestations of research problems also differ markedly from discipline to discipline: bugs in computer programs, unforeseen events in the field, equipment that won't work and so on. In the face of such contingencies, the graduate student must either abandon the project or maintain some degree of faith. Faith involves the belief – or at least the hope – that things will work in the end. Just as natural scientists' accounts include the article of faith that 'truth will out' (Gilbert and Mulkay, 1984), so graduate students need to affirm a faith that their research 'will work out' or that their solutions will 'come out' in the end. Sometimes, given the relative intellectual isolation of young researchers, keeping the faith is the greatest personal demand made of them.

Such articles of faith rest on a fundamental, usually unspoken, faith in disciplinary knowledge. As we have suggested, it is the discipline that provides its members with the resources for such faith. The young anthropologist, whatever the vicissitudes of his or her personal project, maintains a fundamental commitment to the habitus of social anthropology itself. The young biochemist whose experiment will not run properly retains an equally fundamental commitment to the principles of experimentation and laboratory science. They do not entertain radical doubt as to the underlying frameworks of knowledge. Indeed, no scientist – however 'original' or 'creative' – could continue to work without such a bedrock of faith. In fact, it is a characteristic of the social reproduction and knowledge production of academic research that the participants do not engage in radical doubt. For the most part, they function as practical actors, working within the parameters of taken-for-granted knowledge. The intellectual and personal processes of academic socialization are powerful mechanisms whereby the fundamental assumptions about academic knowledge – its divisions and continuities – are sustained. These basic assumptions are largely tacit in nature, tacitly acquired. What 'counts' as research, and what 'counts' as quality or originality are not matters that are explicated or codified. They are for the most part implicit. When academics talk about what they look for in a PhD, as a supervisor or as an examiner, they do not reproduce the kind of checklist with which universities supply external examiners. They do not generate the kinds of 'objectives' or 'outcomes' that contemporary advocates of quality assurance seek to impose upon the processes and products of the contemporary academy. In practice, academics and graduate students work with indeterminate assumptions about what constitutes good work, and what makes for an adequate contribution to knowledge. Explicit coaching in such matters is not a normal feature of work and supervision in the graduate school.

In emphasizing a reliance on tacit academic culture, we are not denying the possibility of 'good practice', or denying the relevance of appropriate training and mentoring. Indeed, we have used many of the lessons learned in this research and elsewhere to summarize many aspects of good practice (Delamont et al., 1997a). In our analysis of supervisors' narratives of supervision (Chapter 8) we stressed how many of them contrasted their own student experience with contemporary practice in order to endorse principles of guidance or training in the current climate of higher education. Nonetheless, it is easy to see that the academic socialization or enculturation of graduate students, and other junior members of the profession, goes well beyond explicit technical know-how. Training in specific research methods, for instance, is hardly a contentious issue at one level, but the complex contingencies and processes of research in practice cannot be predicted and subsumed under such training. Likewise, the 'skills' that are needed to conduct and write up research are not reducible to explicit formulae. The development of academic competence is inescapably a matter of social learning. It is for this reason that we have referred often to the 'enculturation' of graduate students. Theirs is an experience of acquiring a general cultural competence as a prerequisite or as an adjunct to the specialized work of supervised research.

As we have suggested already, these observations can have significant implications for policy and practice in higher education. Our research was intended to be fundamental in character, rather than driven by short-term policy considerations, and there are fundamental lessons to be learned that have broad policy implications. In general terms, the importance of distinctive disciplinary cultures and the role of social enculturation means that the imposition of over-arching bureaucratic methods of management and accountability may be inappropriate. Indeed, it may prove thoroughly ineffectual. The centralizing tendency of academic regulation – within

Disciplines and the Doctorate

institutions and within the national system as a whole – sometimes resembles the efforts of a distant imperial power attempting to impose a unified system of authority on a diverse range of local cultural systems. Such an exercise can superimpose the semblance of order and rationality, while masking the durability of local cultures. Our ethnographic approach has, by contrast, allowed us to concentrate closely on the nature of those local cultures within the academy.

It is clear that we have emphasized the cultural continuity of academic disciplines throughout this book. We have stressed the extent to which graduate students are enculturated into tacit culture and traditions of intellectual work. We have tried to show that graduate student socialization is one powerful mechanism whereby the cultures of the academy are transmitted from generation to generation. In doing so we may reasonably be held to have over-emphasized and over-simplified things to a certain extent. We have done so, perhaps, in two senses. First, we have stressed disciplinary identities to the exclusion of other sources of identity, and with relatively little reference to inter or multidisciplinary research domains. Second, it might reasonably be held that we have stressed academic continuity at the expense of change and development.

It is true that although we studied academics and students in some interdisciplinary fields, including development studies, we have not made much of their experiences. On the other hand, it was striking that many practitioners within such research groups expressed their own 'real' identity in terms of their 'true' disciplinary allegiance. By its very nature, interdisciplinary research seems fragile in these terms. It is a topic that deserves much more detailed attention by sociologists of science and of higher education. Precisely because the subcultures of the academy are strong and enduring, individual work across the symbolic boundaries can prove especially problematic. Practitioners can 'revert to type' and seek refuge in the relative familiarity of their discipline of origin. Likewise, the young researcher who is working at or across the margins may experience even greater isolation, and find even less social and intellectual support than his or her counterpart who is more securely within the boundaries. Working beyond the pale can prove to be a lonely experience. Clearly, such problems are not faced equally by all researchers. It is equally clear that interdisciplinary research does take place and is sustainable. The symbolic order of disciplines and their boundaries is not so rigid that it is impossible to exist outside it. Interdisciplinary groups are not such gross anomalies or monsters that they are excluded totally.

Equally, we must acknowledge that the disciplines and specialisms of the academy are not immutable. Of course, some are, at least nominally, very old. Some departments and faculties can be traced back through the mediaeval universities and beyond, to antiquity. Others are much more recent developments. Of our own research sites, none is ancient. But several have

Disciplines and the Doctorate

been remarkably well established for many years. Disciplines such as geography and social anthropology are developments of the modern university. But they are very well entrenched. Likewise, biochemistry and computer science or artificial intelligence are of relatively recent origin, but now enjoy an unquestioned position within the array of disciplines and departments. There is change. Subjects wax and wane. There are amalgamations and some wither on the vine. New specialisms separate off and form new disciplines. But within a generation or two the appearance of relative stability is soon established.

The work of the graduate student is, in any case, rarely geared towards the radical overhaul of his or her parent discipline. While students may be rebellious, their work is rarely revolutionary to the extent of calling into question the intellectual framework within which they work. So if we have paid undue attention to mechanisms of reproduction, continuity and stability, there are good reasons for it. An additional reason should also be reaffirmed. The stability of intellectual work calls for social explanation just as much as revolutionary change would. To revert once more to the vocabulary of Thomas Kuhn, normal science (in the broadest sense) requires just as much explanation as does revolutionary upheaval. The relative stability of the laboratory sciences (not just biochemistry), for instance, rests in considerable measure on the continuity of their culture and practices. And that continuity is mobilized through the recurrent processes of recruitment and enculturation. Likewise, social anthropology displays a remarkable degree of intellectual stability while experiencing repeated differences in theory and subject-matter. Its very distinctive approaches to enculturation are powerful mechanisms for ensuring such stability.

Our theoretical framework, itself coloured by structuralist anthropologies of knowledge, also tends to capture the stability of symbolic systems. In juxtaposing the different disciplines that we have studied, we have represented the academy in somewhat static terms. We have implicitly represented universities in terms of relatively separate and self-enclosed intellectual and social communities. Obviously, their organization is more complex than that in reality. Likewise, our research design – which sampled across a fairly wide range of departments in different universities – did not mean that we were able to document in depth how graduate training was co-ordinated across faculties or across an entire university. The notion of the 'graduate school' in contemporary UK universities is just one way in which graduate work is promoted beyond departmental boundaries. Our research did not capture such organizational realities. Similarly, generic training programmes in research methods can cross-cut departmental boundaries, and we have little to say about them on the basis of our data. Whether or not such developments will significantly weaken disciplinary boundaries remains to be seen, and certainly remains to be documented. The kinds of cultural and symbolic features that we have documented in the preceding chapters, and the very fundamental differences that we have identified between contrasting subjects lead us to believe that even in the face of integrating policies, differences and distinctions will remain.

Notwithstanding those limitations, our research has pointed repeatedly and forcibly to the strength and relative stability of academic subcultures. Being a scientist or a scholar is not just a matter of what knowledge one happens to profess. It is, at a much deeper level, a matter of personal identity. One's knowledge helps to construct who and what one is. In terms used by Georg Simmel, the academic disciplines construct and distribute *social types*. This does not mean that they reflect personality traits or personal predispositions. Rather, the academy is a highly differentiated and segmented site. Its various subjects and departments produce and reproduce specialized ways of generating and transmitting knowledge. Equally, they have effective means of recruiting actors and of fostering loyalty. In the various chapters of this book we have repeatedly tried to demonstrate some of the mechanisms whereby young natural and social scientists are enrolled into the academic enterprise.

The most 'pure' disciplines that we have discussed – notably biochemistry, social anthropology and geography – display similar phenomena. The patterns of enrolment and identification are similar. They recall what Basil Bernstein has to say about the development of student identities in school systems that are also characterized by the juxtaposition of symbolically bounded segments..Bernstein suggests that in such subjects, students' loyalty and identity is firmly based on the subject itself. The process of socialization is grounded in a protracted and intensive intellectual apprenticeship. The *raison d'être* of that socialization process is the subject itself. Students are progressively initiated into the mysteries of the subject. Their own learning recapitulates the development of the subject itself, incorporating a mastery of classic texts, or classic techniques and demonstrations. The process of initiation is thus akin to a kind of conversion experience. The underlying message systems are tacit, and are treated as implicit in the discipline itself. This is nowhere more evident than among the anthropologists, who repeatedly affirm not just the uniqueness of their subject, but also their personal identification with it. There is a potent combination of personal and intellectual loyalty. Geographers also display a high degree of commitment to their chosen discipline, and their identities are expressed in terms of disciplinary loyalty. The bench and field scientists do not necessarily express their loyalties in quite the same terms, but the biochemists have a high, taken-for-granted loyalty to the core assumptions of laboratory science.

By contrast, we have also seen – less starkly, perhaps – that other domains are not defined in terms of disciplinary loyalties. In inter or multidisciplinary fields, it is not the discipline so much as 'the problem' that defines work and self. Again, one would predict from Bernstein that academic and personal commitments under such circumstances are not implicit in the

Disciplines and the Doctorate

discipline, but explicated through an orientation towards knowledge use. This is what we have seen in domains such as development studies or town planning. Socialization here is not enacted primarily within disciplinary boundaries, but is problem-oriented, and conducted within a more 'profane' symbolic domain, rather than within the 'sacred' domains of the pure sciences.

These different orientations to enculturation underline the ways in which the academy encompasses different styles of knowledge production. The disciplines create and re-create distinctive frameworks of knowledge. They function as epistemic communities, with their own mechanisms for enculturation and social reproduction. The work of the scientist is socially organized and mediated. We should not be surprised, therefore, to learn that his or her experience of academic socialization is also social in character.

Appendix 1
Two Research Projects

This appendix provides a brief summary of the details of our data collection. It is not a sophisticated and reflective account: we have yet to provide any such texts from these projects. The book is based on two linked research projects on doctoral students, their supervisors and their experiences of graduate research. The first of our studies, which was funded under the ESRC's research initiative, on UK doctoral research in the social sciences, was initially conceived in collaboration with a research group from Warwick University, under the direction of Professor Robert Burgess. Designed to be complementary, the two projects, which divided up the total range of social science disciplines between them, had quite different focuses. The Warwick project set itself up as a classic socialization study, concentrating on research students' early initiation into doctoral research. This project targeted sociology, business studies and economics, and concentrated upon the first year of doctoral work.

In contrast, our research, based at Cardiff University, focused less on the practical processes of doctoral socialization and more on the sociology of knowledge. We were preoccupied less with the question of how novices become competent research students, and more with the question of how research students are socialized or encultured into the disciplinary knowledge of their academic subject. While different in this respect, both projects were designed to document key features of the organizational and intellectual lives of research students and their academic supervisors. In our study we targeted social anthropology, human geography, town planning, area, urban and development studies.

A third study within the programme was identified as congruent with the Cardiff and Warwick research. Based at Bristol University, this project which had a particular interest in processes of supervision, targeted education and psychology. Finally, a fourth project, directed by Estelle Phillips, designed to explore issues of 'quality' in the PhD, was also identified by the initiative and its director, Martin Bulmer, as being closely related to the first three. However, in the event, the affinities with that fourth project were more

183

Appendix 1

tenuous. Papers by the investigators from all the projects can be found in Burgess (1994).

The eventual design of the four qualitative projects was a negotiated outcome. We originally proposed to conduct the research through a small number of ethnographic case studies, studying the processes of doctoral research and academic socialization through detailed fieldwork in a few academic departments. The Training Board and the co-ordinator of the overall research initiative had other ideas. They wanted to go for a broader perspective, with a larger number of research sites across the various projects. Thus it was ordained that the four projects, which shared a broadly qualitative approach to research, should strive between them to achieve a 'representative' sample of institutions and departments. It was therefore proposed that the projects should between them represent a geographical spread of institutions across the UK, and include institutions drawn from the main sectors of British higher education: namely, Oxbridge, 'old civic' universities, 'plate-glass' universities, polytechnics (as they were then) and London University. The chosen research sites also included departments that had been subject to sanctions (blacklisted) and those which continued to receive ESRC studentships.

In the event, the sampling requirements that were imposed on us did little to illuminate the expected dimensions of contrast. They did, however, impact on the design and conduct of our own research. Rather than concentrating on detailed ethnographic research in a small number of academic departments, we were compelled to target a larger number of departments. Apart from the purely practical implications for the research, such as the longer series of access negotiations that this required, we were far more thinly spread across departments than we would have liked. This meant we were forced to rely to a large extent upon interviewing academics and students, and had less opportunity for first-hand ethnographic immersion, less scope for participant observation, and a more superficial acquaintance with the settings we visited.

The successful completion of our research on social science PhD work left us with only a partial picture of academic socialization in the UK. Because of this we sought ESRC funding for a further project, concentrating this time on doctoral students and academics in natural science disciplines. No longer constrained by the former sampling requirements, we proposed purposely to select fewer university departments and study these in more depth. Hence we did not attempt to cover all, but intentionally sampled different varieties of 'science'.

We elected to include biochemistry and physical geography because they offered us two major contrasts: first, the contrast between physical geography and human geography (the latter of which had been included in the previous study); and second, the clear distinction between the laboratory-based science of biochemistry and the field-based science of physical

Appendix 1

geography. Our third science, artificial intelligence, was selected to contrast with the first two, as a multidisciplinary domain in which an element of cognitive science and computer modelling is represented.

These disciplines were by no means intended to be 'representative' of the academy, but neither were they randomly selected. They capture distinctively different styles of intellectual work and social organization. Between them they include 'pure' and 'applied' fields, laboratory and field research, single disciplines and multidisciplinary domains. We are acutely aware of our omissions. For example, in an ideal world we would have included research on graduate work in the humanities. Scholarship in many humanities disciplines has traditionally been organized in rather different ways from the natural science disciplines, with a much more individualized approach, which should have proved a useful comparison. However we do note that history, a high-status humanities discipline, was central to the five-nation comparative programme co-ordinated by Clark (1994), and that history was included in the UK study from that same project (Becher et al., 1994). Despite our omissions, within the confines of our research projects – which are substantial in their own right – we feel confident that we captured modes of social organization and academic culture which do cover a wide span of variation and contrast.

In the course of the two projects, we collected data in twenty academic departments between 1990 and 1994. We conducted interviews with a total of 286 PhD students, supervisors and departmental heads. These interviews were supplemented with observation in research laboratories, postgraduate seminars and research group meetings, and of students at their computing workstations. The majority of the interviews were tape recorded. They were transcribed, and the preliminary analysis was conducted using the ETHNOGRAPH software (Seidel, 1988; Tesch, 1990; Weaver and Atkinson, 1994). This assisted us in the process of the thematic coding of transcripts and enabled the collation of coded segments of the data across the entire data set, or from sub-sets, with relative ease. The code and retrieve strategy of data handling is especially useful when dealing with relatively large qualitative data sets, such as the nearly two hundred transcripts with which we were dealing. While constituting a useful tool, the ETHNOGRAPH could not substitute for our own analytic input. We were the ones who identified and developed themes that guided the coding that informed the analysis. The ETHNOGRAPH simply took some of the strain out of it.

Neither did the ETHNOGRAPH exhaust the analytic possibilities afforded by such data, and we have not relied solely upon it in the preparation of this book. Indeed, the data derived just from our research with the anthropologists has been used elsewhere in order to demonstrate the diverse and complementary analytic strategies that may be applied to such qualitative data (Coffey and Atkinson, 1996). We have therefore drawn on a variety of perspectives in approaching the data, and in presenting them in the

Appendix 1

course of this book. In addition to a thematic analysis of the interviews, we have examined aspects of the narrative organization of our interview data. We have also paid attention to the rhetorical features of doctoral students' and academics' accounts of their work and careers.

The methods of negotiating access differed slightly between the first (social science) project and the second (natural science) one. The initial project was announced to vice chancellors in a formal letter from the convenor of the initiative before any departments were approached. Then the individual research teams approached specific departments. The Cardiff team wrote to the head of each department, asking for an appointment in order to introduce and explain our project. Then Paul Atkinson or Sara Delamont saw them and negotiated the access (subject in some cases to ratification by a staff meeting, and sometimes subject to an appearance by members of the research team before such a meeting). If a meeting was requested, then Paul and Odette saw the staff together. If not, then Odette would visit the university, see the relevant support staff and obtain lists of staff and students from which to set up meetings for interviews. The project secretary, Angela Jones, then arranged the appointments. All the interviews were taped unless the respondent objected. Angela Jones transcribed the tapes. Odette then used the ETHNOGRAPH software to organize, code and retrieve the data. When the bulk of the staff had been interviewed, Sara and Paul did a small number of what we nicknamed 'honcho' interviews: visiting senior people, such as pro vice-chancellors with responsibility for graduate affairs, or chairs of the university-wide research committee who might, we felt, 'unbend' more to an 'established' figure or expect to be seen by the grant holders. The one exception to this pattern was Wellferry, where all the interviews were done by Sara.

The science project, untrammelled by the demands of a co-ordinated initiative was more low key. Science disciplines were not facing major policy upheavals, and so there was not seen to be a need for the elite interviews. Access was negotiated directly with departments by Odette and Paul, and Odette then carried out the fieldwork. The interviews were done in the same way as for the first project, but rather more time was spent in the observation of social interaction and talk among members of the chosen research groups.

These two projects on the occupational socialization of PhD students should be seen in the context of previous studies conducted by the authors. Over a twenty-year period Atkinson (1981, 1997) has studied the socialization of doctors; Parry (1988, 1994) the socialization of journalists; Delamont the experiences of doctoral students in education (Eggleston and Delamont, 1981, 1983) and in chemistry (Galton and Delamont, 1976). In Cardiff, Atkinson and Delamont have also worked with a number of colleagues studying occupational socialization; much of that research is collected in Coffey and Atkinson (1994). The implications of this work for

Appendix 1

the supervision of higher degree students are drawn out by Delamont et al. (1997a). The sociological perspectives outlined in Chapter 1 of this book are among the guiding ideas of this local tradition of research.

Appendix 2
The Policy Context

Although this book is based mainly on empirical research that we conducted in British universities, its relevance far exceeds its contribution to the understanding of higher education in the UK. The fundamental social processes of enculturation in the academy go beyond the specific institutional arrangements of departments and universities. This book, therefore, is not just an account of the local experiences of postgraduate students and their supervisors. Through the exploration of social and intellectual processes whereby academic knowledge and academic disciplines are created and recreated, it makes an important contribution to our understanding of the construction and reproduction of knowledge within the contemporary academy. Nevertheless, it is important to set the research in context and to account for our own research experiences in other people's laboratories and departments – to provide for our own experiences 'in the field' among our academic peers.

The academy does not operate in a vacuum. At the time of our research the climate of postgraduate research was influenced by very specific research and policy interests which focused on doctoral study in the UK. The research on which the book is based, which was funded by the Economic and Social Research Council (ESRC), derived directly from these policy interests. The first of the two studies which we undertook on doctoral research focused on the social sciences. This formed part of a national research initiative which itself had originated from a proposal of the ESRC's Training Board within the Research Council itself. The ESRC, which has limited resources at its disposal, is severely restricted in the number of research students which it can fund. The majority of students are funded from other sources, including the universities themselves, or are self-funding. Although not the major funder of PhD study in the UK, the ESRC does however exert a disproportionate influence over postgraduate training. This is in part because it is the only central, UK-wide source of social science funding, and consequently its studentships carry a symbolic value beyond their purely practical impact. Landing an ESRC award is an indication of esteem for both the academic host department and the recipient student.

Appendix 2

Competition for studentships is keen, and success in the national competition is a considerable achievement for the candidate.

Prior to the research initiative under which our research was funded, the ESRC implemented some of the recommendations of the Winfield Report (1987), resulting in policy innovations which had considerable impact on the UK social-science community. They constituted a far more direct Research Council intervention into postgraduate research training than ever before and were the subject of considerable debate (Delamont, 1989). The two main innovations were the introduction of a sanctions policy, and prescriptive guidelines for research training and doctoral study. Through the sanctions policy the ESRC set institutional targets for PhD completion rates. It became a requirement for students to submit their PhD theses within four years of initial registration, and institutions whose submission rates fell below the official threshold ceased to be eligible for postgraduate research support. This policy of sanctioning, which was commonly referred to as blacklisting, had considerable national impact. It was potentially divisive, not only between institutions but between departments within the same institution: a whole university could lose its entitlement to Research Council studentships because of poor completion rates in just one or two of its social science departments.

The policy of sanctions against institutions with poor completion rates was complemented by a system of positive recognition from the ESRC of institutions and departments eligible to receive postgraduate studentships. Eligibility became a function of both completion rates and the quality of research training, especially training in the methods of social research, being offered to doctoral students. The traditional British emphasis had, up until that time, been on students' individual research and on the thesis as the sole outcome of the research training period. This was now questioned as the best way to produce social scientists competent to carry out research other than doctoral work.

Panels of subject specialists were commissioned to design 'training guidelines' (ESRC, 1991; revised edn, 1996), which were divided into generic requirements and those specific to the subjects supported by the ESRC. From then onwards departments had to apply for ESRC recognition by demonstrating their capacity to deliver formal research training that met the general and subject-specific guidelines. The receipt of doctoral studentships was dependent upon the formal recognition exercise and its outcome. Since 1992, a department wishing to receive ESRC-funded studentships has had to comply with the training guidelines to provide formal research teaching accounting for about 60 per cent of a student's first year of their doctoral study.

Reflecting the prevailing political climate, the ESRC responded not only to a moral panic concerning PhD completion rates, but also to their own agenda concerning the replacement of social scientists in British higher

Appendix 2

education. They realized that when university teachers recruited in the 1960s and 1970s reached retirement age in the early years of the new century there would be a need to recruit substantial numbers of suitably trained social scientists. The ESRC's policy therefore balanced, on the one hand, reprisals for poor completion rates and, on the other, a positive approach to the introduction of formal research training, with particular emphasis on training in research methods.

It was against this backdrop of change towards its 'client institutions' and their respective departments that the ESRC's Training Board established a programme of research into UK doctoral research in the social sciences. The programme was the outcome of a competitive bidding process. Although we locate our first project, on the social sciences, in the context of the ESRC recognition exercise, this exercise itself was embedded in a broader UK policy context. We need to clarify this, because while our research was first and foremost a contribution to basic research in the sociology of knowledge, there are key points where it engaged directly with significant issues and debates around the organization and support for doctoral research in the UK more generally. It is certainly a contention that policy formation and debate in this area have been insufficiently informed by the type of detailed understanding of academic cultures and organization that research such as ours would have provided (see Parry et al., 1994a; Delamont et al., 1997b).

We can date the wider policy context of our research by reference to the Winfield Report (Winfield, 1987; Delamont, 1989). Although its remit was restricted to the social sciences, Winfield's recommendations to the ESRC about the funding of doctoral research were far-reaching. They set the tone for policies introduced subsequently by the other Research Councils and the British Academy, and affected the sciences and the humanities. Although detailed implementation has varied between disciplines, the general tone of policy has been consistent across the entire subject spectrum. (For a full account of this, see Becher et al., 1994; Hockey 1991.)

The ESRC were the first UK body to be so prescriptive about postgraduate research training, but they were not alone. All the Research Councils had been exercised by the question of doctoral research. As early as 1982 the then Advisory Board to the Research Councils (ABRC) identified three problems relating to the British PhD. These focused on the optimum balance between generic research training and the individual's unique doctoral project, the length of time between initial registration and submission of the PhD thesis, and the relationship between time spent on general research training and submission rates. The ABRC report recommended that the normal full-time PhD candidates should complete in four years, ideally leading to a timescale of six to seven years from initial matriculation for a first (bachelor's) degree to PhD completion. In international terms this is an extremely compressed timetable. The report concluded that two major barriers to a four-year submission were students' lack of background knowl-

Appendix 2

edge and technical skills, and the choice of research project being too broad and over-ambitious. These problems applied to physics and biochemistry as well as to geography and economic history.

In the natural sciences, the issues raised by the ABRC report were equally important, though less politically sensitive. In the late 1980s, the Natural and Environmental Research Council (NERC) introduced its own sanctions against departments with poor completion rates. The NERC were also at that time entertaining the proposal for a new national higher degree (MRes), to be inserted between the existing undergraduate programme and the PhD with the aim of teaching research skills.

The British Academy and the Science Research Councils (which had been reorganized in the early 1990s) continued to stress the importance of doctoral completion rates, and entertained the need for training in research techniques before or during the PhD registration. These policies provided the background and the mechanisms for the concentration of doctoral research in the UK. The promotion of doctoral research could be seen as a collective, organizational issue rather than as one dependent on the individual student and his or her supervisor. A concomitant emphasis on the quality of the research environment and its appointed training programme laid the foundations for future consolidation of research training in a restricted range of settings.

The Research Councils' interest and intervention in the universities' provision of doctoral training parallels other modes of surveillance, regulation and differential funding. Teaching Quality Assessments and the recurrent Research Assessment Exercises that are conducted every four or five years in the UK are themselves part of the same process. The provision of research training and the evaluation of research performance reflect the same sets of assumptions. At their heart is the notion of the research context, culture or environment. The concern over postgraduate research is but one part of a wider preoccupation with research productivity in UK higher education. It is frequently assumed that the size and vigour of a research-student population, even a 'graduate school', are in themselves performance indicators of a flourishing research culture. A lively research culture is equally often assumed to be the sine qua non for the training of successful postgraduate students.

These assumptions have influenced, and been reinforced by, the recent UK policy statement on postgraduate education – the Harris Report (1996). The Harris Committee was established in 1995 by the Higher Education Funding Council for England (HEFCE), the Committee of Vice-Chancellors and Principals (CVCP) and the Standing Conference of Principals (SCOP). Its remit was to review taught postgraduate courses as well as higher degrees by research. The report contained a number of recommendations including issues relating to the resourcing of taught postgraduate students, responsibility for quality assurance for postgraduate

191

Appendix 2

provision, and the provision of a code of practice for postgraduate research education.

For the purposes of this book, the most significant of the specific issues covered by Harris is that of 'critical mass'. Harris asserts that effective doctoral study takes place where there is 'a critical mass of research activity'. This is a key observation which is in keeping with a relatively long period of UK policy formation in promoting concentration and selectivity in research and research training. Indeed, there seems to be a consensus, over a decade of assessments and selectivity exercises, that a concentration of research training and the achievement of critical mass is desirable (or at least inevitable). It is, at the very least, notable that the proposals concerning 'critical mass' received relatively little challenge in the public debates in 1996, in contrast to other aspects of the Harris Report (e.g. *Times Higher Education Supplement*, 7 June 1996, 28 June 1996).

Most policy statements and intervention in higher education have been insensitive to differences in disciplinary cultures. This has increasingly led to common, universalistic frameworks of regulation, training needs and timetables (Coffey and Atkinson, 1997). Although the ESRC laid down subject-specific sets of training guidelines, their emphasis on core skills and competencies suggests they see themselves as responsible for the production of 'social scientists' rather than subject specialists. Precisely because the Training Guidelines set out to promote general, decontextualized research skills they have been accused of transforming the British PhD into a 'driving licence', rather than the older ideal of a 'licence to explore' (Bernstein, 1996). In a similar vein, Natural Science Research Councils pushed for the MRes because they not only identified generalized research skills but also endeavoured to introduce them as a quasi-discipline in their own right.

The introduction of the MRes as a universally recognized degree, and as a prerequisite to doctoral and further research, has been resisted more strongly than the social scientists resisted the ESRC Guidelines. Nevertheless, the general tenor of policy pronouncements in the past ten to fifteen years has been consistent. The emphasis on explicit, decontextualized research skills, and on the concentration of research through differential recognition and selectivity, has been remarkably consistent. The pronouncements have also been remarkably congruent with broader developments in higher education policy in the UK over the same period.

References

Abir-Am, P. (1982) 'The discourse of physical power and biological knowledge in the 1930s', *Social Studies of Science*, 12, pp. 341–82.
Adam, A. (1995a) 'Artificial intelligence and women's knowledge: what can feminist epistemologies tell us?', *Women's Studies International Forum*, 18, 4, pp. 407–15.
—— (1995b) 'Embodying knowledge: a feminist critique of artificial intelligence', *European Journal of Women's Studies*, 2, pp. 355–77.
Ashmore, M., Myers, G. and Potter, J. (1995) 'Discourse, rhetoric and reflexivity', in S. Jasanoff, G. Markle, J. Petersen and T. Pinch (eds) *Handbook of Science and Technology Studies*, London: Sage.
Atkinson, P.A. (1981) *The Clinical Experience: The Construction and Reconstruction of Medical Reality*, Farnborough: Gower.
—— (1984) 'Wards and deeds: taking knowledge and control seriously', in R.G. Burgess (ed.) *The Research Process in Educational Settings*, London: Falmer, pp. 163–85.
—— (1985) *Language, Structure and Reproduction: An Introduction to the Sociology of Basil Bernstein*, London: Methuen.
—— (1990) *The Ethnographic Imagination*, London and New York: Routledge.
—— (1992) *Understanding Ethnographic Texts*, Thousand Oaks CA: Sage.
—— (1995) 'Bernstein's structuralism', in A. Sadovnik (ed.) *Knowledge and Pedagogy*, New York: Ablex.
—— (1996) *Sociological Readings and Re-Readings*, Aldershot: Avebury.
—— (1997) *The Clinical Experience: The Construction and Reconstruction of Medical Reality*, 2nd, expanded edition, Aldershot: Ashgate.
Atkinson, P.A. and Delamont, S. (1985) 'Socialisation into teaching: the research which lost its way', *British Journal of Sociology of Education*, 6, 3, pp. 307–22.
Atkinson, P.A., Reid, M.E. and Sheldrake, P.F. (1977) 'Medical mystique', *Sociology of Work and Occupations*, 4, 3, pp. 243–80.
Ball, S. (1981) *Beachside Comprehensive*, Cambridge: Cambridge University Press.
Barley, N. (1983) *The Innocent Anthropologist*, London: British Museum Publications.
Barnes, B. (1974) *Scientific Knowledge and Sociological Theory*, London: Routledge and Kegan Paul.
Becher, T. (1989) 'Physicists on physics', *Studies in Higher Education*, 15, 1, pp. 3–21.
—— (1990) *Academic Tribes and Territories*, Milton Keynes: Open University Press.

193

References

Becher, T., Henkel, M. and Kogan, M. (1994) *Graduate Education in Britain*, London: Jessica Kingsley.

Becker, H.S., Geer, B., Hughes, E.C. and Strauss, A.L. (1961) *Boys in White*, Chicago: Chicago University Press.

Behar, R. and Gordon, D. (eds) (1995) *Women Writing Culture*, Berkeley CA: University of California Press.

Bernstein, B. (1975) *Class, Codes and Control*, vol. 3: *Towards a Theory of Educational Transmissions*, London: Routledge and Kegan Paul.

—— (1977) *Class, Codes and Control*, vol.3, revised edition, London: Routledge.

—— (1990) *Class, Codes and Control*, vol.4: *The Structuring of Pedagogic Discourse*, London: Routledge.

—— (1996) *Pedagogy, Symbolic Control and Identity: Theory, Research, Critique*, London: Taylor and Francis.

Bloor, D. (1976) *Knowledge and Social Imagery*, London: Routledge and Kegan Paul.

Bosk, C. (1979) *Forgive and Remember: The Management of Medical Failure*, Chicago: University of Chicago Press.

Bosley, K. (1989) Introduction to *The Kalevala*, Oxford: Oxford University Press.

Bourdieu, P. (1975) 'The specificity of the scientific field and the social conditions of the progress of reason', *Social Science Information*, 14, 5, pp. 19–47.

—— (1988) *Homo Academicus*, Cambridge: Polity Press.

Bourdieu, P. and Passeron, J-C. (1977) *Reproduction*, London: Routledge.

—— (1979) *The Inheritors*, London: University of Chicago Press.

Burgess, R.G. (1983) *Experiencing Comprehensive Education*, London: Methuen.

—— (ed.) (1994) *Postgraduate Education and Training in the Social Sciences*, London: Jessica Kingsley.

Callon, M. (1986) 'The sociology of an actor-network', in M. Callon, J. Law and A. Rip (eds) *Mapping the Dynamics of Science and Technology*, Basingstoke: Macmillan.

Campbell, J.K. (1992) 'Fieldwork among the Sarakatsani, 1954–55', in J. de Pina-Cabral and J. Campbell (eds) *Europe Observed*, London: Macmillan.

Chapman, M. (1992) 'Fieldwork, language and locality in Europe, from the North', in J. de Pina-Cabral and J. Campbell (eds) *Europe Observed*, London: Macmillan.

Clark, Burton, R. (ed.) (1993) *The Research Foundations of Graduate Education: Germany, Britain, France, United States, Japan*, Berkeley CA: University of California Press.

Clarke, A.E. (1998) *Disciplining Reproduction*, Berkeley CA: University of California Press.

Clarke, A.E. and Fujimura, J.H. (eds) (1992) *The Right Tools for the Job*, Princeton NJ: Princeton University Press.

Clifford, J. (1997) *Routes*, Cambridge MA: Harvard University Press.

Clifford, J. and Marcus, G.E. (eds) (1986) *Writing Culture: The Poetics and Politics of Ethnography*, Berkeley CA: University of California Press.

Coffey, A. and Atkinson, P. (eds) (1994) *Occupational Socialization and Working Lives*, Aldershot: Avebury.

—— (1996) *Making Sense of Qualitative Data*, Thousand Oaks CA: Sage.

—— (1997) 'Analysing documentary reality', in D. Silverman (ed.) *Qualitative Analysis: Issues of Theory and Method*, London: Sage, pp. 45–62.

Cohen, A. (1982) *Belonging*, Manchester: Manchester University Press.

References

—— (1992) 'Self-conscious anthropology', in J. Okeley and H. Gallaway (eds) *Anthropology and Autobiography*, London: Routledge.
Collins, H. (1974) 'The TEA Set', *Science Studies*, 4, pp. 165–86.
—— (1985) *Changing Order*, London: Sage.
—— (1990) *Artificial Experts*, Cambridge MA: The MIT Press.
—— (1994) 'A strong test of the experimenters' regress', *Studies in the History and Philosophy of Science*, 25, 3, pp. 493–503.
—— (1995) 'Sociology and artificial intelligence', in S. Jasanoff, G.E. Markle, J.C. Petersen and T. Pinch (eds) *Handbook of Science and Technology*, Thousand Oaks CA: Sage.
—— (1996) 'Embedded or embodied: Hubert Dreyfus's *What Computers Still Can't Do*', review essay, *Artificial Intelligence*, 80, 1, pp. 99–117.
Collins, H. and Pinch, T. (1993) *The Golem*, Cambridge: Cambridge University Press.
—— (1998) *The Golem*, revised edition, Cambridge: Cambridge University Press.
Cortazzi, M. (1993) *Narrative Analysis*, London: Falmer.
Delamont, S. (1987) 'Three blind spots', *Social Studies of Science*, 17, 1, pp. 163–70.
—— (1989) *Knowledgeable Women*, London: Routledge.
—— (1992) *Fieldwork in Educational Settings*, London: Falmer.
Delamont, S. and Atkinson, P.A. (1990) 'Professions and powerlessness', *The Sociological Review*, 38, 1, pp. 90–110.
—— (1995) *Fighting Familiarity*, Cresskill NJ: Hampton.
Delamont, S., Atkinson, P.A. and Parry, O. (1997a) *Supervising the PhD*, Buckingham: The Open University Press.
—— (1997b) 'Critical mass and pedagogic continuity', *British Journal of Sociology of Education*, 18, 4, pp. 533–50.
Douglass, W. (1992) 'Anthropological methodology in the European context', in J. Pina-Cabral and J. Campbell (eds) *Europe Observed*, London: Macmillan.
Downey, G.L. and Lucena, J.C. (1997) 'Engineering selves', in G.L. Downey and J. Dumit (eds) *Cyborgs and Citadels*, Santa Fe: School of American Research Press.
Dreyfus, H. (1979) *What Computers Can't Do*, New York: Harper and Row.
Dreyfus, H. (1992) *What Computers Still Can't Do: A Critique of Artificial Reason*, Cambridge MA: MIT Press. .
Dreyfus, H. and Dreyfus, S. (1986) *Mind Over Machine: The Power of Human Intuition and Expertise in the Era of the Computer*, New York: Free Press.
Durkheim, E. and Mauss, M. (1963) *Primitive Classification*, London: Routledge.
Eggleston, J. and Delamont, S. (1981) *A Necessary Isolation? A Study of Postgraduate Research Students in Education*, Cardiff: Social Research Unit, Department of Sociology, University College, Cardiff.
—— (1983) *Supervision of the Students for Research Degrees*, Kendal: Dixon Printing Company for British Education Research Association.
Economic and Social Research Council (1991) *Postgraduate Training Guidelines*, Swindon: ESRC.
Economic and Social Research Council (1996) *Postgraduate Training Guidelines*, revised edition, Swindon: ESRC.
Evans, C. (1988) *Language People*, Milton Keynes: Open University Press.
—— (1993) *English People*, Milton Keynes: Open University Press.
Fardon, R. (ed.) (1990) *Localizing Strategies*, Edinburgh: Scottish Academic Press.

References

Fleck, L. (1979) *The Genesis and Development of a Scientific Fact*, Chicago: University of Chicago Press.
Fujimura, J. (1997) *Crafting Science*, Cambridge MA: Harvard University Press.
Fulton, O. (1996) 'Which academic profession are you in?', in R. Cuthbert (ed.) *Working in Higher Education*, Buckingham: The Open University Press.
Galison, P. (1987) *How Experiments End*, Chicago: University of Chicago Press.
Galton, M. and Delamont, S. (1976) *Final Report on PhD/PGCE Chemistry Courses*, Leicester: Leicester University School of Education for the DES.
Getzels, J.W. and Jackson, P. (1963) 'The highly intelligent and highly creative adolescent', in C.W. Taylor and F. Barron (eds) *Scientific Creativity: Its Recognition and Development*, New York: Wiley.
Gilbert, N. and Mulkay, M. (1984) *Opening Pandora's Box*, Cambridge: Cambridge University Press.
Granfield, R. (1992) *Making Elite Lawyers*, New York: Routledge.
Grillo, R. (1985) *Ideologies and Institutions of Modern France*, Cambridge, Cambridge University Press.
Gumport, P. (1993) 'Graduate education and research imperatives: views from American campuses', in R. Burton Clark (ed.) *The Research Foundations of Graduate Education*, Berkeley CA: University of California Press.
Hacking, I. (1992) 'The self-vindication of the laboratory sciences', in A. Pickering (ed.) *Science as Practice and Culture*, Chicago: Chicago University Press.
Hagstrom, W.O. (1965) *The Scientific Community*, New York: Basic Books.
Hammersley, M. and Atkinson, P. (1995) *Ethnography: Principles in Practice*, second edition, London: Routledge.
Hargreaves, A. (1984) 'Contrastive rhetoric and extremist talk', in A. Hargreaves and P. Woods (eds) *Classrooms and Staffrooms*, Milton Keynes: Open University Press.
Harris, M. (1996) *Review of Postgraduate Education*, vol. 1: *The Report*, vol. 2: *The Evidence*, Bristol: Higher Education Funding Council for England.
Hess, D. (1997) 'If you are thinking of living in STS', in G.L. Downey and J. Dumit (eds) *Cyborgs and Citadels*, Santa Fe: School of American Research Press.
Hockey, J. (1991) 'The social science PhD', *Studies in Higher Education*, 16, 3, pp. 319–32.
—— (1994) 'Establishing boundaries: problems and solutions in managing the PhD supervisor role', *Cambridge Journal of Education*, 24, 2, pp. 293–305.
Jackson, A. (ed.) (1987) *Anthropology at Home*, London: Tavistock.
James, A., Hockey, J. and Dawson, A. (eds) (1997) *After Writing Culture*, London: Routledge.
Jamous, H. and Peloille, B. (1970) 'Professions or self-perpetuating system?', in J.A. Jackson (ed.) *Professions and Professionalisation*, Cambridge: The University Press.
Jenkins, R. (1992) *Pierre Bourdieu*, London: Routledge.
Jenkins, S. (1998) Speech to the Annual Meeting of the British Association for the Advancement of Science, *Times Higher Education Supplement*, 11 September 1998, pp. 19–21.
Kadushin, C. (1969) 'The professional self concept of music students', *American Journal of Sociology*, 75, pp. 389–404.
Knorr-Cetina, K. (1981) *The Manufacture of Knowledge*, Oxford: Pergamon.

References

—— (1995) 'Laboratory studies', in S. Jasanoff, G.E. Markle, J. Peterson and T. Pinch (eds) *Handbook of Science and Technology Studies*, London: Sage.
—— (1999) *Epistemic Cultures*, Cambridge, MA: Harvard University Press.
Kuhn, T.S. (1962) *The Structure of Scientific Revolutions*, Chicago: University of Chicago Press.
—— (1977) *The Essential Tension*, Chicago: University of Chicago Press.
Kuper, A. (1973) *Anthropologists and Anthropology: The British School 1922–72?* Harmondsworth: Penguin Books.
Lacey, C. (1970) *Hightown Grammar*, Manchester: Manchester University Press.
Latour, B. and Woolgar, S. (1986) *Laboratory Life*, 2nd edition., Princeton NJ: Princeton University Press.
Lynch, M. (1985) *Art and Artefact in Laboratory Science*, London: Routledge.
McAleese, R. and Welsh, J. (1983) 'The supervision of postgraduate research students', in J.E. Eggleston and S. Delamont (eds) *Supervision of Students for Research Degrees*, Kendal, Cumbria: Dixons Printing Company for the British Educational Research Association.
Merton, R.K., Reader, G. and Kendall, P.L. (eds) (1958) *The Student Physician*, Cambridge MA: Harvard University Press.
Miller, C.M.L. and Parlett, M. (1976) 'Cue-consciousness', in M. Hammersley and P. Woods (eds) *The Process of Schooling*, London: Routledge and Kegan Paul.
Mulkay, M. (1985) *The Word and the World: Explorations in the Form of Sociological Analysis*, London: George Allen and Unwin.
Myers, G. (1990) *Writing Biology: Texts in the Social Construction of Scientific Knowledge*, Madison: University of Wisconsin Press.
Newell, A. (1990) *Unified Theories of Cognition*, Cambridge MA: Harvard University Press.
Nye, A. (1990) *A Feminist Reading of the History of Logic*, London: Routledge.
Olesen, V. and Whittaker, E. (1968) *The Silent Dialogue*, San Francisco: Jossey Bass.
Parry, O. (1983) 'Uncovering the ethnographer', in N. McKeganey and S. Cunningham-Burley (eds) *Enter the Sociologist*, Farnborough: Gower.
—— (1988) *The Journalism School: The Occupational Socialization of Graduate Journalists*, unpublished PhD thesis, University of Wales, Cardiff.
—— (1990) 'Fitting in with the setting: a problem of adjustment for both students and the researcher', *Sociology*, 24, 3, pp. 417–30.
—— (1992) 'The production and reproduction of news', *International Journal of Qualitative Studies in Education*, 5, pp. 215–30.
—— (1994) 'The reproduction of an occupational community', *British Journal of Education and Work*, 6, pp. 45–56.
Parry, O., Atkinson, P. and Delamont, S. (1994a) 'Disciplinary identities and doctoral work', in R.G. Burgess (ed.) *Postgraduate Education and Training in the Social Sciences*, London: Jessica Kingsley.
Parry, O., Atkinson, P., Delamont, S. and Hiken, A. (1994b) 'Suspended between two stools?', in A. Coffey and P. Atkinson (eds) *Occupational Socialisation and Working Lives*, Farnborough: Avebury.
Phillips, S.U. (1982) 'The language socialization of lawyers: acquiring the "cant"', in G. Spindler (ed.), *Doing the Ethnography of Schooling*, New York: Holt, Rinehart and Winston.

References

Pickering, A. (ed.) (1992) *Science as Practice and Culture*, Chicago: Chicago University Press.
Pinch, T. (1981) 'The sun set: the presentation of certainty in scientific life', *Social Studies of Science*, 11, 1, pp. 131–58.
—— (1986) *Confronting Nature*, Dordrecht: Reidel.
—— (1993) 'Turn, turn and turn again', *Science, Technology and Human Values*, 18, pp. 511–22.
Pinch, T.J., Collins, H.M. and Carbone, L. (1996) 'Inside knowledge: second order measures of skill', *The Sociological Review*, 44, 2, pp. 163–86.
Polanyi, M. (1958) *Personal Knowledge*, London: Routledge and Kegan Paul.
Pylyshyn, Z. (1984) *Computation and Cognition: Towards a Foundation for Cognitive Science*, Cambridge MA: MIT Press.
Rapport, N. (1992) 'From affect to analysis: the biography of an interaction in an English village', in J. Okely and H. Callaway (eds) *Anthropology and Autobiography*, London: Routledge.
Riessman, C.K. (1993) *Narrative Analysis*, Newbury Park CA: Sage.
Scott, S. (1985) 'Working through the contradictions in researching postgraduate education', in R.G. Burgess (ed.) *Field Methods in the Study of Education*, London: Falmer.
Shibutani, T. (1967) 'Reference groups as perspectives', in J.G. Manis and B.N. Meltzer (eds) *Symbolic Interaction*, Boston: Allyn and Bacon.
Seidel, J. (1988) *The Ethnograph: A User's Guide*, Littleton CO: Qualis Research Associates.
Spencer, J. (1989) 'Anthropology as a kind of writing' *Man*, 24, pp. 45–64.
Strathern, M. (1981) *Kinship at the Core*, Cambridge: Cambridge University Press.
Tesch, R. (1990) *Qualitative Research: Analysis Types and Software Tools*, London: Falmer.
Tobias, S. (1990) *They're not Dumb, they're Different*, Tucson AZ: Research Corporation.
Traweek, S. (1988) *Beamtimes and Lifetimes*, Cambridge MA: Harvard University Press.
Wakeford, J. (1985) 'A director's dilemmas', in R.G. Burgess (ed.) *Field Methods in the Study of Education*, London: Falmer.
Walford, G. (1981) 'Classification and framing in higher education', *Studies in Higher Education*, 6, pp. 147–58.
Weaver, A. and Atkinson, P. (1994) *Microcomputing and Qualitative Data Analysis*, Farnborough: Avebury.
Whittlesea, C. (1995) *Pharmacy Doctoral Students: Thesis Writing Skills and Strategies*, unpublished MSc Econ thesis, University of Wales College of Cardiff.
Winfield, G. (1987) *The Social Science PhD*, 2 vols, London: ESRC.
Woolgar, S. (1988) *Science: The Very Idea*, London: Tavistock.
Wright, J. (1992) *Selection, Supervision and the Academic Management of Research Leading to the Degree of PhD.*, unpublished PhD thesis, University of Nottingham.
Young, K., Fogarty, M.P. and Mcrae, S. (1987) *The Management of Doctoral Studies in the Social Sciences*, London: Policy Studies Institute.
Zuckerman, H. (1977) *Scientific Elite*, New York: The Free Press.

Name Index

Abir-Am, P. 17
Adam, A. 107, 110
Albright, C. 65–6, 67, 69
Anderson, M. 170
Angelworth, I. 66, 67, 159
Ashmore, M. 43, 53, 135
Asmara, L. 57
Atkinson, P.A. 8, 10, 19–22, 23, 28, 32–3, 35, 43, 54, 56, 62, 95, 118, 136, 155, 185, 186, 192
Avril 103–4

Ball, S. 156
Barley, N. 75–6
Barnabas 148
Barnes, B. 58
Barsington 65, 102, 103, 159
Batchelor, C. 132
Becher, T. 3, 43, 64, 131, 133, 135, 140, 154, 185, 190
Becker, H.S. 43, 154
Behar, R. 95
Bernard, C. 56
Bernstein, B. 7–9, 14, 152, 153, 155, 169, 174, 181, 192
Bettman, E. 84, 94, 95
Bloor, D. 58
Boatman, A. 102, 104–5, 131
Borringer 26
Bosk, C. 177
Bosley, K. 34–5
Bourdieu, P. 1, 5–7, 9, 14, 43, 45, 100, 134, 173, 174; good taste 42; guidance 72; legitimate membership 34, 35, 50; normative behaviour 68; proximity/remoteness 18, 23, 28; recruitment 116; thesis 152
Brande 41–2, 142
Bulmer, M. 183

Burgess, R.G. 135, 154, 156, 183, 184

Caldecot 161
Caldwell, D. 132
Callon, M. 68
Campbell, J. 76
Challoner 83, 144–5
Chapman, M. 74
Clark, B.R. 26, 154, 185
Clarke, A.E. 17, 54
Clifford, J. 76, 95
Coffey, A. 33, 62, 118, 136, 185, 186, 192
Cohen, A. 74
Collins, H. 12, 54, 56, 58, 62, 63, 68, 109, 111, 123
Coltness 139–40, 145–6
Conroy, P. 102–3, 104, 113
Cooper, E. 90–1
Cortazzi, M. 135
Coughlin, E. 86, 88, 96
Creighton, H. 47
Crupiner 134, 138, 140

Danberry 58, 131, 133
Danson 141
de Manuelos 46, 101
Deladier, S. 61, 167
Delamont, S. 10, 23, 28, 32–3, 35, 36, 39, 43, 53, 54, 56, 135, 157, 160, 162, 178, 186–7, 189, 190
Dewry 41, 43–4, 57, 58, 130, 158
d'Hiver 147
Dorroway 98
Douglas, M. 7, 45, 79
Douglass, W. 74
Downey, G.L. 153
Dreyfus, H. 112
Dreyfus, S. 112

199

Name Index

Drummock 45, 82, 87, 91
Dumont, G. 44, 49, 80–1
D'Urfey 87
Durkheim, E. 5
Durtham 44
Duval 62, 69, 124, 130

Eggleston, J. 39, 157, 162, 186
Enright, N. 97
Evans, C. 43

Fardian 130–1
Fardon, R. 73, 74
Faul, B. 167, 168
Feering 74, 76
Ferguson, M. 69
Feste 85, 90
Fitton 44–5, 77, 78, 93
Fleck, L. 54
Fonteaux 160
Fouteaux 66
Frome, L. 83
Fujimura, J.H. 16, 54, 59
Fulton, O. 3, 4, 9
Fustian 77, 83, 95, 98

Gaisbrook 40
Galison, P. 13, 64
Galley 95
Galton, M. 186
Gantry 41, 64, 65, 69, 131, 159
Garnette 57, 67, 124–5, 158, 168
Geodrake 80, 87
Getzels, J.W. 56
Gideon 76
Gilbert, N. 42, 58, 63, 70, 135, 177
Gilchick 77
Godlee 85, 143
Gordon, D. 95
Granfield, R. 43
Grillo, R. 73
Gumport, P. 42–3, 157
Gunderson, K. 157

Hacking, I. 13, 16, 54, 55, 63, 70, 132, 167
Hackington 109
Hagstrom, W.O. 68
Hakapopoulos 147–8
Harcourt 85
Hargreaves, A. 123, 137
Harme 108

Hatchett 109–10
Helsgood, C. 108–9
Herrick 75
Hess, D. 54
Hockey, J. 135, 154, 190
Hughes, E. 10
Hurrell 19–20, 95

Ianello, S. 48
Ingersoll, J. 47
Ireland, S. 132
Ives, C. 39–40, 44, 50–1, 81, 92

Jackson, A. 73, 74
Jackson, P. 56
James, A. 95
Jamous, H. 35, 62
Jannerat 80
Jelf 149, 150
Jenkins, R. 5
Jenkins, S. 56
Jones, A. 186

Kadushin, C. 43
Kaltenbrun, V. 48
Kanelos, T. 48
Kenway 137
Kettering, H. 50, 85
Knorr-Cetina, K. 11–12, 59, 115
Kuhn, T.S. 15–16, 54, 56, 115, 173, 180
Kuper, A. 72
Kylie, J. 48, 110–11

Lacey, C. 156
Latour, B. 43, 59, 68, 135
Lester, E. 49–50, 95
Loomis, B. 82
Lucena, J.C. 153
Lundgren, J. 47, 49, 92
Lynch, M. 43, 135

McAleese, R. 135
McAlister, S. 131, 160
McQumpha 42
Madson, G. 81–2
Maitland-Maine 45–6
Mallory, C. 48, 106, 112, 131
Mandrake 41
Mannheim 118
Marcus, G.E. 95
Mardian 42
Martins, R. 107–8

Name Index

Mauss, M. 5
Meade 146
Menakis, N. 168
Merton, R.K. 154
Miller, C.M.L. 39
Mincing 143–4
Mohr, E. 67, 160
Moliner, R. 47
Montoya, L. 49, 50, 78, 80, 82, 89
Morrow 149–50
Mulkay, M. 40, 42, 58, 63, 70, 135, 177
Munsey 139
Myers, G. 69

Nagle, H. 109, 110
Nankivell 138–9, 154
Netley 139
Newell, A. 107
Nuddington 138
Nye, A. 112

Olesen, V. 43

Paget 35–6, 39
Palinode 148–9
Panthing 146–7
Parlett, M. 39
Parry, O. 19, 20–2, 24, 27, 28, 30–1, 32–3, 62, 63, 154, 186, 190
Passeron, J-C. 42
Passington 107, 112
Peloille, B. 35, 62
Pendleton, F. 48
Perrin, G. 64, 129, 168
Perrini, J. 168
Phillips, E. 183
Phillips, S.U. 43
Pickering, A. 54, 55
Pilgrim 101–2, 106, 146
Pinch, T. J. 12, 54, 56, 63, 68
Polanyi, M. 62
Portland 37
Pylyshyn, Z. 107

Quayne 44, 65, 68, 125–6

Ramilles 38
Rapport, N. 74
Rennie 139
Ridgeway 36
Riessman, C.K. 135
Ross, W. 48–9, 105

Rowlandson 38–9

Savanake 38
Schroeder, P. 167
Scott, S. 135
Scott-Windlesham, T. 77
Scovil, M. 158
Seidel, J. 185
Shannon 141–2
Shibutani, T. 117
Silva 40
Simmel, G. 181
Snow 40
Soczewinski, W. 126–7
Sopwith 28
Spencer, J. 95
Staley, B. 160
Stayman, M. 43, 57
Stottle, A. 159
Strathern 74
Subonadier 107

Talisman 77, 83–4, 118–19
Tatley, H. 167–8
Teague 91
Tesch, R. 185
Throstle 88
Tobias, S. 54, 56, 153
Travers, D. 74, 78–9, 80, 83, 88, 94
Traweek, S. 12, 68, 135
Trevithick 86
Tyrone, E. 66, 128–9, 132

Upton, M. 47

Verney, S. 47
Viera, A. 157, 158
Vorhees, J. 130

Waite 105–6, 108
Wakeford, J. 135
Walford 160
Walworth, R. 80
Weaver, A. 185
Welsh, J. 135
Wenzel, S. 58
Whittaker, E. 43
Whittlesea, C. 69
Winfield, G. 154
Wishart 37–8, 140–1
Woodrose 36–7, 142–3
Woolgar, S. 43, 59, 68, 135

Name Index

Wright, J. 135
Wynyard 37, 38
Wyston, B. 92

Yeager, N. 86, 88, 92
Young, K. 135

Zuckerman, H. 123

Subject Index

access negotiations 21–2
achieved roles 152
Advisory Board to the Research Councils (ABRC) 190–1
algorithmical model 62
ambition 53
anonymity 25–6
anthropology 15, 19–21, 117, 133; biographies 118–24, 125; failure 45, 50, 96–7, 177; fieldwork 72–99, 114; intellectual equality 156; isolation 45, 96, 162–4; peer groups 166; qualitative methods 46–7; societies 168–9; students' biographies 126–8; students' dreams 48, 49; supervisors' views 44–5; supervisory relationship 163–5; *see also* social anthropology
area studies 24, 155
artificial intelligence 29, 155, 171, 175, 180, 185; modelling 100–15; multidisciplinary work 169; students' dreams 48
ascribed roles 152
Association of Social Anthropologists 168–9
autonomy 138–50, 151, 163, 176

Biochemical Society 69, 167–8
biochemistry 1, 15, 29, 130, 167–8, 180, 181, 184; laboratory work 53–71; research group 157–8; students' biographies 128–9; supervisors' biographies 124–6; supervisors' views 42, 43–4
biographies 118–30
black boxing 55
Boarbridge University 22–3
Boys in White 154
brevity 39

British Academy 191

Carnegie Survey 3
classification 5–6, 7–8
CNAA *see* Council for National Academic Awards
coherence 37–8, 39
Committee of Vice-Chancellors and Principals (CVCP) 191
comparative approach 28
computers *see* artificial intelligence
conceptual net thesis 55
conferences 69, 70, 167, 168
confidentiality 25–6
connectionism 107–8
consensus 111
continuity 70, 179; groups 102–3; pedagogic 56, 152–72
contrastive rhetoric 123, 137, 149, 150
convergent thinking 56
converts 73
coping strategies 10
core set 123
Council for National Academic Awards (CNAA) 23, 40
critical mass 192
cue-deafness 39, 44
cultural capital 14, 76
CVCP *see* Committee of Vice-Chancellors and Principals

deadlines 15
defensiveness 27–8
descent groups 123
descent systems 117
development studies 24, 27–8, 155, 182; examiners' views 36–7, 40; fieldwork

203

Subject Index

72, 98; multidisciplinary departments 170
differentiation 6, 9
disciplinary culture 155
discipline 14–15
discipline proximity 24
discrimination 6, 42, 43

Economic and Social Research Council (ESRC) 19, 22, 25, 27, 31, 90, 140, 183, 184, 188–92
enculturational model 62
enthusiasm 48–9
environmental sciences 42, 45–6, 53, 154, 169, 171
epistemic community 115
epistemic cultures 12
epistemology 24
ESRC *see* Economic and Social Research Council
essential tension 16, 54, 55, 152, 174, 176
ethics 26, 31
ethnographic monograph 20, 73, 86
examiners' views 35–41
excitement 36
expert systems 109–11, 113–14

failure 2, 32, 176–7; anthropologists 45, 50, 96–7, 177; biochemistry experiments 56–9, 60–2; fieldwork 86
faith 114–15, 177
familiarity 18, 23, 24, 28, 32
fieldwork 19, 45, 47, 72–99, 114, 162–4, 175–6
flexibility 82–3
framing 8
funding 166
funding bodies 15

genealogies 116–33
generations 116–33
geography 29, 167, 168, 169, 180, 181; postdocs 160; students' dreams 47; *see also* human geography; physical geography
geology 130–1
groups: continuity 102–3; meetings 165–6; size 160, 166

habitus 7, 9, 96–8, 116, 157
Harris Report 191, 192
hidden curriculum 10

Higher Education Funding Council for England 191
human geography 22–3, 24, 163, 166; fieldwork 72, 83, 95, 99; joint supervision 165; qualitative methods 46–7
humanities 17, 185

identity 3, 7–9, 73–82, 97, 126, 153–4, 172, 179, 181
identity-formation 4
incongruity 56–8
independence 91, 92–3, 139–40, 141, 176
indeterminacy 82–94
indeterminate criteria 35, 36, 37–8, 39–41, 43, 178
indeterminate knowledge 62–3
individualized research 161–7
innovation 16
Institute of British Geographers 167, 168
intangibility 80
interdisciplinary research 179
intervention 138–50, 151
isolation 42, 176; anthropologists 45, 96, 162–4; modelling 113; multidisciplinary work 169–70, 179; social science 155, 157, 161

joint supervision 164–5
journals 167
judgement 36, 42–3

Kingford 39
knowledge acquisition 10
knowledge-based systems *see* expert systems

laboratory work 11–12, 13, 53–71, 114, 135, 175–6
learning the ropes 10
length 35–6, 38–9
library research 75–7
liminal state 176
loneliness 42, 44, 50
loyalty 4, 8–9, 96, 153, 170, 181

modelling 100–15, 175
modesty 40
multidisciplinary research 154–5, 169–71, 179, 181
myths 154

Subject Index

Natural Environmental Research Council (NERC) 104, 191
Natural Science Research Council 192
natural sciences 153; ABRC report 191; biographies 124–6; examiners' views 41, 153; failure 176–7; genealogies 123; research groups 157–61; supervisors' narratives 134–51
negative results 41
NERC *see* Natural Environmental Research Council
networks 166, 167
neural networks 107, 109
Nobel prize 40, 123
normative science 68

organizational context 3–4
organizational culture 7, 8–9
originality 16, 36, 37, 38, 46, 174
ownership 158

paradigm shift 20
paradigms 15–16, 54, 115, 173
participant observation 86–7, 89, 93
pedagogic continuities 56, 152–72
pedagogic stability 70
pedagogy 8
pedigrees 117, 118–30
peer groups 131, 166
peer research 18–33
peer review 18
personal modes 152, 153, 154, 155, 161, 169, 171
physical geography 53, 65, 100–6, 113, 129, 130, 132, 184–5
physics 12, 42–3, 157
positional modes 125, 152, 153, 154, 155, 161, 167, 169, 171
postdoctoral researchers 64, 65, 67, 70, 130–1, 132, 159–60
posters 69
Postgraduate Training Guidelines 90
pre-established knowledge 63–70
proximity 18, 23, 24, 28, 32
publications 36, 37, 41, 68, 69

qualitative methods 25, 46–7, 82–3, 86
quality 51

reality shock 56, 70
reflection 29
remoteness 23, 32

Research Assessment Exercise 191
Research Council Training Guidelines 25
research groups 12, 102–5, 113, 129–33, 138, 153, 155–6, 157–61
research methods training 81, 82–93
risk 177
rites de passage 4, 79, 93, 97–8, 116
robotics 48, 105–6, 108
Royal Economic Society 167
Royal Geographical Society 168
Rushberry 26

Sampo 34–5, 46
Science and Engineering Research Council (SERC) 41
Science Research Councils 191
sciences: laboratory work 11–12, 13, 53–71, 114, 135, 175–6; research groups 130–3, 153, 155–6, 157–61; student biographies 128–9; *see also* environmental sciences; natural sciences; social sciences
scientific ambition 53
scientific knowledge 11–14
scientific method 8, 24–5
SERC *see* Science and Engineering Research Council
sites of secondary knowledge production 169
situational learning 10, 13
social anthropology 24, 28, 180, 181; fieldwork 72–99, 175–6; unsuccessful students 50; *see also* anthropology
social difference 5, 6
social location 24
social organization 11–14
social sciences 17, 153, 154, 155, 156; examiners' views 38, 40–1; individualized research 161–7; isolation 155, 157, 161; loneliness 42; supervisors' narratives 134–51
social types 181
societies 167–9
sociology of knowledge 5, 7
sociology of scientific knowledge (SSK) 11–14, 54, 55, 111
Spencer Foundation 26
stability 13, 53–4, 55, 56, 70, 71, 117, 180–1
Standing Conference of Principals (SCOP) 191
status passage 4, 10

205

Subject Index

strangeness 18, 23, 24, 28, 32
The Student Physician 154
subcultures 3, 9, 10
succession 130–3
symbolic violence 50

tacit knowledge 62, 63, 70, 80, 98, 103, 175, 178
Teaching Quality Assessments 191
team work 64–7, 70, 138, 154, 155–6
technical knowledge 62–3
technical qualities 35, 36, 40–1
tension 16, 54, 55, 138, 152, 153–4, 158, 174, 176–7

time factors 15, 133, 145
town planning 27–8, 29, 154–5, 170, 182; examiners' views 35–6, 37, 38, 40; fieldwork 98; group meetings 166
training 46–7, 134, 178; fieldwork 81, 82–93; laboratory work 55–6, 57, 59, 64–7, 130

urban studies 23, 24, 36, 72, 98

Winfield Report 189, 190
writing-up 142–3; anthropology 79, 91–2, 94–6, 164; social science 162–3

Made in United States
Orlando, FL
21 January 2024